THE RESURRECTION OF THE BODY

Themes of Theology

THE
RESURRECTION
OF THE BODY

by

H. CORNÉLIS, O.P.

J. GUILLET, S.J.

TH. CAMELOT, O.P.

M. A. GENEVOIS, O.P.

Translated by

SISTER M. JOSELYN, O.S.B.

FIDES PUBLISHERS, INC.

Notre Dame, Indiana

Published originally in France, 1962, by Les Éditions du Cerf, Paris, under the title *La Résurrection de la Chair*.

In the Themes of Theology Series:

God Speaks
God Among Men
The Theology of Sin
The Theology of Sex in Marriage
A Mission Theology
The Resurrection of the Body

CONTENTS

DO YOU BELIEVE IN THE RESURRECTION OF THE BODY?

Every day when we say the Creed we repeat with the Church, "I believe in the resurrection of the body and life everlasting." Do we really mean these words? If so, would not our entire attitude toward life and the world be different? How many of us are imbued with the kind of hope in the resurrection that the first disciples and the martyrs exulted in?

We invite all our readers to ponder this question. To assist them, we present here interviews with four well-known personalities, who were asked to discuss these three questions:

1. Do you believe in the resurrection of the dead?
2. How do you imagine the "heavenly Jerusalem"? Do you think our human ties of affection will be continued in heaven?
3. Hope in the resurrection seems to have faded greatly since the first centuries. How do you explain this?

Paul Claudel: Human love will continue.

1. Our Saviour's assurance is formal: "There where I am, you also will be." Our life after death will thus be His life. In the world beyond we shall not be exiled; there will be no radical change. We shall pass from the world of effects to the world of cause. Instead of seeing reality in terms of its effects, we shall see it—in God—in terms of cause.

1

We shall be in our Father's house; as St. John says, we shall be at home with God, members of His household.

2. I myself have not the slightest doubt that human love will continue after death, for God will not change man essentially. The feelings between father and son, for instance, are so deep and so permanent because they have their root in God Himself.

God gives us those we love so that we may love Him more. I therefore believe that our love for those who have helped us attain to glory will be stronger than ever. We shall love each other in the full truth then, not in partial ignorance or by chance as we do now.

I believe that every human being constitutes a whole. After this life we shall not be mutilated; we shall remain intact. Note the text of Osee: "I will draw them with the cords of Adam." Human ties not only will remain but will be put to a special use in life eternal. St. Paul says: "That which has been conceived in corruption shall be exalted in glory." So we shall not be changed, we shall be glorified, which is something entirely different.

I believe that memory and sensibility will continue to exist. St. Luke speaks of a condemned rich man who observed his descendants' evil behavior. Thus one world does see the other; even the damned, the reprobate, see it, and how much more the elect?

After death, even as separated souls awaiting the resurrection of the body, we shall continue to do good and to receive good. This is the tradition of all the saints. Did not St. Thérèse of Lisieux say: "I wish to spend my heaven doing good upon earth"?

So we shall remain in touch with those we loved on

earth. The Bible says, "What therefore God has joined together let no man put asunder." Death itself destroys neither the ties nor the obligations of love.

Human love will continue to exist. . . . Our human obligations do not alter when we change our dwelling place. Living in a different condition will not free us from our duties to those we loved.

3. One can hardly say enough of the future life. There is not enough preaching on the subject, unfortunately. As St. Thomas says, the beatific vision is rarely spoken of by the clergy. But we must speak not only of the beatific vision but also of the deific vision. We shall, so to speak, put on God the better to know Him and to love Him. We must love God with the very strength of God.

Christ's discourse at the Last Supper, " . . . that they may be one in us . . . " should be preached more often.

If we read the Bible attentively, if we read the Fathers attentively, we shall learn much more than we ordinarily hear.

We should not be always speculating about the after-life. Nevertheless we must have *in this life* some conception of what our future will be.

St. Paul says: "Eye has not seen nor ear heard what things God has prepared for those who love Him." We can still desire what we have neither seen nor heard, and we have the duty to desire it.

Gabriel Marcel: The world today can be endured only if one's spirit is riveted on this hope.

1. For us Christians living today, something especially influences us to belief in the resurrection of the body:

what we know the body endured in the concentration camps. One feels that human flesh has undergone such intolerable outrage that it must receive some kind of reparation in glory.

If this question must be asked, it should be asked in this way: "Does belief in the resurrection of the dead hold an important place in your life or is it merely a formula of your 'Credo' that you murmur only with your lips?" To such a question, I answer, "For me, this belief is fundamental. It seems to me one of the most important truths of Revelation. . . ."

For I am convinced that the body greatly surpasses all that science can say of it and even what human perception can grasp of it.

Obviously, if we accept the theories of scientism and Cartesianism, which view the body as only a machine or apparatus, the resurrection must appear to be a marvel indeed. Yet is not this the attitude of our time? And if preachers themselves have had difficulty with the subject, is it not because they too are influenced by scientism? What we need, then, is a sound philosophy of the relationship between soul and body. If the body were thought of as a subjective reality, a mediator, it seems to me we would be more ready for belief in the resurrection.

In any case, I believe life today is unendurable if one's spirit is not rooted in this hope of our Creed. If this hope were shared by a greater number, perhaps a respect for the flesh and for the body, so terribly lacking in our time, would be restored.

2. I believe that all that is positive in human feeling

will continue in the afterlife. But what is positive? And what is negative? From the outside one cannot tell. Yet, if we are honest with ourselves we know we sometimes feel something unworthy in us and which will disappear, and, on the other hand, we experience something directed toward God which will live on.

For a long time I have considered whether true communication between this world and the next is possible.

I have no doubt of the authenticity of certain miraculous apparitions, for instance. And yet I do not think we can speak of anything like "communication" in the ordinary sense. The dead do not communicate with the living as I communicate familiarly with my neighbor. But perhaps under some other and incomprehensible form . . . .

Some people experience intuitions or consolations. I know of a woman who was watching beside the body of a loved one, when suddenly, at two in the morning, she was seized by a kind of extraordinary joy. Later, a neighbor said to her, "Did you not experience, a little while ago . . . ?"

We need neither deny these things nor seek them. Such signs, such consolations, God gives gratuitously, through grace. To seek them out deliberately is to risk falling quickly into dangerous curiosity.

3. The reintroduction of a supernatural dimension into our existence should certainly show effects in our daily life. The hope for an absolute brotherhood contained in the dogma of the Mystical Body seems to me to provide a tremendous impetus toward the beginning of true brotherhood on earth.

Abbé Michonneau: Christian people live as if they no longer believed in the resurrection.

1. How can they not believe? Is not a Christian defined as one who is on his way to heaven?

In order to go to heaven we must die. But we ought not to disconnect death and resurrection. Rather we should think of death as being the resurrection. The moment of the resurrection of Christ is the very moment of His death.

2. It is individuals and real individuals who are in heaven. We shall continue to love each other in heaven in a very human manner, but this love will be elevated by and centered on the love of God. As to the glorified body of which the Church speaks, I certainly believe that this is not merely a metaphor. But how will our body be resurrected? A mystery, though a necessary mystery; to try to penetrate it would be vain curiosity. We must have faith. Our Saviour does not forbid us to think of the future but He does not wish us to penetrate it fully; He asks us to live in the present.

Heaven is prepared for on this earth. It is in time that man must be made fit for heaven.

I believe that the dead remain at our side and that they yearn for the salvation of the world, something like people who stand on a wharf helping those in a boat by encouraging cries and prayers.

3. We do not live with the afterlife sufficiently in mind. We do not think enough of death; we do not have enough courage before it. The idea that one cannot say to a Christian, "You are going to die," and rejoice with him, is scandalous.

Preaching, perhaps, is responsible. For centuries there

was an exaggerated insistence on the fear of hell and on the punishments of the afterlife, and death became very terrible. Instead of a perspective opening up before us, heaven came to be a kind of consolation prize. Half of the faithful think of heaven both too materialistically and too spiritually: they imagine it as an immense theater where each of the elect has the right to a special seat. On the other hand, for a decade or so our young priests, as a reaction, have not been too concerned with the future life. "Teach us how to live before you teach us how to die," the faithful say. They have been taught to live, but they forget that to live is to prepare to die, that is, to prepare for the resurrection.

Fortunately, we see the outline of a movement of return to an authentic eschatological vision of the universe. And it is about time, for our Christian people have absorbed paganism into their thinking as well as into their morals. They live as if they no longer believed in the resurrection.

R. P. d'Ouince: The point of view of the theologian.

1. The point of view of the theologian is to return to the Gospel.

For the Christian, the resurrection is integration in the Body of Christ, which is something wholly different from the seasonal renewal of vegetation.

Basically, we believe in the resurrection of the dead because Christ rose again. St. Thomas has correctly noted the unique character of the resurrection of Christ, at once a miracle and a mystery.

The resurrection of Lazarus was indeed a miracle, a historic event, beyond the common laws of nature, but Lazarus, though resurrected once, was still subject to the universal law of death.

The resurrection of Christ possessed the double character of being historic and mysterious. During the forty days following His resurrection, the Saviour appeared to His disciples with a visible, tangible body. But at the same time He had ended His history; His earthly mission was completed. He showed Himself alive to His disciples only to confirm their—and our—faith in life eternal.

2. When Christ returns, He does not speak of *sheol* nor of paradise. And this knowledge should give us enough light to change our lives. Still, the Saviour did not say that the future life has no relation to our life on earth. On the contrary, we take our works with us. If He said to the woman who had had seven husbands, "At the resurrection they will neither marry nor be given in marriage, but are as the angels of God in heaven" (reread Matt. 22:30 and ff.), He also said that the Apostles would still be Apostles. Thus He in no way asks us to impair our personality.

Two ideas can, moreover, orient our conception of the future life. The first is that, unlike the abode of the dead imagined by the pagans, the Christian heaven is a place of intense life, the feast of recovered innocence: in the light, those invited to the banquet will be reclad in their nuptial robes and their souls will be transparent. The most penetrating statement on heaven is that of St. Paul: "Then I shall know even as I am known."

The second idea is that we shall be truly resurrected only when the Mystical Body of Christ has attained its fulness, that is, when the last human being has died.

3. The loss of hope in the resurrection is related to our sense of faith. There is too strong a tendency to reduce faith to a purely moral and sociological content.

We are too preoccupied with the social consequences and the moral obligations of religion and not enough with the religious vision of the world which it imposes upon us, with the revelation of mysteries.

We see the resurrection too much as a reward, a little like children who expect a good mark after they have done their work well. But the resurrection is a religious and not a moral thought. It is the Saviour resurrected, it is creation redeemed, it is "the restoration of all things in Christ."

No matter what the strength of our conviction, it must be said that faith does not exclude suffering, and that human suffering continues up to death.

To transform the anguish of annihilation into the certitude of paradise requires constant effort, a necessary leap of the will into the unknown.

An unfailing certitude, but at the extreme limit of the self; a seamless garment of certitude but one bearing in its folds the weight of our sorrows and our wounds.

One

THE RESURRECTION OF THE BODY AND PRIMITIVE CONCEPTIONS OF THE LAST THINGS

An examination of the majority of beliefs concerning the state of man after death shows certain rather well-defined trends which could serve as a kind of consensus of the religious thought on this subject.[1] However, the resurrection of the body, though not contradictory to these common views, is not found among them and is scarcely—or very equivocally—prefigured. The very ancient belief in a certain survival of the individual clashed with the evident and apparently irremediable corruption of the body. Seeking to evade this obstacle rather than confront it directly, thinkers found themselves in an illogical position. Wise men, reflecting on the nature of man, came to distinguish that which thinks (with the cosmic order as principal object), that which dreams, that which makes man live, which "animates" and is like breath, if not identical to it, and finally that which differentiates the individual and is closely linked with the body, if it is not the body itself. From these ideas stem the complexity and the multiplicity of

[1] Van der Leeuw, in his opuscule, *Onsterfelijkheid of Opstanding*, rightly underscores the community of feeling in regard to the "totality" of the vital phenomenon which exists among primitives and Christians, but the terms he uses are deliberately extremist because of the thesis of the nonexistence of a "separated soul" which he and other Protestants defend: "The faith of primitive peoples is comparable to that of Christians in this, that neither distinguishes the soul from the body. In the Old Testament and in the Gospel this distinction does not appear. Where there is question of the soul it is the whole man—but in his true being—that is designated; 'existential' man, as we would say today" (p. 31).

11

the notions of "the soul" which we meet in primitive religious societies, and hence also arise the multiple possibilities of survival after death (envisaged by these groups).

Sometimes several of the elements combining to make up man are thought of as able to survive independently of each other. Because the remembrance of the dead person retained by those who lived with him, his presence in their dreams and their imagination, weakens with time, what is basic to the individuality of the dead is thought of as becoming enfeebled to the point where it blends into the indistinct mass of ancestors. Because intimacy with the dead was often dreaded, certain ceremonies at a definite date had for their object the "expulsion" of the dead, more or less politely, from the society of the living.[2] This same enfeeblement of memory doubtless led to a conception of life after death as a partly erased copy of earthly life. It should be added that even the life of the living individual in primitive societies remained at a low level of personal differentiation. Thus the contrast between the feeble individuality of the dead and the hardly more marked individuality of the living is decreased. The vague mass of "ancestors" functions as the guardian of the traditional values by which the tribe lives, and is the clan's most "conservative" element.

The rituals and myths connected with the funeral obsequies of the chief offer only an apparent exception, because the chief while alive was given the privilege of "personality" only in order to go beyond it by hypostatizing the function of sovereignty in the tribe. "Person-

[2] *R.H.R.*, 1954-2, p. 111, review by Mircéa Éliade of Uno Harva, *Die religiöse Vorstellungen der Mordwinen.*

ality" did not belong to him any more than it did to
the least of his subjects. Only when his seignorial privilege begins to be extended—first to the "great" and then
to all, as in the Egypt of the pharaohs—was the idea of a
personal survival conditioned by the particular events in
the life of an individual gradually affirmed. But even in
this case the figure of the dead person remained submerged in a *type,* that of the "blessed" or the "hero."
This led the living to alter the memory of the deceased
and bring it into conformity with his "legend." We may
quote here what Paul Mus says of the social categories
in which the notion of transmigration is presented as it
existed in pre-Buddhist India: "Asia was civilized in
societies centered on the person of the chief or the
father: This person epitomizes the whole group, 'consumes' it; that is to say, possesses it by right. The individual, such as we conceive him, is thus annihilated in
two ways, by default or by excess. Real only in their
chief, the dependents are less than individuals; the chief,
who 'devours' them, is more. Conceived in this way the
supreme entity will be God and World at once. One may
define this entity, so different from our personal God,
as *a complete way of life,* abstract because it is a system,
concrete because it is life. Thus the world, a kinship of
life with itself in all beings, is fragmented into innumerable communcations, possessions, reincarnations. The
complete theory of transmigration, the major discovery
of Indian thought, is only the systematization of this
folklore. The whole from the beginning formed a great
bloc of life, composed in detail of lives and deaths, in
which circulated only one impulse, life itself. It is always
the community which is the true value and in which

individuals are registered as simple events" (*Esprit,* June 1956, pp. 959-960).

The "Osirization" of the pharaoh or the "apotheosis" of the Roman emperor comes at the end of a somewhat different development, but shares in the same initial sociological situation, the hypostasis of the group in the person of the chief. One must interpret similarly the sacrifice of the spouse and servants who had to accompany the chief into the tomb. The chief bore within himself all the meaning of their life and without him they could only exist here on earth like widows in most ancient societies, as living dead.[3]

Ancient and modern societies widely use two principal funerary modes, cremation and burial. Can we draw some light from this fact? The insistence of Christians, dating from the early days of the Church and never gainsaid, upon condemning cremation should prompt us to ask: is there in the beliefs of the buriers a positive preparation for the dogma of the resurrection? Put in this way, the inquiry proves to be full of interest. One fact seems to emerge from archeological evidence: the

[3] Leenhardt in the *Encyclopédie Quillet,* t. I, p. 136, stresses the importance of the consequences of this identification and confusion of the person with the society, in an ensemble of the living and the dead, for the interpretation of primitive symbolism. He recalls the speech of a Kanake to a missionary who thought he had brought spiritual ideas to this people: "Not at all, what you have brought us is the body." He meant by this that the notions of the spirit and of a mystique were not unknown, but that conscious control and the domination of their person, delimited by the contours of their body, was a novelty. The person, scattered in the socio-mystical realm, emerged to limit itself. The Kanake grasped that his being was not diffused in nature but incarnated in the body of a man (p. 137).

See also the subtle analysis by a Siamese, Marsi Paribatra, of the distance which still remains from this point of view between the Orient and the Occident, in *Esprit,* July-August 1956, p. 42.

bronze age, which frequently cremated its dead, broke with a more ancient neolithic custom which, however, it never succeeded in completely obliterating. There is beginning to be agreement among scholars on the main characteristics of this neolithic culture, the appearance of which marked such a great step toward the liberation of man from the caprices of nature. Attentive observation of the seasonal rhythms and of vegetative life led men to the cultivation of food plants which could be preserved in storage. These communal efforts required the establishment of human and relatively stable groups in which it was necessary to organize strictly the distribution of reserves. This culture must have been particularly brilliant in the Nile delta, in the Ganges basin and in Mesopotamia. As is still the case in certain archaic societies, woman must have enjoyed in these communities an authority which came to her both from her skill in the works of cultivation and from her character as procreatrix, whose rhythms of fecundity paralleled those of nature herself.

A certain number of beliefs concerning the condition of the dead are naturally tied to this rather clearly circumscribed cultural complex, but there are also facts which resist this classification, while they can be grouped easily around another very general theme, that of initiation.[4] One should not, however, consider the matriarchal

---

[4] Gordon in the *Histoire des Religions* of Brillant and Aigrain, v. I, p. 222: "It is (initiation) which loosed dynamic forces on the world, forces which undergirded and enveloped the material universe. . . . It led to the *ritual of death and resurrection*. To be reborn into a higher universe, which is that of immortal life, it is necessary first to die to the world of sensation, by observing strict discipline . . . which constitutes the discipline of the underworld."

and the initiation themes as complementary, for it is very evident that initiation existed in widely diverse types of societies, including the dominantly matriarchal neolithic society whose chief characteristics we have sketched. Nevertheless, grouping the facts around these two centers of interest offers the advantage of revealing a complete view of the known contribution of primitive societies which lived on the margin of history. Moreover, it documents two conceptions of survival in which we hope to recover the antecedents of belief in the resurrection of the dead.

Because of their "transcendence" to terrestrial fortunes and the regularity of their course, the stars have, since the earliest times, been the chosen object of men's meditations. Man discovered in the heavens the best of himself: his need for order, regularity and law. He projected himself upon the screen of the heavens in order to read there more easily the meaning of his own existence. The parade of the heavenly bodies is led by an impressive pair, sun and moon, which play a capital role in the organization of the mental world of man. But above these are the heavens themselves, occupying a supreme place in the pantheon of the most primitive peoples and retaining in the course of religious development a certain secret importance not revealed by any ritual nor narrated in any myth. This undeniable importance is affirmed despite the usurpations and outrages to which the "heavenly father's" turbulent offspring subject him. This very turbulence united the god-sons to the dramatic destiny of men, themselves engaged in a struggle between life and death. The role of "mediator" between the impassible world of the heavenly gods and the changeful world here below is providentially played by the moon. Once one has perceived the ties that unite the phases of the moon to feminine physiology and vegetative life in general, a multitude of life and death rhythms group themselves around these fundamental relationships. The date of the Jewish Passover, feast of the first fruits, was regulated according to the arrival of spring. In the Christian context this feast became that of the resurrection.

The civilization of the hoe and the furrow, whose great sacrament undoubtedly was the *hieros gamos,* the sacred marriage of heaven and earth "represented" by the king-priest and his spouse on the field or in the temple *cella,* has enriched humanity's mental images with a complex highly important to our subject: that of the seed which must "die" to be "reborn." Some like to stress the dark aspects of this "cerealist" culture, as it is sometimes called. They see the more spiritual religious sense of an earlier culture giving way to sexual orgies, blood sacrifices, and superstitious magic, the earlier, more noble conceptions thus being reduced (in order to survive) to transmission by initiates, as a result of occult traditions.[5] This view is probably too much influenced by the ritual excesses characterizing some decadent cultures. These rites retained the outlines of very venerable religious thought, though degraded by long usage and emptied of spirit. Doubtless the anathemas

---

[5] "The hierogamic union which at the end of the neolithic period, in social groups profoundly influenced by the matriarchate, was the sacramental act par excellence, that which reconstituted the state of wholeness proper to supernature and was completed by the resurrection, continued almost exclusively under aberrant forms. But a great many tribes did not forget that the marriage was connected with the disciplines of initiation" (Gordon, *op. cit.,* p. 222).

of the prophets of Israel against the similar remains of a past epoch profoundly embedded in Chanaanite culture, still account for some of our hostile reaction to the religious values of this level. We should not forget, however, that numerous human groupings were only possible from the time of this "village" culture which assured the regularity of vital resources.

The community is for its members a maternal "womb" —whose protective limits are identified with the enclosure surrounding the communal dwelling. The Latin word *gremium* evokes simultaneously a sheaf of corn and the breast and from its Indo-European root derives the Sanskrit *grama,* designating a village agricultural society, basis of the Ganges civilization. It has not been sufficiently stressed that, despite the prophets' condemnation of excesses, the Israelite community in the Promised Land absorbed many Chanaanite religious values which proved perfectly assimilable to the religion of the jealous God. Without the neolithic foundation of Chanaanite culture, the poetry of the Canticle of Canticles would be unimaginable. And does not the Catholic meaning of tradition for its part teach us that it is only in the womb of the Church that the seed of the Word carries out its fecundating work and engenders life?

But the agricultural mentality, which lives in intimate communion with the immanent laws of the cosmic order and shows a profound sensibility to the most concrete life values, risks losing sight of the "heavens." Heaven is now thought of only in terms of its act of fecund and intimate union with earth.

Does not the myth of the revolt of the children of a primordial couple arise precisely from the "suffocation" human beings undergo in such a society, crushed in this tight grip? Life and death succeed each other without respite in their regular alternation. Death, which replaces life, is felt to be the condition of life. Moreover, it does not really remove the deceased from the communal life; it only causes him by a happy exchange to enter the cycle of the mass of natural energies which permit perpetuation of the group.

A neolithic custom still surviving in Africa requires that the head of the dying rest on the lap of a woman of his family.[6] In ancient Chinese symbolism the bean put in a pot to germinate symbolizes the head.[7]

[6] In the famous account of Savitri in the *Mahabharata,* the dying husband rests in the arms of his wife, his head on her breast. The persistence of such images in the tradition affords "existential" depth to the expression of realities of a different order. Thus the return of the Son to the "bosom" of His Father, frequently evoked by ancient ecclesiastical writers, for example: "Quod si vis audire quid profuit Christo . . . Inclinasse caput super gremium Patris et tradidisse spiritum" (Origen, *In Mat. ser., P. G.* 13, 1789).

[7] "The rites concerning vegetable food are justified, because the fruit of the earth is the flesh of the ancestors; naming a child with an ancestral name affirms that the child is the substance of the forefather, and that he is furthermore, by virtue of the name, the same person as the ancestor, etc." (Leenhardt, in *Enc. Quillet,* I, 136).

Insofar as one can attain to some certainty about these dogmas, it seems that the Phrygian religion would be among those which best retain the archaic structure of the neolithic religion. A certain continuity of doctrine has existed from Chanaan to Phrygia passing through Ras Shamra. All three retain the custom—condemned by the Mosaic legislator—of cooking a goat in its mother's milk, a ritual in which the goat probably represents the god's son. This religion developed the "mysteries" in the course of which the mystic (probably identified with the god) declares: "Goat, I have fallen into the milk." This mystical death had the value of resurrection to a new life by a "return to the mother." These conclusions, which are those of Ramsay in an *E. R. E.* article, "Phrygians," 902 b, are in good part hypothetical, supported, however, by a common type of Phrygian epitaphs grouped around temples and appearing in the form of dedications in which the deceased is assimilated to the divinity. Still, Cumont adds prudently: "In truth, we scarcely

Such things show the very widespread belief that the newborn descends in a strict line from a primordial ancestor, the principal agent of all conception within his clan. To accuse the cerealist culture of materialism is nonsense. On the contrary, it is steeped in a religious valuation of all the gestures of the life it tightly encloses. The "sacred" is present everywhere; it is immanent in the smallest acts, for the least action is profoundly stamped by traditional values. It sets to work, more or less strongly, the generative powers which reside in the tribe. In this society, constantly bent over the cradle and the tomb, birth is an act permeated by the sacral. And death is of exactly the same order. Moreover, the dead were usually buried in the very earth of the house, and, in the most ancient Chinese custom, in the most distant and dark corner, where the seeds were stored and the marriage bed was set.

The idea that the soul—or one of the souls—of the dead seeks, more or less immediately after death, for a womb in which to reincarnate itself probably belongs to the same context. Very possibly it is only the "soul of life" which carries on this change of habitation; the "soul of death," on the contrary, remains near the

---

know in what manner the Phrygian priests imagined the happiness of the world beyond" (*Rel. Orient.*, p. 56).

"In several Hallstatt cemeteries in France dating from before the Merovingian period, one finds the dead decapitated, the head placed upon the lap" (Wernert, in *Enc. Quillet*, I, pp. 53-72). On the Chinese ideogram for "head," cf. *Anthropos*, 1950, 4-6. In the Polynesian archipelago there exists a mystique of the "decapitated head," related to sexual love, fertility, and happiness in the next world.

As we shall see later, this complex of rituals and of "agrarian" beliefs is still recognizable in the background of the religions of Egypt and Mesopotamia.

body in the tomb. The former is less strictly individualized than the latter, and was often represented as the "breath," itself communicating with and participating in the great cosmic breath which unites all the living to the rhythms of the universe. According to other, similar conceptions of the meaning given to this common power of life, this soul returns to a "reservoir" of souls, imagined sometimes as the heavenly storehouse of the world or as an underground storage pit out of which a redistribution of life will be made *in tempore opportuno*. The "remembrance" of the dead is attached, on the contrary, to the soul of the dead or, better, the surviving soul. This soul keeps its earthly attachments and prowls around the places with which its past loves and hates are connected. But in itself its life gradually weakens, as does its memory in the minds of those who live on. Abandoned by its own, it suffers from hunger and thirst and seeks in the filth of gutters and latrines for something with which to sustain its miserable existence. Becoming spiteful, it sometimes plays outrageous tricks, which can be prevented by observing the prescriptions for the worship of the *manes* offerings of food placed in some familiar corner of the house or on the threshold. One must sometimes go to the length of killing this burdensome vestige of the dead—but without violence! These souls will so voraciously satisfy what remains to them of hunger for life[8] that they will quickly rejoin the mass of fecundating forces diffused in nature. By libation rituals or types of baptism one may obtain for the dead—and at the same time for the living—the tranquil forgetfulness which the Greeks attributed to the waters of Lethe.

[8] Buddha passed into *nirvana* as a result of indigestion.

The accounts of the trials that souls had to undergo before attaining the final stage of their rest belong to another cycle of beliefs that can easily be grouped around the idea of initiation.[9]

These beliefs, unlike those just described, which are valid for all, apply only to a privileged category of the dead, the initiates. This initiation can be accomplished by the funeral rites themselves, or else an initiate—a shaman —undertakes to accompany the soul on its final and dangerous voyage. The dead who are accorded this privileged destiny are thus in some way the "elect," the "heroes," and the process carried out for this end can be considered a "heroization." In it, fire often plays an essential role in its quality of most noble element, present in the stars and supremely victorious. In opposition to the funeral libations, fire serves to exalt, to "purify" as quickly as possible from its perishable ties the divine and immortal part of man. Cremation is connected to the line of "burning" ascesis (*tapas*) in which the yogi devoted themselves to drying out between four fires the "humours" which keep the soul in collusion with the impermanence

---

[9] Among the Ojibway, "when an individual dies, he makes his way toward the abode of the dead until he comes to a huge strawberry. If he tastes it, all return to the land of the living will become forever impossible for him. . . . Innumerable accounts of this type describe incidents which are happening or have happened in those closed-off places where the initiate dwells 'dead to the profane world,' and where the visitor, if he gains admittance, must observe very strict rules. It is especially necessary for him to abstain carefully from touching food or drink which is offered him, otherwise by this ingestion of a divine substance that penetrates to the heart of his being, he will be incorporated forever into the sacred and can no longer obtain permission to return to the regions of ordinary mortals" (Gordon, *op. cit.,* v. I, pp. 254-255). The pomegranate seed of Persephone must have had this significance.

of things of earth. There is not now question of promoting the natural flow of vital power into the pent-up wave of rebirths, but on the contrary of making every effort to escape from it. Schematicizing to an extreme degree, one could say that these two great types of beliefs in an afterlife have the same relationship as the moon and the sun, the lunar sphere marking the limit of the turbulences proper to the biosphere, and the one beyond that beginning the reign of the "immortal" heavenly bodies.

It would be rash, although tempting, to claim that those cycles gave birth to opposite notions of the divine, with the conception of the cremators progressing toward a transcendent god and those practicing burial feeling the principle of the "sacred" as immanent. Though the divine for the cremators has taken a heavenly habitation, it is nonetheless also situated at the interior of the universe. It has only been concentrated in the "head" of the cosmos by correspondence with the mental step which gave value to the human activities situated in the head, mainly sight and hearing, the most "spiritual" of the senses and the ones best able to conquer total cosmic space to the profit of the infinitesimal space where the consciousness is situated. Thus an anthropology and a cosmology for the use of princes, sovereigns who claimed universal hegemony, took their rise. Mankind nevertheless hesitated on the threshold of these celestial palaces, as the poem of Gilgamesh demonstrates. Is it not an act of "hybris" par excellence for man to pretend to pass through the fiery portals of immortality?

By the correspondence established between microcosm and macrocosm, by the elevation of the "high" in relation to the "low," the method of ascension becomes the central symbol of this religious mentality. It is obviously difficult to determine how and why the esteeming of heavenly and immortal things is connected to the practice of an initiation ritual. "Cerealist" societies, moreover, have never been entirely impervious to such rituals. There were societies where girls were initiated, although this was much rarer than the initiation of boys. Some have wanted to see in initiation the essential theme and the key to universal religious phenomena. Without going that far, we can admit that the theme of initiation opens up a special approach to the understanding of a great many religious facts. The neophyte has access to a new life based on values which had previously been concealed from him or grasped only in formless confusion with wholly profane values. From the initiation trial arises a new man. Initiation is a second birth. Up to a certain point—the painful character of the initiation ordeals is evidence—the scale of profane values is reversed. What attracts becomes dangerous; what terrifies becomes desirable. The horrors of the first age are found to be surmountable through the grace of the ritual which, as it symbolizes the death of the candidate, gives him the courage to face the event. The initiate thus achieves the right to be seated at the table of the gods, he shares the food of immortality, he has passed beyond the human condition. Death itself, experienced symbolically in the initiation drama, has become a sacrament of life. Salvation becomes metaphysical.

The rite is not only the entry into the mystery but also its culmination. The weight of its meaning extends to the dimensions of the whole. By it, man takes possession of the world and becomes man. If man is a world in miniature, the world in its turn is thought of as "macranthrope." Death ceases to have power over the one who knows this. All the philosophy of the Upanishad concerns the establishment of these correspondences which confer upon the individual the permanence of the cosmic order. Rapport between man and the world is established by the intervention of a middle term, the ritual. The development of rites permits man to espouse integrally the rhythms and the modes of life of the cosmos. Obviously, it is easy to associate these views with the agrarian conceptions of the "eternal return" of the cycle of vegetative life. Nevertheless, the idea of initiation supplements them by a not unimportant element of religious psychology. The initiate is one who has taken possession of his destiny by knowledge. He has taken its measure in thinking of himself as dead. A more or less strict parallel is thus established between the development of rituals which follow the mystical death of the candidate and the events marking the voyage of a soul after death, death itself being thus assimilated to a *rite of passage*.

According to whether the initiation rite required a journey into usually forbidden lands or an ascent to "heaven" up the side of a cliff or a post with notches— often seven in number—the soul was thought to penetrate after death into a strange region in search of the place of its repose or to mount to heaven by traversing the interplanetary stages in the course of its dangerous ascent. One of the aims of the funeral ceremonies was the sending of assistance by the living to the dead person along his difficult route. The funerary sacrifice was as it were a screen through which the most essential objects were permitted to follow the deceased[10] into the next world. But often the world of the dead is thought of as having characteristics opposite to those in the world of the living. A sacrificial animal or one killed in the hunt returns to the country of his ancestors and serves them as game. If they in their turn have good hunting and scrupulously observe their rituals in the world beyond, the reproduction of the animals will be assured regularly in this world and the tribe will have no famine. The arrow of the dead warrior is broken because to be useful in the world of the dead it must be unusable by the living. This idea of an introduction by violence into the "kingdom of the heavens" is perhaps at the basis of the ancient religious conception of the penalty of death. This penalty is usually thought of as a satisfaction adequate to atone for the fault committed, a fault which by its nature would exclude the guilty one from the community and thus from the benefit of the vital forces of which it is the bearer. These vital forces are, however, again made accessible to him who promptly submits to the penalty of death, for it offers deliverance from the malediction incurred and gives a person access to the community of his ancestors, to the "sacred" society.

Dying on the Cross, that is to say by an ignominious death which was felt to prolong His "excommunication" into the world beyond, Christ nevertheless arose gloriously, and it was for nothing less than this that His disciples (themselves under the threat of the same excommunication) kept up the hope of being seated at the Messianic feast promised only to the members of the

[10] Cf. *Histoire des Religions*, Brillant and Aigrain, v. I, pp. 279 and 289; *Enc. Quillet*, v. I, p. 155.

initiated community of the sons of Abraham. It was thus entirely natural that the Christian initiation rite evoked in St. Paul the opprobrium of the Cross and that he used it forcefully in his disputation against the Galatians, who were tempted to give up their hope in the Law (Gal. 2:15—3:1). And if he used it also in the mythic category of the new Adam it is because it was certain to arouse in his hearers an echo conditioned by the ancient religions of mankind accustomed to contemplate in initiation rituals the reproduction of events marking the "typic" life of the ancestor. By an "initiatic" inversion of values, it is the death of the new Adam which becomes the origin of eternal life.

The ladder of Jacob, the value accorded to the memory of the forty years in the desert, the mystique of the "going up" to Jerusalem, show that the great initiation images of an ascension to heaven and a pilgrimage to the "center" of the earth had found an audience in Israel. By circumcision, Israel declares itself a people of initiates. The Pharisees' hope in the resurrection is based upon the sacred solidarity established by the covenant between the God who gives the breath of life and His chosen people. Christian hope, based upon the baptismal initiation, would only have to transpose these categories to find its traditional expression.

The tendency of initiation religions toward an "ascensional" mystique, which usually related them to monotheism by means of "heavenly" gods, sometimes had the consequence of making the divine so remote and so incommensurable with the human condition that it was necessary to make appeal to mediators who could bridge the chasm. The "hero" was one of these mediators. The alternation of the values of life and of death which is at the basis of the "cerealist" culture gives to the cult of heroes a dramatic power and a capacity for poetic creation which is not granted in the same measure to the serene religions whose regard is fixed on the things above. We have pointed out from the beginning of this study the importance of the chief in reincarnating in himself the tribe's destiny. When the chief dies, the tribe itself in some way dies. Thus it is imperative that the chief be resurrected, even though in another world, in such a state that his function in life continues to be carried out. On the one hand the chief reincarnates part of himself in his descendants; and on the other hand he rejoins the gods, or at least his forefathers, in a place where he continues his beneficent action. Because this function is primarily to give life, it is to the solar divinity, source of all life, from whom the chief had, even in life, obtained his power, that he becomes assimilated by the funeral rituals. The theology of heroes is usually a solar theology. M. Éliade has shown that it unites certain "sublime" elements in the cult of the "heavenly" gods with more dramatic elements whose central theme is struggle between light and darkness. Celestial gods and solar gods had in common a certain mysterious aspect which permitted them to preside over the fate of the dead as well as of the living. We find a good example of such a theology in Egypt.

It should be pointed out that the solar gods, as distinct from the celestial gods, are not creators but only organizers of the cosmos. Richer in myth, the sun gods are also daily more present to men's imagination than the celestial deities, who are more remote. Also, they are more often savior gods, themselves "saved" through a victory of truth over the dark works of an enemy of cosmic dimension. Complex ties, sometimes quite close (as seems to be the case in Chanaan), attach them to the fertility cults. The dramatic action in which they find themselves engaged makes them strongly delineated personalities, even where the gods, as in the Indo-Iranian domain, had a general tendency to be only hypostatized functions. See, for example, the portrayal of the personage of Indra in the Indian veda and of Mithra in Iran. When, through these "mysteries," the faithful participate in the glorious deed of a god, this can lead in principle to a more individualized idea of the salvation of souls after death. If the god undergoes a "death" and a "resurrection," his devotee becomes capable by participation of reproducing the divine victory over death. But this generally complete and coherent outline can be utilized as a valid explanation only here and there, where one can assemble proof that the progress of concrete religious thought has indeed developed along this line, and there seems to have been no case in which the proofs have been completely established.[11] At best we can arrive at more or less strong presumptions, and that is true in most situations of this kind. In fact, this is one of the main types. At any rate, in this schema a relation between the faithful man and his god is not brought about by a conversion of heart but more by an "engagement" of

---

[11] M. Éliade, *Traité d'Histoire des Religions,* section 46, pp. 135-138. The discussion of this thesis in regard to Osiris, Adonis, Eshmoun, Asklepios, Melqart, Attis, Mithra, and Dionysos can be found in Fr. Nötscher, *Altorientalischer und alttestamentlischer Auferstehungsglauben,* Würtzburg, 1926.

a military type or by a demonstration of loyalty towards the head of the State representing on earth the god-protector of the city. The privileged condition of the "soldier" who dies on the battlefield, known in the ancient epic of Gilgamesh, is guaranteed, even outside the case of a strictly "heroic" death, to those who have prepared themselves by the "sacrament."

This rapid survey has permitted us to view the main categories which historians of religion utilize when trying to determine the religious context in which the idea of the resurrection, as taught in Judaism and then in a profoundly modified version in early Christianity, especially by St. Paul, could have been born. It remains to examine the extent to which the historic religions with which the Judaeo-Christian tradition was in contact had developed beliefs which could have prepared or suggested the idea of the resurrection of the dead and also to what extent, in each case, borrowing of this type is probable. As we have pointed out, Mazdaism is the only one of all these religions which had a belief in the resurrection really comparable to that of the Bible. Its case is thus the most important and the most difficult. We shall discuss it a little more fully at the end of this first chapter.

Before Abraham left Ur of the Chaldees the wise men of Egypt were already seriously speculating on the meaning of human existence. Toward the middle of the twenty-third century B.C., a wave of scepticism infiltrated religious thought, throwing into question both man's origin and his state after death. This occurred at the end of the sixth dynasty, when the culture of the Nile already had behind it a rich past. At least in lower Egypt the prehistoric foundations can be considered with assurance to have been of the "cerealist" type we described above. Without doubt, the people there lived intimately with the dead. The conception of the tomb as the dwelling place of the dead, so tenaciously held in Egypt, and the related custom of making repeated offerings to serve the dead person as provisions probably date from this period. There is little possibility of error here when one traces back to this date and this milieu the first roots of the cult of Osiris, evidently connected with the periodic rebirth of vegetative life caused by the river's flooding. Later we shall describe briefly its fully developed form.

The appearance of the "negative confession" and heaviness of heart in funerary texts of very early date raises questions. Undoubtedly these texts are witness to an undercurrent of belief, whose first traces go back to before the sixth dynasty, in a judgment by God upon the actions of men. This belief exists independently of the various local cults which annexed it. If the most explicit example, the *Book of the Dead,* is a manual of magical practices planned to permit a dead person to escape punishment through a clever speech that deceives the judges but is only a lie, one cannot conclude that such was the original or general conception. And the mere fact of the care with which the "negative confession" is minutely related in the text suffices to prove that even unscrupulous magicians could not in the least prevent an exalted idea of the divine exigencies from entering the thought of a blessed future. The stereotyped form of these "negative confessions" only indicates that, as so often happens, social conformism had weakened the religious sense, and that the dead person was supposed to comply by a facile gesture that did not involve a very deep change of heart. There is no indication that the Pharisees' belief in the resurrection of the just, conceived as a moral sanction, was ever influenced by the Egyptian idea of the judgment of the soul. If Egyptian belief had any influence on the formulation of the eschatalogical beliefs of Judaism and Christianity, it was in the elaboration of the idea of a particular judgment. This is a possibility, at least in relation to the Alexandrine theology of the last things.

The worship of Osiris and its corollary, the "Osirization" of the dead deserves more attention. It seems to have developed dramatic myths around the tomb of the Thinite kings at Busiris in the delta, and its practice became general in the predynastic period. In Egypt, a royal tomb is par excellence a monument of immortality.[12] More clearly than elsewhere we find here the religious phenomenon of the "heroizing" of the chief. The strongly centralized social structure of Egypt is paralleled even in the afterlife. The forms of the pharaoh's sepulture and the rituals for his embalming have not merely an individual and topical interest; they are a true, collective representation of the values fundamental to the Egyptian fatherland.

[12] The blessedness of the dead "Osirized" in Amentis was certainly doubted at some date, but the apologetic note in certain funerary inscriptions from the middle of the fourteenth century suffices to prove, contrary to Nötscher, that the hope of the faithful was genuine, since it experienced the need to "give witness to" the faith. Here for instance is a text from a Theban tomb:

All ye excellent nobles, the Ennead of the Mistress of Life,
Hear ye how praises are made to the god's father,
With homage paid to the excellent noble's efficacious soul,
Now that he is a god living forever,

Thus it is noteworthy that it was around a royal tomb that the Osirian drama was represented. We shall limit ourselves to a review of its essential characteristics, those which help to penetrate the meaning of the myth of the resurrection of the god.

Osiris, son of the earth-god and the heaven-goddess, succeeded to the government of this world. He was a victorious king who brought to an end the conflicts that broke out in various places. Isis, who was both his sister and his wife, took over the functions of ruler while he was at battle. But Seth, his brother, who was jealous of his success, was able to draw him into an ambush. According to the Hellenistic (and thus later) version of the story, Seth had a chest built to the measurements of Osiris and then offered it during a banquet to the one who would fill it most exactly. When Osiris accepted the challenge, the chest was closed and thrown into the Nile. Osiris was cast upon the shore at Byblos, where

---

Magnified in the West.
May they become a remembrance for the future,
For all who come to pass by.
I have heard those songs which are in the ancient tombs
And what they tell in magnifying (life) on earth
And in belittling the necropolis.
Why is it that such is done to the land of eternity,
The right and true, without terrors?
Quarreling is its abomination,
And there is no one who arrays himself against his fellow.
This land which has no opponent—
All our kinsfolk rest in it since the first day of time.
They who are to be, for millions of millions,
Will all have come to it. (Reprinted from *Ancient Near Eastern Texts,* ed. James B. Pritchard, by permission of Princeton University Press, 1950, pp. 33-34.)
What must be retained from Nötscher's thesis is that real hope was not devoid of feelings of anguish and uncertainty (E. Otto, *Ägypten,* p. 79).

Isis found him at the end of a tearful search. (According to an older version, the body was found in the mud of the Nile, already putrefied.) Thanks to the help of various gods, among whom we should note Ra, the sun, Osiris was brought back to life. The ancient, wholly Egyptian versions of the story restore him to life in the mythical region of the "West"; it is Hellenistic humanism that brought him back to live among ordinary human beings.

In the predynastic period, the faithful of Osiris hoped to be born again with the god in his Western paradise.[13] It is very remarkable (see p. 15) to note that their chief occupation there was essentially the cultivation of corn of a gigantic size with a stalk taller than that of palm trees and ears exceeding the size of a man! The requirement for attaining to this blessed state was the enactment for the corpse of the dead person of the same rituals which had resurrected the body of the god.[14] Neither this Osirian conception of immortality, nor the solar conception we shall soon describe succeeded in supplanting in men's minds the older idea of the survival of the

[13] F. Daumas, "The Significance of Gold in Egyptian Thought," *R. H. R.*, January, 1956, pp. 6 ff., shows how this divinization of the pharaoh and later of all those who shared his privilege in demonstrated by the simple fact of the importance given to gold, or to the color yellow substituted for it, in the sarcophagus and the tomb. Gold is the flesh of the gods. "Your body is enriched with gold," was recited before the mummy. Osiris owed his incorruptibility to his golden body. Gold had so sacred a character that private individuals had to be contented with a posthumous, participated divinization, not theirs by essence as with the god-king.

[14] Some have wished to find in Osirian teaching the origin of the mysterious expression (very rare in the documents of contemporary Judaism), the "bosom of Abraham," used by Christ to describe the resting place of poor Lazarus (Preuschen-Bauer, in Kittel, *T. W. N. T.,* s.v. Κόλπος), but this thesis is based on that of the *refrigerium,* interpreted as a funeral banquet presided over by the "Osirized" dead person.

deceased in the tomb. The combination of these divergent notions occurred without any particular logic, as often happens with beliefs about the afterlife.

The other "immortalizing" current in Egypt centered in the figure of Ra. But before this topic can be pursued, we must consider the development of a myth from the last creative epoch of religious significance in Egypt, the troubled period at the end of the sixth dynasty, whose importance we sketched earlier. Ra had become old— during the period of the pharaohs—and rebellious men caused his throne to totter. He then sent the lion-goddess Sachmet to destroy this ungrateful race. But he soon changed his mind and through a ruse avoided the total destruction of humanity. A similar theory of universal "crisis" and thus of "apocalypse" appears in a myth of the Osirian cycle in which it is Atum, the creator, identified with the evening sun, who plays the chief role. Atum decides to reduce the universe by a flood to the original state of chaos from which he had once drawn it. Only Osiris safely passes through this cataclysm. Originating in a period of Bedouin incursions and the dismemberment of the kingdom, these ideas had been brought up to date by the time of the invasion of the Hyksos, which is thought to have resulted in the migration of the tribe of Jacob. We may be able to distinguish some trace of these ideas in the account of the

---

While it is very probable that Egypt had a certain influence upon Jewish and Christian funeral rituals, it is much less clear that this influence was extended to the conception of eschatological hopes. For instance, the expression *domus aeternitatis,* borrowed from Egypt as a decoration for tombs, does not involve borrowing the idea of survival in the tomb, from which the expression originated.

Egyptian plagues. The latter are of interest here because they suggest, as does the account of the flood, that the end of one world can be the beginning of another for the whole of mankind. When resurrection is thought of, as it is in Judaism, as the beginning of a *new creation* (according to the general rabbinic idea of rebeginnings of the divine work; the flood, the passage through the Red Sea, etc.) the parallel here, however vague, is worth noting.

"The believers in the solar doctrine began to develop a funerary doctrine within the framework of their theology at the beginning of the fifth dynasty with the advent of a royal house originating in Heliopolis and holding its own special beliefs. They first associated the doctrine with the king, to whom they accorded a different state from that of ordinary mortals, like that which the religion of Osiris had allowed to its faithful. Just as the rituals of embalming, by transforming the dead into an Osirian removed him from the power of the earth-god in order to introduce his soul into the West, so the special lustrations, a kind of baptism of the dead, conferred upon the king's spirit the dignity of a Heliopolitan and gave him access to the empyrean. He was admitted into the ship of the sun" (Drioton, *Hist. des Rel.,* Brillant and Aigrain, III, p. 114). The eighteenth dynasty, which interred its dead in the famous Valley of Kings, for the first time separated the tomb from the temple where the cult of the divinized pharaoh was observed. All the decoration of the tomb strongly emphasized the solar immortality conferred upon the dead. Meanwhile, in this period, the pharaoh's privilege was already being shared by anyone able to be admitted to the royal cemetery, which had at first been reserved to the highest court dignitaries but was gradually extended to all functionaries. The bath of natron continued to be the proper ritual of "solarization." Nevertheless, even in the royal tombs, so full of evidences of a celestial immortality, the dead *dwelt,* as is proved by the abundance of funerary furniture and many other indications.

When we remember the close and prolonged relation between Israel and Egypt during almost all periods in the history of the chosen people, we can only be surprised that there is so little similarity between their eschatological conceptions. Surely the idea of survival in the tomb existed throughout the "fertile crescent," but it had been only slightly elaborated in Phoenicia, under the immediate influence of Egypt: Osiris was cast up at Byblos, according to the Hellenistic account. In Phoenicia, the dead were placed in a stone sarcophagus shaped like the Egyptian but without its furnishings and decoration. The account of the return of Joseph's bones to the promised land is evidence that Israel was acquainted with Egyptian customs, but the cave of Machpelah does not have the same significance as the Nile tombs. It bears witness to the settling of the Hebrews, in the persons of their ancestors, in the land which God had destined for them. We should note, however, that the two peoples had a similar idea of the dignity and the importance of the *body* in assuring the survival of the "individual" after death. Neither the Egyptians nor the Jews, moreover, practiced cremation.[15]

---

[15] "When, under the republic, the Alexandrian mysteries spread into Italy, no religion had yet brought such an explicit promise of blessed immortality to man and this is what attracted them irresistibly. In

Cretan culture, particularly where funerary rituals are concerned, occupied a kind of position ahead of Egypt in the direction of Greece. Ancient Crete had devoted its principal worship to the Great Mother, whose domain included both the living and the dead. As a result, the conception of the afterlife of the dead was very closely connected with that of the ever-renewed fecundity of the earth. The parallel between belief in an afterlife and the state of seed planted in the earth played an important role among the Cretans. Moreover, the very spiritualized symbols of the chrysalis and the butterfly are also found in the decorations of Cretan tombs.[16] For their part, the Indo-European invaders who founded Mycenaean civilization seem to have had more gross ideas. Dead princes were not divinized, like those of Crete and Egypt, but were "heroized." The respect surrounding their tombs resembled a little that which the Israelites accorded those of the patriarchs. The "founders" of the Greek cities were buried *intra muros,* close to the gates of the city. There they received libations intended for the good of all, to preserve what they retained from the life of the city. The worship given them is that which, more fully developed, was given to every head of a family returning to his ancestors. In structure, the Mycenaean tombs resembled those of the Scythians. The ideas on which they were based were essentially the same as those under-

place of the irresolute and contradictory opinions of the philosophers on the soul, Serapis (or Osiris-Apis) offered a certainty based upon a divine revelation and corroborated by the faith of unnumbered generations who had been devoted to it" (F. Cumont, *Les Religions Orientales,* p. 92).

[16] Cf. *Enc. Quillet,* v. II, pp. 20-23, and p. 188.

lying the building of burial mounds in Gaul. The needs of the dead were imagined as similar to those of the living.

We should not confuse the area of beliefs concerning a subterranean world with those related to fertility.[17] Despite their frequent contacts, these cycles were not necessarily connected. We must avoid any classification that unduly simplifies the observable facts. One may direct this criticism to those religionists who divide all the Mediterranean evidences on the afterlife into two sets, one connected with the "Orphean" mystique with its individualistic tendencies, the other with an Irano-Judaic apocalyptic whose preoccupations are mainly collective.[18] This approach is part of the development of a new and popular trend in the domain of the science of religions: the vogue of shamanism. In particular, Orpheus, a figure upon whom opinion is still extremely divided, is the mythic model of a shamanistic tradition imported from Thrace and Scythia, but inspiring Empedocles and even Plato. In this view, Zoroaster also was a shaman. These explanations are attractive at first glance but certainly require that the "shaman" concept be subjected to an adequate preliminary treatment: so far, the definition is cut to measure. In his remarkable book, *The Greeks and the Irrational,* Sather locates belief in metempsychosis in this area and even makes of it one of the essential features connecting Plato with shamanism. A no less competent Iranist in his field than Sather, Nyberg has made Zoroaster a shaman, although there is not the slightest evidence in the *Gatha* in

[17] Nilsson, *op. cit.,* p. 191.
[18] Buonaiuti defends this thesis in *Eranos-Jahrbuch* 1936, pp. 165-166.

favor of the doctrine of metempsychosis. Such occurrences should make us cautious. One cannot help feeling that there is a certain relationship among these diverse evolutions, when one tries to see as a whole the modifications in the religious conceptions of Greece and the Orient of the sixth century before Christ. If we were more sure of the period in which Zoroaster lived—one of the most common opinions places it in the sixth century—these relationships could perhaps convince us that a religious propaganda originating north of the Crimean-Caspian-Pamir line, simultaneously reached Greece through Asia Minor, Iran through Khorassen and India through Gandhara. Bands of enthusiasts who practiced rigorous austerities traveled through towns and countryside astonishing their audiences by their thaumaturgic gifts. There are striking resemblances between the oldest type of bacchants and the brotherhoods of *vratya* found in certain regions in the north of India. About the same period transmigration became a presupposition common to all Indian religions. But the evidence remains too scattered and the relationships too tenuous for us to be able to build solidly upon such a hypothesis. Let us note in passing that the bands of prophets who lived in Israel from the time of Saul show some of the shamanistic traits described here, though this fact need have no significance as far as Israelite beliefs about the next world are concerned. If we alluded to the devotees of Dionysus, it is because a famous myth, which tells how the body of the god was devoured by the Titans (from whose ashes men were born), can serve as a point of departure for the belief that a divine spark was buried in the grave with the body, a doctrine which, under the

term Pythagorean, played a great role in Plato's idea
of the state of man after death.

The conclusion after many debates and innumerable
hypotheses is that we still have arrived nowhere in
determining the origin of the ideas of metempsychosis
which apparently developed simultaneously in different
places.[19] Where these ideas arose, belief in the survival
of a more "spiritual" part of the composite human being
developed into a systematic outline tending to provide
an answer to some of the most importunate questions
which human life presents. The striking differences between the lot which falls to men from birth, the unde-
served sufferings they undergo, and especially the scandal of the wicked who end in pleasure a life passed in
destroying the happiness and the life of others—all this
finds an explanation that satisfies our sense of justice if
we admit that the spiritual principle, burdened with the
moral past of the individual whose continuity it assures,
is reincarnated after death in this or that womb according
to the merits accumulated during its earlier lives. According to Josephus, historian of the Jewish wars, who
perhaps wishes to present the Jewish belief in the resurrection in a way more understandable to the pagan
mentality, the Essene sect taught this mode of eschatology. The influence of Pythagoreanism on Essenian

---

[19] The fundamental idea, of which the concept of metempsychosis is
only a special application, is the distinguishing of a more "divine" element in man which escapes from the vicissitudes of corruptible flesh.
This element, sometimes thought of as a separate entity, gave birth to
the conception of a *daimon,* given to man at birth and leaving him
only after conducting him to the tribunal where souls are judged. The
Platonic myths greatly enhanced these conceptions which, moreover,
became very popular, to the extent of providing the most light on pagan
funerary symbolism of the Christian era.

teaching is generally recognized, for both show a horror of bloody sacrifices consistent with the belief in the migration of the soul into the bodies of animals. Others have seen in this last point a connection with Zoroastrian teaching on religious respect for the life of pure animals, but in this case we must give up any parallelism in eschatological matters, for we have no evidence of a belief in metempsychosis in Mazdaism.

Before leaving our examination of metempsychosis in its relation to Judaism, we must ask to what extent this doctrine, broadly speaking, would have given the Jews the idea of the resurrection of the dead. For those who have had studied the texts, this hypothesis seems absolutely unconvincing, because the resurrection of the dead is not an opinion independent of any religious context, or one proceeding mainly from anthropological speculations. It is an essentially religious doctrine drawing all its meaning from a fundamental notion of a justice to be re-established by God on a day chosen by Him for releasing His people from opprobrium and restoring— to the living as well as the dead—the benefit of the unfailing Covenant He had made with them. The doctrine of metempsychosis, on the contrary, derives from a well-developed view of the constituent elements of the human personality, and while the idea of a just retribution can become so deeply engrafted upon it that it ends, as in India, by becoming identical with it, the justice which the law of karma affirms remains essentially *immanent,* and has nothing to do with the intervention of a transcendent God since it functions very well without Him. On the other hand, even on the level of anthropology, metempsychosis assumes that the transmigratory part of man bears with it his total personality; but it is only too evident that Jewish anthropology ignores such conceptions. This will be even more true with the Fathers of the Church, who made use of various opinions of the Hellenistic school when trying to define the idea of man which Christian teaching professes. For the apologists of the resurrection, Pythagoreanism sometimes seems an ally, but a dubious one, to be used only with caution. One point, the idea of a reincarnation of the soul as the moral sanction of an earlier life, could have had some influence on the way in which St. Paul explains the proportion between the appearance of the glorified body and the spiritual splendor of the soul. In the expressions used by the Apostle to convince the Corinthians (1 Cor. 15:39-40), if the argument drawn from the adaptation of each animal's body to its own proper milieu presupposes a Stoic background, that concerning the degrees of brightness of the stars is designed for those spirits imbued with the belief—largely vulgarized—in astral immortality, revived from the "Pythagorizing" Platonic myths which taught metempsychosis. On the other hand, those who became propagandists of this doctrine were also those who—like Plutarch, for example—defended the truth of oracles, and the same arguments served as a basis for both opinions. But one of these arguments, that based on memory, appears even in rabbinism, where it is used to support the opinion that a child in its mother's womb enjoys a knowledge of the universe which it will be deprived of at birth. In India as in Greece, it was always on these "second states" of dream and ecstasy that the partisans of transmigration claimed to base their opinion. The "oracle" received in dream is attested to even in the New Testament. What is completely absent from the Judaeo-Christian tradition is the use made of memory by paganism to render plausible the pre-existence of a soul or previous lives.[20] When the rabbis admitted the pre-existence of the soul created in the beginning by God and held in reserve until the day of birth, this pre-existence was conceived as inactive, the faculties of the soul remaining latent.[21]

In the Jewish mentality what is radically opposed to pagan views on transmigration is that the latter presuppose a belief in the eternity of the world. In the pagan views, present existence appears as a moment in an indefinite process without beginning or end. This conception cannot be reconciled with that of the sovereign act of a God, Creator and Providence, who determines each person's state after a probation sharply delimited by birth and death. The Jewish idea of the resurrection of the body, firmly based on the notion of judgment and a decision which cannot be appealed, is thus, despite cer-

[20] In the Judaism of Christ's time the opposition between flesh and spirit began to play a role but did not lead to a sharp dualism.

[21] Metempsychosis provided paganism with an answer to the problem of the apparently unjust differences in condition that divide men from birth. This problem was known to Judaism and there it took on an aspect even more difficult, because in Judaism God is unique, all-powerful and transcendent in relation to His creation. Rabbinism, which had known and sometimes adopted the idea of pre-existence, never used it to absolve God of responsibility for the inequality in the destiny of helpless infants. Philo, who worked out the Gnostic solutions, admitted that God, in the case of men, did not create alone but entrusted the completion of the work to angels, who were responsible for its imperfections. In Palestine, the solution was sought in the prescience of God and in free will; but if one attempts to resolve the problem of bad will thus, innocent suffering remains inexplicable. That is why Origen would combine the Palestinian solution with that of metempsychosis to develop his peculiar eschatological doctrine.

tain appearances, at the opposite pole from a doctrine of successive reincarnations each of which is a sanction upon the acts of the preceding one. These conceptions are irreconcilable, as an immanent justice contradicts the idea of a judgment of a transcendent God. The genesis of the Greek ideas on retribution in the afterlife will permit us to clarify this.

Although it is almost the Christian era before Judaism reveals the first traces of a dualist conception of man, contrasting body and soul, these ideas were, on the other hand, very old in Greece, where in the end they everywhere dominated the idea of man. Even among the Stoics, a certain "Platonism" was introduced, although they did not conceive the "pneumatic" part of composite man as absolutely immaterial. We explained earlier why we generally place in about the sixth century the contribution which oriented all Hellenistic anthropology in this way. At bottom probably lay the experiences of the "liberation" of the soul thanks to some "second state" subsisting in sleep or in induced ecstasy. Philosophy had as its ideal the freeing of the soul from bodily ties. This ideal thus strangely resembles that of the yogi. The rule of its ascetic effort is already the *agere contra,* with the aim of untying the bonds enchaining the spirit. Paradoxical formulas began to condense this new wisdom; for example, "To die is to live and to live is to die." About the sixth century B.C. we find both in Greece and in India conditions favorable to the development of a doctrine of *karma,* with its extreme ascetic consequences, but Greek humanism instinctively rejected certain Indian excesses, because it never ceased admiring the beauty of the body, no matter how strong its contempt for all that was perishable.[22] For a Greek, the beauty of forms is as imperishable as an "idea," while for an Indian all form is an obstacle to the reign of the "absolute." Beyond a common wish to escape from becoming by a separation between the spirit and fleshly life tormented by its passions, another presupposition of the doctrine of retributive reincarnation—personal responsibility—is thrown into relief about the same time in India as in Greece. In India it is evidenced in the teachings of Buddha and Jina, which follow a moral evolution that can be dated from about the sixth century. In Greece, Solon, the contemporary of Ezechiel, citing a law affirming the traditional principle of collective responsibility, comments on it by saying that the "innocent" pay for the guilty. The expression used, *anaitioi*, is a mute protest against past errors, and implies a profound change in mentality. In exile, Israel itself had deepened its moral conceptions in the same way, and there are evidences that Iran shared in the same movement of ideas.

But in Israel the idea of evading the risk of acting in the flesh by a flight into abstract ideas, or into the blissful unconsciousness of deep sleep, never arose. Neither the fusion of the *atman* in the *brahman* nor contempla-

[22] Greece saw the peculiar quality of the spirit to be intellectual activity, not purely receptive passivity, as in India. Contemplation of the harmonies present in the most divine parts of the cosmos was thought of as beatifying for the intelligence, which was drawn from the same substance as the heavenly bodies. The Gnostic mentality would more clearly approach the Indian conception, according to which the best in man is absolutely stranger to this world. Plotinus' chief complaint against the Gnostics would be their blasphemy of the divine stars. For a Greek, to blaspheme the mathematical beauty of celestial motions was to disavow that in man which rendered him fit even for the divine.

tion of the ideas was the object of the preaching of Yahweh's prophets, as a way of delivering man from the burdens of his destiny. Also, the ardent questioning of why the just man suffers will find, in the little Jewish world, as immediate response, only Job's protestations of innocence or the apparently endless alternations of Coheleth. The solution of late Judaism, in which the resurrection formed an integral part, has nevertheless now been initiated and is gradually developed in the oracles of Joel concerning the judgment of the peoples in the valley of Josaphat, to reach its termination in the revelation of the existence of the famous "Books" of Daniel in which all the acts of men would be found inscribed (Dan. 7:10). This is a judgment not only of nations but of every individual. The dead are called to it as well as the living. Thus it is necessary that they arise (Dan. 12:1-2). The revelation of personal responsibility, given at about the same time to the Greeks, to the Indians, and to the Hebrews, thus led to three different conceptions of man's state after death. Greek philosophy took refuge in the knowledge of the universe and of the universal and fixed its beatitude in the stars; Indian asceticism sought to go beyond good and evil and seek the conquest of the immanent absolute or its negative equivalent, nirvana; the Jewish prophet did not seek an escape from his anguish but preserved his faith in the transcendent justice of God, and it was thus that slowly, gropingly, the universal last judgment and the resurrection of the body was revealed to him. If the Israelites avoided the stumbling block of mysticism it was also because of the small importance to them of anthropological and cosmological speculation, in connection with problems that are essentially religious and moral.[23] Israel found neither in man nor in the universe a place of escape where the justice of God did not have access.

To those who would wish to establish a parallel between the hopes of an individual resurrection which the Eleusian mysteries or others of like kind awakened among their initiates and the resurrection as it is conceived in the Judaeo-Christian tradition, it is sufficient to recall that if the pagan mind had really been prepared for the apostolic teaching on this point, St. Paul would not have been confronted by mockery on the Areopagus and Augustine would not have had to declare three and half centuries later that the dogma of the resurrection was still the Christian teaching most violently rejected.

Since neither Egypt nor Greece afford us valid evidence in favor of the influence of their eschatological conceptions on belief in the resurrection, it is appropriate that we turn to the third great culture with which Israel had close relationships. Ties uniting the Semites of the west and the country between the rivers were numerous

[23] "The nucleus of belief in the resurrection was not found in the opinion of a school on immortality, but in immediate relation with concern for the personal salvation of each individual. This seemed guaranteed only by the thesis of a bodily resurrection. That is why the stress placed there is so strong that the Mishna declares: 'Those who say that the resurrection is not affirmed by the Law will have no part in the age to come.' If the Sadducees denied the resurrection and even immortality, they at the same time completely rejected the Messianic hope, at least under the form that later Judaism gave it" (Schürer, *Gesch. des jüdischen Volkes,* II, 458). "Hope of a resurrection and Messianic hopes were not at first independent and later harmonized; on the contrary, the desire to have a part in the Messianic kingdom gave birth to hope in a resurrection of the body" (*ibid.,* p. 633, no. 60).

and close. Abraham had begun his migration from Ur of the Chaldees, and Haran was a major stage in his itinerary. At a period much more important for our subject, the exile had led the chosen people of Israel to the banks of the rivers of Babylon. But it is near the time of the exile or shortly afterwards that there appear among the prophets those images of a rebirth of the nation which mingle poetic fiction and the realism of an extraordinary hope. We shall discuss the Mesopotamian and Semitic religions together, although Sumer and the first Phoenicians were not sons of Sem. The union between Sumer and Akkad on the one hand and between Tyre, Sidon, Byblos and the western Semites on the other was so close and so ancient, however, that from the point of view of eventual influence on Israel's thought, distinctions between the beliefs proper to each race are not only difficult to ascertain but in this case serve no real purpose.

In the thought of this culture, extending from the shores of the Mediterranean as far as Iran, death was not only the term where life ends.[24] Death and life are two powerful rivals which simultaneously exercise their sovereignty over each existence and with their contrasting colors compose the entire spectrum of reality. This conception, a grossly dualistic one, which comes to light on several occasions in the course of the history of religious thought in the Orient, can, however, just as well

[24] For this part of our explanation we are utilizing principally the works of Dhorme, but also the remarkable communication of the Dutch Assyriologist, Liagre-Böhl, to the Royal Flemish Academy of Belgium, October 18, 1947.

evolve as monism, because in it life is conceivable as springing up from the very womb of death, whose depths are thus not sterile.

Although the kingdom of death has its broad domains underground or in the ocean's depths, it is, nevertheless, able to make incursions into the world above. Is not the sun itself, the giver of life, just as capable of bestowing death? The god associated with the sun could thus neutralize from his own advantage the opposition—absolute at first glance—between the two realms of death and of life. It is, however, common in this cultural context to believe that the infernal empire is under the authority of a divine personage, a jealous keeper of the world of shades, of dust, of silence, and of thirst, who will never release those who once cross the gates of his domain.

In Babylonia, it is a goddess, Ereshkigal, who performs this function, but it is noteworthy that she has a husband, Nergal, in whom the character of the sun god, who gives life and also death, is still discernible, because he has two fathers, heaven (Enlil) and the abyss (Apsu). The ocean's large expanse of bitter waters—the Apsu—always seemed terrifying to the mainland Semites, and represented for them the enemy par excellence of the god whose victory put the universe in order and preserved life. Death is thought of as a return to the primordial qualities of dryness or moisture, since Enkiddu on the one hand returns by death to the filth of the original chaos, exactly as did the world itself in the course of the deluge which gave it new life, while on the other hand the shades of *sheol* are mainly thirsty, and the most useful service they await from the living is the funeral libation. There was thus an idea that the shade that left the body went to the dark fire reigning in the deepest underground places, while the buried remains gradually disintegrated into the element of water. In connection with this rudimentary anthropology, we should note the place bones occupy in the Semitic mentality. The eschatological significance of the figure of the lion arises without any question from the fact that it breaks even the bones of its victim; thus it has a power analogous to fire or the sun, and becomes a symbol of such power. As long as the bones exist, something of life also subsists, and a "spirit of life" can give them back flesh and breath and bring them to life again. It is these bones that one wishes may rest in peace, so that they will escape from fire or worms, which represent the radical destruction of the remains of the *individual*.[25]

The conflict between life and death takes a particularly dramatic turn when an exceptional personage, a god, goddess, or hero, joins the infernal power in single combat. It is thus admitted that some personages, like Ishtar, succeeded in returning from hell, or at least, like Gilgamesh, almost achieved immortality by their exploits.[26]

[25] A destruction that leaves no traces behind it seems to the Hebraic mind to be without remedy: 2 Kings 23:16-18; Is. 38:13; Dan. 6:17. The fire and the worms in Is. 66:24 represent this absolute curse, which is opposed to the image of a peaceful "sleep" of the bones; cf. Jud. 16:17; Sir. 7:17. Nergal, the Babylonian god of the underworld, had the lion for his sign.

[26] Enkiddu, the companion of Gilgamesh, failed in his "descent" to the underworld because he did not observe the advice of his friend: to show himself there only in the mean guise of one who stoops to the dust. Ishtar penetrated hell only after despoiling herself of all glory. Hades could be conquered only by observing its laws. This specifically Semitic idea is a kind of distant adumbration of the victory of Christ through the Cross. Cf. I. Mendelsohn, *Religions of the Ancient Near East, Sumero-Akkadian Religious texts and Ugaritic Epics*, pp. 111-113, 120-122.

The meaning given in the Stoic philosophic myths to the figure of Hercules doubtless was inspired by Semitic ideas. Thus Hercules appears on the sarcophagi of the Hellenistic period as the vanquisher of death.

It is not difficult to see how suggestive are these Semitic facts for those attempting to establish the origins of belief in the resurrection of the dead. On this point, Father Lagrange wrote in his great work, *Religion des Sémites:* "The idea of the resurrection is found everywhere, just as the idea of renewal is universal in mythology. More than once there are cases in which the power of the infernal gods having been broken, hell casts up its prey. One of these perspectives was doubtless not very sympathetic to the living, the one in which escaping spirits came to trouble humans; a soul badly cared for by its descendants could become as baneful to them as a demon—and what about general invasion of spirits into the realm of the living? But there was a more sublime hope, that real life might be given back to the dead. Among the ancient Semites, only the Babylonians and the Hebrews have left us writings posing these serious problems. We have almost no ancient materials from the other Semites and their literature from the early period could have been influenced in a contrary sense by materialistic ideas. We can conclude nothing positive about them. But if one thinks of the extraordinary influence exercised by the Chaldeans in the religious domain and of the number of rather exalted beliefs common to all the Semites, one will not be far wrong to place the resurrection of the body among the ideas prevailing in the Semite world about 2,000 B.C., and the care taken with sepulture finds in the hope of resurrection a still more complete explanation. . . ." pp. 294-295).

Since Father Lagrange wrote these optimistic lines, new facts are changing the picture. It remains true that the Semites all held cremation, which was widely practiced in the other sectors of the ancient religious world, to be repugnant. But through the discoveries of Ras-Shamra we now possess rather extensive remains of a religious literature whose redaction antedates the Bible and which offers evidence about the religion of a Semitic branch adjacent to the Hebrews. Deciphering these remains is difficult, but so far nothing decisively favoring belief in the resurrection of the dead has been found in them. On the contrary, what is more and more confirmed is the profound homogeneity of religious sentiment throughout the whole Semitic world. The great images which epitomize the religious sensibilities of these peoples remain substantially the same throughout space and time. This common foundation is so constituted that the appearance of belief in a resurrection of the dead should immediately have found an enthusiastic response.[27]

The myth of the death of the warrior Mot confirms in effect what is known in the Semitic realm (through

[27] The conclusion of Bousset, *Rel. des. Jud.,* p. 594, insists upon the heterogeneous character of the elements Judaism integrated for its eschatology, while praising the genius of the apocalyptic writers and the rabbinical theologians who succeeded in outlining a valid synthesis from strange and chaotic fantasies. To us, it does not seem possible to explain the development of Israel's eschatological beliefs in this way, which assumes a massive and unreflective borrowing by popular acclaim, followed by a difficult work of elaboration and assimilation by thinkers. The borrowing, although occurring through popular channels, was not blind. Each borrowed feature was taken up because it answered a question that had become urgent by contact with another religious culture and only because, to the religious consciousness of Israel, it seemed at least in its

late accounts of the worship of Adonis) about the god of vegetation who dies and comes back to life. Here as in Egypt, on a common basis of neolithic culture, stories and dramatic rituals flourished, centered on the figure of a god who is son and husband, in whom death and life alternate by his "passion" and his "resurrection." In this view, as we explained above, death and life are on exactly the same level; they are religious values which are opposite but of the same genre. But there is no clear evidence that the resurrection of the god was a prototype of the rebirth of man, as it evidently was for vegetal life. The same situation exists in Babylon, in Ishtar's escape from the underworld where Ereshkigal wished to imprison her. The impression is that if a goddess as powerful as Ishtar could escape this misfortune only by great suffering, there was no hope that men could ever escape from the grip of the infernal powers. The poem of Gilgamesh, as a whole, leaves precisely the same impression.[28] Nevertheless the whole poem centers around

bare essence, if not in the organic place it occupied in the culture from which it was borrowed, to accord with the fundamental Mosaic revelation. Moreover, one must insist more than Bousset did upon the peculiarly Semitic character of many of the features appearing later in the development of Judaic eschatology. Hidden for a time by the deliberate austere expression of a Yahwism not yet assertive enough to employ freely the myths borrowed from pagan recollection, these latent traits reappeared after the exile, when the religious conscience of Israel, forged in sorrow, had less to fear from pagan licentiousness than from a narrow legalism against which the expansion of the apocalyptic spirit was surely a healthy reaction.

[28] "Although celestial powers play a role there, it is man who holds the chief place, and not the gods. The axis upon which the epic turns is man's fear of the inevitable: sickness, old age, and death; and his desire for the unattainable: perpetual health, glory, and immortality. These are the eternal problems which make this literary *chef d'oeuvre* an immortal monument" (I. Mendelsohn, *op. cit.*, p. 47).

the problem posed by man's death. This question certainly haunted the Semitic spirit. The first pages of Genesis, exactly like the myth of Adapa, have no other aim than to work toward a solution. In both accounts, immortality and perfect knowledge appear incompatible in man. Adapa loses his immortality in a manner somewhat resembling the way Adam lost his, but while there is food which Adapa (like Adam) may take or not take, Adapa seems to be, in the end, the innocent victim of a quarrel among gods and not a sinner responsible for his condition. The problem is succinctly stated. Though believing it extravagant for man to presume to eternal life the Semite, on the other hand, thinks that man naturally tends to immortality and that he would be capable of it if an accidental circumstance in the relations between man and the gods had not fixed him in his mortal condition.

Nevertheless, as we have said, except in the case of unusual divine or semidivine personages, no one was thought to escape the confines of Hades. This suggests both a providential action peculiar to the realm of Semitic culture which provides a human means of expression for the future revelation of dogma, and at the same time the unique quality of the privilege of Israel, for whom alone these foreshadowings bore fruit. These observations are valid only for the people of the ancient Orient, including the Semites, whose conceptions of the state of the dead we have already studied. The question of the Iranians remains open. But, up to the present, the fact that the people best known to Israel by race and culture provided a "natural milieu" where belief in the resurrection could develop reduces the chance that this belief came to Israel from a nation like Iran, whose religious categories were much stranger to Israel than those of Egypt, Phoenicia, or Babylonia.[29]

The condition lacking in the common Semitic foundation for the development of a doctrine of the resurrection of the dead comparable to that of Judaism is the idea of a judgment of God, progressively extended to "all flesh."[30] But the development of the idea of judgment in Israel shows a continuous line leading from the "Day of Yahweh," the simple settling of an account with a turbulent neighbor, to the cosmic views of the late apocalyptics. When the idea of a universal judgment developed, it was normal that the preparatory elements, diffused through the images of "life" and "death" that Israel drew from a common Semitic foundation, should crystallize in the doctrine of the resurrection, a corollary of the universal nature of this judgment.

One question remains unsettled, however. Even though we find no trace of a general resurrection of the dead in Semitic literature, does the possibility of such a resurrection remain open, and is it somehow required by the

[29] Nergal, spouse of Ereshkigal, the original solar god, like Apollo or Rudra who kills and vivifies and descends to the kingdom of the shades at the winter solstice, became the performer of the sublime deeds of the divine court. But his "justice" never dominates the religious horizon as "Yahweh's justice" dominates Israel's.

[30] "This precise example (the myth of Phaeton having a common Semitic basis with that of Is. 14) shows the attitude of Biblical authors toward mythology, an attitude both critical and positive. It is critical in rejecting everything in the myths which contradicts the fundamental beliefs of Israel and positive in accepting certain religious and sapiential ideas (compatible with their faith) conveyed by the myths, the first expressions of groping human thought" (Grelot, *R. H. R.*, January, 1956, p. 48).

internal logic of Semitic religious feeling toward death?

Because he believed that, on the basis of the translations of the tablets containing fragments of the epic of Gilgamesh, it is possible to answer this question very positively, Father Lagrange (as we said earlier) was openly optimistic about the Semitic origin of the resurrection of the body, to such an extent that he concluded: "Thus there is not a solid foundation for assuming a whole evolution in which the cult of the dead diminished. And it is the same with another hypothesis in which the hope of a resurrection is thought to have been a borrowing from the Persians or a late fruit of the unshakable hope of the Jews in a definitive victory in their war against the Seleucid. These ancient beliefs have the deepest roots among mankind, and ancient Babylonia was pleased to invoke its god as he who raised the dead to life."[31] Nevertheless, Father Lagrange remains cautious in interpreting the texts, and he does not share the conviction of Jensen, who, refuting the "heroic" interpretation of the epic of Gilgamesh, adds: "Gilgamesh is not at all a Babylonian Hercules; we do not have here an heroic epic. No, it is a matter of answering anxious questioning on the subject of life and death and the world beyond, and of the fulfilment of a joyful hope of resurrection through the resurrection of Enkiddu which is assumed in the conclusion."[32] To this, Father Lagrange has already replied: "Jensen gives to this conclusion an interpretation conforming to his general theory. . . . It is more appropriate in the context to imagine the two

[31] *Études sur la Religion des Sémites,* p. 295.
[32] *Th. Lit. Z.,* 1901, p. 34.

heroes bent over the aperture which leads to the underworld."[33] This opinion has become general among recent translators. Moreover, Father Lagrange bases his personal conviction not only upon the *conclusion* of the poem but on another passage that it is well for us to examine.[34] The Sumerian version of the poem anticipates survival after death in the infernal regions, a life that was unenviable but could be relieved by the constancy of a large posterity in regularly offering sacrifices for the dead. The Akkadian version rises to the notion of a redivision of the dead into classes, according to their conduct on earth. Here is the passage which seems to illustrate these points:

> Do we build houses for ever?
> Do we seal (contracts) for ever?
> Do brothers divide shares for ever?
> Does hatred persist for ever?
> Does the river for ever raise up (and) bring on floods?
>
> . . . . .
>
> Since the days of yore there has been no [permanence];
> The *resting* and the dead, how alike [they are]!
> Do they not compose a picture of death,
> The commoner and the noble,
> Once they are near to [their fate]?
> The Annunaki, the great gods, foregather;
> Mammetum, maker of fate, with them the fate decrees:
> Death and life they determine.
> (But) of death, its days are not revealed.[35]

Do these enigmatic phrases suggest a resurrection? Recently Langdon joined full force with Father Lagrange

[33] Lagrange, *op. cit.*, p. 320.

[34] Note this conclusion: "He whose shade has no one to care for it, you have seen — I see — he eats the food left at the bottom of a pot, the food which has been thrown into the street."

[35] Reprinted from *Ancient Near Eastern Texts,* ed. James B. Pritchard, with permission of Princeton University Press, 1950, pp. 92-93.

in a positive opinion: "The fate of all is not similar, since there must be judges, and their judgment is not arbitrary, it is based on past life; moreover, what is fixed, though unknown, is the time of death; it must be followed by life, although one cannot say whether there is question of a privilege for some or of a general resurrection."[36] For our part, the tone of this fragment seems especially to recall that of Ecclesiastes and to exhibit the same prudent scepticism. One thing is certain: nothing on earth lasts. Thus death will certainly follow life. Sleep already unites, in a fraternal attitude strangely like death, human beings who otherwise seem destined for a different lot. The gods have determined men's fate beforehand and Mammetum in particular fixes the number of their days, a secret never revealed to anyone. If our interpretation is correct, the text is only a *memento mori*. What makes one see more in it is the feeling that the divine decision has bearing on the afterlife, but it seems that the text yields better sense if there is question only of earthly destiny.[37]

Riesenfeld, basing his belief on the works of the school

---

[36] *Enc. Quillet,* v. I., p. 404.

[37] According to Th. de Liagre-Böhl, the author of the poem is opposing a naturist synthesis of eschatological trends such as the "solar" type, seen in the worship of Marduk (see p. 64), in which one re-enters life through death itself. Gilgamesh did not seek a higher life, but simple immortality, excluding death, and even this was denied him. Yet Böhl argues that the twelfth tablet, translated from Sumerian, offers another solution: there is a world beyond which has its proper laws and a very special life in which all men, not only some privileged ones, may share. One's state in this afterlife does not depend upon the number of one's sons or of the sacrificial practices, but on the way one has lived. Immediately before the passage quoted above, which completes the poem and the twelfth tablet, one reads: "He who dies in combat, you have seen him — I have seen him — his father and his mother raise his head, and his wife is at his bedside."

of Upsala and reacting against those who attribute to Iranian influence the late introduction of a hope in a resurrection into Judea, has defended the opinion that this belief was born in Semitic territory proper but originated in the seasonal drama performed on the occasion of the New Year in the temple of the god who overcame death. To assume such practices in the temple of Jerusalem before the Babylonian exile and to build a case upon them is a rash hypothesis that arouses serious reservations on the part of Father de Vaux.[38] However, it seems possible that myths of this type left their traces, at least literary ones, among the chosen people. These images derived from a distant cultural past could have given a traditional background to certain pages of Ezechiel or the Deutero-Isaias. The martyr-nation could have come to take the place of the son of the god in the old agrarian myth brought up to date to serve an absolutely new religious idea of suffering as reparation for a *fault* and preparation for a "resurrection." Thus the privilege of "Osirization" instead of being gradually extended from the king-god to his privileged subjects, as in Egypt, would have been transferred from a mythic "son of god" to the entire nation. In a very ancient past whose memory was still preserved in some stereotyped literary formula, the "chief" had played this role in a liturgical drama. It is not even necessary to go back to the obscure tribal chiefs antedating David. There had also been enough successors of David who had sought the favor of Baal (included among the "abominations" condemned by the prophets) so that his cult remained rooted in the imagina-

[38] *R. B.,* 1950, p. 157.

tion. We know elsewhere of infants being sacrificed to Moloch; the perpetuation of the rite of a paganized New Year would not be as abominable. The difficulty that Father de Vaux opposes to this scaffold of hypotheses is that we have to assume (without evidence of the continuity of a tradition) that the rituals found among neighboring peoples nearly a thousand years before the regular organization of the temple worship in Jerusalem could have come to life again. But it can be replied that literary forms, at least in the Orient, are very long-lived —for example the "priestly" account of the creation preserving the literary form of a poem read in a Mesopotamian temple on the occasion of the New Year. Finally, even if we eliminate the Israelite liturgy from the frame in which Riesenfeld places his hypothesis, we can at least admit the probable permanence of ancient and common Oriental images in the tradition which set in motion the collective hope of salvation among the chosen people. Thus a bridge would join the great text of Ezechiel about the resurrection of the dry bones and the old agrarian myths of Babylonia and Phoenicia.

In Babylonia as in Egypt, there exists beside the agrarian current an immortalist current whose mystique is the "sun-victorious-over-the-shadows" type and which is especially associated with the divinization of the royal person. At certain periods in Egypt as in Babylonia there were temptations to synthesize the two currents around the divine personages who furnished protection to a dynasty practicing enlightened despotism. From this point of view, what Ammon was in Egypt, Marduk became in Babylonia. Something similar could have happened to Baal, although in his divine essence he was more like Osiris than Ra. "In spite of his name, meaning the master, Baal is not the first among the gods, but only the lord of the land, its nourisher. Like Osiris in Egypt and for the same reasons, he is, however, very popular, and in a dangerous emergency, *for example when the end of the world seems imminent,* it is to him one turns by choice, for he is closer than any other to the human condition."[39] If the "eschatological" intervention of Baal can thus be connected with the victorious action of Yahweh on His "Day," the judgment of Bousset, champion of the Iranian origin of belief in the resurrection, who does not believe that any ideas underlying the "apocalyptic" current are met with in Babylonia, must be challenged.[40] Bousset spoke only of Babylonia because he did not yet know the Ugaritic texts, but in eliminating the possibility of Semitic influences, he urges the Iranian origin of this type of eschatology. Virolleaud's interpretation of the figure of Baal should give us pause, because if the Semitic world at an ancient time knew the theme of the intervention of a god when the threat of destruction weighed upon the entire universe, the Iranian religion itself could very well have borrowed this theme and later developed it within the framework of its own theology.

When it is observed that the priestly milieu, whose influence is dominant during peaceful times, in general developed agrarian tendencies, while the milieu of the warriors and the nobles imposed a theology of the heroic and solar type, during troubled periods, one can only be

[39] Virolleaud in the résumé of the communication made to the *Société E. Renan,* in *R. H. R.,* January, 1956-I, p. 137. Cf. a slightly different interpretation of the myth by Dussaud, *Enc. Quillet,* v. I, p. 365.

[40] *Rel. des. Jud.,* p. 577.

struck by the remarkable character of Mithraism. This religion, whose main themes are borrowed from Iran, nevertheless absorbed a large share of Babylonian "Semitisms." The religion of soldiers who sought to conquer the Roman empire in the third century A.D., clearly solar in its general character, Mithraism had nonetheless taken important elements from the agrarian religions. Mithra, however, not only brings his aid to the soul in the course of the perilous journey it takes through the heavenly spheres after death, but, assimilated to Phaeton, is the author of the final conflagration and, redescending to earth on this occasion, raises men to life, giving immortality to the good and finally destroying the wicked. We must examine the extent to which the traits of this eschatology sprang from Iran but we can observe that from then on the gods who—like Baal and Mithra—realized in their divine person a synthesis of the two currents (agrarian and solar) are conceived as consummating a story by an act of corporal punishment whose instrument is fire. But this action is, nevertheless, thought of as the beginning of a renewal. Only, as distinct from the hope of the agrarian theology, this renewal is conditioned by a moral discrimination and the new life bestowed upon the good is eternal. In the case of Baal, this schema is only outlined, and one can reconstruct it only with the same certainty as for Mithra. But of Marduk, another god whose theology unites the two tendencies, it is said,

> They had made his grave, at a banquet . . . .
> The Babylonians saw that (Marduk) had restored [his] life.
> All mouths praise [his] greatness.

> "Who commanded it, who accomplished the vision of the
>   deity?
> In whose mind is the going (freely) on one's way realized?
> Apart from Marduk, who revived his lifeless state?
> Besides Sarpanit, what goddess conferred life unto him?"
> Marduk is able to revive in the grave.
> Sarpanit knows how to deliver from destruction.[41]

The assemblage of texts which (except for one doxology)
the above lines conclude, is supposed to acknowledge the
benefactions of Marduk to one of the faithful whom ill-
ness had brought to the verge of death and who says:

> ". . . he has made me live again. He has saved me [from
> distress]. He has brought me across [the infernal river]
> Hubur. Marduk has taken me by the hand."

It appears that Marduk can explain characteristics of
the Mithra figure which the Indo-Iranian Mithra does not
explain.

There is general agreement that the state of Judaic
eschatology assumed by the Evangelists was the result
of late developments in the postexilic faith. But agreement ends when a retracing of the history of this development is begun. According to some, it is sufficiently explained as a maturation of ancient beliefs proper to
Judaism; for others, it took this precise turn only because of an important accretion of Iranian origin.
But there is not much agreement, even among those who
see a predominant Iranian influence on the development
of eschatological beliefs in the Iranian religions themselves. Iran is a varied and constantly changing religious
world where many varieties of belief can exist simultaneously. Thus, until we are able to set the question of
the reciprocal influence of Judaism and Mazdaism on a

[41] Reprinted from *Ancient Near Eastern Texts,* ed. James B. Pritchard,
with permission of Princeton University Press, 1950, p. 437.

firm chronological basis, all conclusions should be regarded as tentative.

For example, finding a compendium of Iranian eschatology comparable in form and content to the fourth book of Esdras, principal source of medieval ideas of the afterlife, means returning to the *Bundahish,* the existing text of which derives from a period after the establishment of Islamism in Iran. Yet in this all agree in acknowledging that many of the traits of this late literature are very old, and doubtless go back to the Sassanian *Avesta.* This *Avesta* in its turn is a traditional work and contains many archaic passages, some of which, the *gatha,* can be attributed to Zoroaster himself, while others go back to pre-Zoroastrian times. However, the chronological analysis of these traditions has not been completed, and on some points, apparently including eschatology, we cannot hope to attain certainty. What developed over fifteen to twenty centuries must be reconstituted from a very small number of accurately dated landmarks.[42] Even the hypotheses generally accepted by scholars are not invulnerable to rigorous criticism. These hypotheses are utilized, however, because we must establish some groundwork for a historical study strikingly lacking in definite facts. For instance, we continue to refer to the works of Söderblom, despite the fact that

[42] The life of Zoroaster himself is not always dated with certainty by Iranists. The most recent effort of this type is that of F. Altheim and Ruth Stichl, *Z. F. Rel. U. Geistesgesch.,* 1956, I. It confirms the frequent placing of the prophet's activity towards the second half of the sixth century and dates his death about 522. But there are still partisans armed with defensible reasons for dating the life of Zoroaster 400 years later. The opinion of Father Lagrange, who thought he found Hellenistic influences in the *gatha,* and extended this date almost up to our era or even beyond, is no longer generally accepted.

they are outdated since progress has been made in the readings of the texts, because of the general time scheme in which he placed them. This last point—the most important—remains the most difficult to ascertain. On these disputed matters there is a desperate lack of studies, especially research devoted to establishing the relative chronology of texts and beliefs and definitely locating in time and place precise and important information.

Moreover, these uncertainties exist in other domains than the Iranian. Ezechiel is the great prophet of Israel in exile. He probably shows traces of a polemical attitude toward Iranian dualism, a fact proving his knowledge of this type of religion. But although some are prepared to recognize Ezechiel as the initiator of the doctrine of the resurrection,[43] others go as far as to affirm that he "has not even presented the doctrine of a retribution beyond the tomb."[44] When a renowned specialist declares in another connection that "the true meaning of the Zoroastrian eschatology still remains obscure,"[45] we must

[43] Proksch, *Theol. des. A. T.,* p. 704.

[44] Auvray, *Ézéchiel,* fasc. of the "Bible of Jerusalem," p. 16.

[45] In a recent and very important article, which makes this point in the area of our knowledge of Iranian religions, Widengren several times expresses regret at the inadequacy of our information or the lack of serious studies on points of prime importance:

"We still do not have an historical analysis of all the elements which make up the middle-Persian apocalypses" (*Numen,* 1954, 43).
"A description of the ethics of Iranian religion is lacking" (*ibid.,* p. 83).
"We still do not have any study devoted to the religious conception of the soul in ancient Iran" (*ibid.,* p. 31).
"What remains particularly obscure here is, first, certain particular problems, like the concept of Saoshyant, besides the true meaning (*die eigentliche Bedeutung*) of eschatology and dualism" (*Numen,* 1955, 76).

We shall make frequent use of these articles, which we simply cite under the abbreviation *W. N.* I and II.

admit that we do not feel encouraged to draw definitive conclusions. On such slippery ground, how have serious scholars arrived at definitive positions, positions which still completely dominate the thinking of one segment of biblical criticism?

This springs from a profound conviction in the minds of certain scholars: they think that the internal logic of Iranian dualism should lead to the particular form of eschatology characteristic of both Judaism and Mazdaism, while, on the contrary, this would be inexplicable starting only with religious postulates found in pre-exilic Yahwism. We saw earlier that one can defend the existence of a purely Semitic progress toward the notion of the resurrection of the dead. However, two elements are still lacking in this preparation before the dogma can flower into its Christian structure: a clear vision of the participation of the faithful, after death, in the privileges of their dead and risen god, and the relationship of the resurrection and the judgment. On this last point, the internal evolution of Judaism offers sufficient explanation. Nevertheless, we need not exclude a priori the idea that it was speeded up and directed by an external influence, Iranian in type. One cannot entirely escape the deep impression which Bousset's arguments in favor of an Iranian influence made in their time. What remains intact is the similarity of structure of the Jewish and Iranian apocalypses. A cosmic catastrophe, preceded by signs in the heavens, serves as the background of a last universal judgment in which the works of each person are openly manifested. At the end of this judgment the good will be definitively separated from the evil. A general resurrection unites the soul which has endured pain or received reward in a provisional state, to the body whose matter is restored from the four elements. The resurrection is thus consummated in order to permit the public manifestation of the sentence of judgment and also to integrate the material world, purified by fire, into the final victory of goodness. This resurrection has for its author Saoshyant, the eschatological savior, held in reserve in the form of a golden seed in a lake where the virgin who gives it birth bathes. Saoshyant begins by awakening the "sleeping" heroes who will help him in his final struggle against the forces of evil.[46]

[46] Chantepie, *Handbuch,* II, 225. We give here the passage of the *Bundahish* concerning the resurrection, according to an Italian translation of P. Messina, in *Orientalia,* 1935, 269:

In the same way as Masi and Masani, when they germinated from the earth first drank water, then partook of plants, then of milk, then of meat; and just as men approaching the time of their death abstain first from meat, then from milk, then from eating of bread, and without appetite on the threshold of death, drink only water, thus, in the millenium of Usetarmah, the strength of men's appetites will decrease in such a way that after having eaten only one meal, they will remain satisfied for three days and three nights. Afterwards they will abstain from eating meat and from eating vegetables and from drinking water. During the ten years before Sassans comes, no one will eat, but no one will die. Finally Sassans will move the body, according to that which is said: "Zarathustra asks Ormazd: 'A body which the wind has carried, which the water has transported, of what will you remake it, and how will the resurrection take place?' And he answers: 'If the heaven, of the substance of the ruby, supports itself without pillars in the power of the spiritual permanence of the light of the vast spaces, if I have created the earth, which carries the whole material world and has nothing outside itself to support it, if I have put the sun, the moon, and the stars in motion under the form of shining bodies in the middle of the atmosphere, if I have created the barley, in order that it may be seeded in the earth and may grow and multiply anew, if I have created all sorts of colors among the plants, and if I have created in the plants and in other things a fire that does not burn, if I have created a son in the maternal womb, if I have created the many kinds of hair, of skin, of nails, of blood, of fat, of eyes, of ears and other things, if I have created feet for the water that it may run, if I have created the cloud like the spirit which carries with it the water of the world and rains where it pleases, if I have created the air which, visibly, by the force of the wind transports on high what is found below, without anyone's being able to hold it with his hands, certainly each of these things was more difficult to create when it was brought about, for with the resurrection I have the help of that which exists and, on the contrary, when I created these other things, there was nothing in existence that they had been.

" 'Behold, if I have created what was not, why is it not possible to re-create that which has already been? For in that time I shall again demand the bones from the spirit of the earth; from that of the water, the blood; from that of the plants, the hair; from the wind, being, in the same way that they received them in the first creation. To begin, Sassans will move the bones of Gayomart, then those of Masi and Masani. . . .

" 'Then, when they shall have given back to the material world their whole body and form, they will give them their property. Of that light which is with the sun, they shall give half to Gayomart, the other half to the rest of men. Afterwards men will recognize themselves in such a manner that soul will recognize soul, and body, body. . . .'

"In this time, Ormazd will bring his work to its conclusion: creation will be such that he will never have to do any more work in it after they have re-created the dead. Sassans with his helpers will make a sacrifice for the re-creation of the dead, and they will immolate the bull Hadhayosh in sacrifice; from the fat of this bull and of the white Hom they will make ambrosia; they will give it to all men and all men shall be immortal."

This text deserves a long commentary. We shall limit ourselves to a few observations. The gradual decrease in nourishment corresponds to a spiritualization of material being and implies a certain contempt for the body. It is very old in Iranian eschatology for it exists in the Bahman *Yasht* in a slightly different form. It recalls the Buddhist idea that men were first given "ethereal" bodies, which became coarse only because they consumed increasingly gross food to satisfy their lusts. This also recalls an Indian ascetical method according to which the daily portion of food is decreased during the time the moon is waning in order to gradually increase the amount again while the moon waxes. The affinities of this part of the text are thus Indian, involving a strongly dualist anthropology with a contempt for the body, at least in its present state.

On the other hand, the resurrection apologetic resembles rabbinical teaching and the Jewish apocalyptics as much by its appeal to the omnipotent creator as by its solicitude that each element restore what it possessed of the body. The spirits appointed to the elements were known in the synagogue and in the Fathers of the Church, but were probably of Iranian origin, because they correspond very closely in function to the "fravarti," types of celestial hypostases of earthly realities. In the Upanishad there is an idea like that in the *Bundahish* which has each

Most of the details of this picture evoke images familiar to those who know the traditional Jewish and Christian accounts of the last things. As Bousset, who founded in this observation the basis of his conviction of the historic dependence of one of these doctrines upon the other, puts it, nowhere except in Iran and in the Judaeo-Christian tradition does there exist a combination of these three eschatological elements: the destruction of the world by fire, the resurrection of the dead, and the last judgment.[47]

One cannot deny that this is remarkable. Need one necessarily conclude that it is the result of a massive borrowing? Could it not result from fairly numerous coincidences plus some borrowing of detail? Is there even the possibility of a complete, basic independence of these currents, but also of a borrowing (because of competition) by the Iranian apocalypse in its final version of some ideas from Moslem eschatology, which in turn was itself strongly impregnated by Judaeo-Christian conceptions? All these questions are very difficult to resolve accurately in the present state of the documentation and its scientific analysis. But the similarity between the two doctrines is so striking that the principal facts on which the theses rest should be analyzed as far as possible. Despite the uncertainty remaining at all

---

part of the body at death rejoin a cosmic being to which it corresponds, with the characteristic notion that the hair grows into plants. The idea of plants as distinct "elements" is also Indo-Iranian. The importance of the wind as that which recalls each being is exactly like that of the breath (*prana*) in similar Indian literature. In short, Indo-Iranian ideas dominate this picture, but the comparison with India provides a parallel neither for the fact of the resurrection strictly speaking, nor for the transcendent action of Ormazd, its instigator.

[47] *Rel. des Jud.*, p. 581.

levels of this comparative study, it nevertheless retains a lively interest, and it necessarily leads to a broadening of the discussion to the fundamental structures of the two religions, in order to decide which one originated the complex eschatology they possess in common.[48]

As soon as one tries to examine more closely any one of the three parallel elements supporting Bousset's thesis, it appears that the main evidence dissolves. This is due partly to the rarity and the obscurity of the most ancient

---

[48] There are few questions upon which opinions are as divided as the relationship between Parseeism and Judaism in the matter of belief in the resurrection of the dead. Henry, *Le Parsisme,* pp. 195-210, is convinced of the borrowing by Judaism of an ancient Iranian belief preserved as an archaism in a dualist doctrine which ought to have repudiated it. F. Cumont considers the resurrection to be one of the Mazdaean ideas diffused in the Mediterranean world by the spokesmen of the Jewish and Persian settlements, the effect of Persian doctrine appearing to him undeniable, however difficult it is to perceive the cause of this diffusion. (*Rel. Orient.,* pp. 127-130). Nötscher, *Altorientalischer u. alttestament-licher Auferstehungsglauben,* believes that the Persia of the Achaemenidae professed a general resurrection, or at the very least, a resurrection of all the faithful Mazdaeans. To him, Jewish borrowing seems possible but undemonstrable. E. Schürer, *Gesch. des Judischen Volkes,* v. II, p. 587, sees especially in the immediate personal retribution following death, the major characteristic of Persian eschatology and understands the introduction of this belief into late Judaism to be a sign of the influence of Mazdaism. Beyond this, it does not seem to him that the anteriority of Iranian eschatological beliefs to those of the Israelites is demonstrated and he believes the Persian influence, if it must be admitted, remains marginal and does not affect the fundamental originality of Judaism. Dawson, *The Ethical Religion of Zoroaster,* thinks that the resurrection, which does not appear in the *gatha,* was introduced into Persia through Egyptian influence. Though Proksch, *Theologie des A. T.,* p. 704, like many Old Testament specialists, agrees that Persian eschatology could have colored the forms of Jewish apocalyptic, he believes that all the essential aspects of Jewish eschatology are sufficiently explained by the development of a purely Hebraic faith, and Volz, *Eschatologie des Jud. Gemeinde,* p. 231, has preceded him in this path. Masson-Oursel in *Enc. Quillet,* III, p. 35, who stresses the diversity of burial rituals existing in Iran, accepts as evident the Jewish influences on Sassanian Mazdaism. The last Judgment and the Messianism of the Sassanian apocalypses de-

evidences, precisely the ones that should be decisive. The whole question comes down, in a word, to deciding how much the late and explicit evidence, like that provided by the *Bundahish,* rests firmly on an ancient and explicit Iranian tradition with the same meaning.

The point of departure for such research is usually provided by the *gatha,* compositions which are certainly of ancient origin and were probably composed by Zoroaster himself. The value of certain recent studies, like those of Wikander and Widengren, has been to demonstrate that the eschatological ideas of Zoroaster, while departing from past Iranian religious beliefs, nevertheless were to a large extent conditioned by this past, and further, that certain pre-Zoroastrian characteristics were reintroduced into Mazdaean orthodoxy in the course of its millennial development. There are two criteria by which the pre-Zoroastrian character of a Mazdaean doctrine can be judged: one, it has a discernible parallel in Vedism and two, it is not in the direct line of the pure Zoroastrian spirit. Although agreement on the first point is relatively easy, opinions on the second diverge widely, depending on the interpretation given to the figure of Zoroaster.

The *gatha* constitute a precious document and the only

---

rived from the synagogue. As to the figure of Sassans, Masson-Oursel follows the opinion of Przyluski, but Abegg, on the other hand, thinks that Buddhism, Hinduism and Parseeism developed their Messianic figures independently of any exterior influence. Scheftelowitz, finally, advocates the total independence of Judaism from Iranianism. As for the Iranists, the overwhelming majority accept as obvious the influence of Mazdaean eschatology upon Judaism but are more or less reserved on the details and circumstances of the borrowings. Some go so far as to make Iran the source of all the new religious forms which spread through the Hellenistic world.

decisive one in determining the meaning of the Zoro-astrian reform, because they are the only part of the entire *Avesta* not reinfiltrated by traditional polytheism. These texts are brief and obscure and do not deal directly with eschatological questions. They do, however, make certain the Zoroastrian origin of certain elements that are enshrined in later accounts of the last things. But it would appear—though the point has been questioned—that the *gatha* do envision a judgment of the world by fire. Even if we restrict the texts referring to a "last revolution" and a "trial by fire" to the establishment of a kingdom of justice[49] on earth whose prophet Zoro-aster is, and to the ordeal by molten metal submitted to by all the faithful who are conscious of being in the truth, it remains that such expressions lent themselves to a development of natural meaning in a community which did not immediately see the conversion of all to the preaching of its founder. But certain texts can be read more naturally on the hypothesis of a cosmic judg-ment by fire than on that of a simple ordeal:

> For those sinners, of whom you know very well what they
> leave behind them, wise Lord,
> None should declare himself initiate
> If he wishes to have the reward which, as we know,
> Is given at the time of the decision by molten metal.
>   (*Yasna,* 32, 7)

[49] Hope for this kingdom, the *Khshathra vairya*, occupies an important place in the *gatha*, in which it already assumes a transcendent aspect along with its terrestrial one. Cf. Chantepie, *Handbuch*, II, 192; Duchesne-Guillemin, *Zoroastre*, p. 139, who concludes: "Zoroaster an-nounces a regeneration of the world, the coming of the kingdom of God. He is the earliest, by far, of the authors of the apocalypses. Nyberg was right to insist on this point" (p. 142).

The fire of divine justice is the instrument for the distribution of different rewards to the good and the wicked. Thus it evokes that *ignis sapiens* which the Fathers after Philo took from the Stoics, and it has exactly the same function in Origen. But who is to say that they themselves did not borrow it directly from the Magians? The question is not easy to resolve because in the ancient Stoa fire had a cosmological rather than a moral function. Not until Seneca did it purify the earth of its crimes. Yet, among the Hebrew prophets from the eighth century on, divine fire punished the impious. What seems peculiar to the Zoroastrian fire is that it brings about the distinguishing of the good and the wicked. This is in accord with the Zoroastrian idea of a radical, initial choice whose consequences extend to the final end of all existence. From before Zoroaster the Indo-Iranians seem to have known a periodic destruction and renewal of the world by fire, but like the ancient Stoa, they understood it in a purely cosmological sense.

Although at the end of this inquiry the fire of judgment really seems to be, in the *Bundahish,* an authentically Zoroastrian category, it is still impossible to conclude with certainty that the place of fire in the Jewish apocalyptic was a borrowing from Iran, for the fire of the holiness of Yahweh is affirmed as far back as the earliest biblical accounts, and its evolution into an eschatological fire can be explained as an internal development, not needing any contribution from outside.[50]

[50] E. Schürer, *op. cit.,* II, 638, takes pains to show that the Judaeo-Christian doctrine of eschatological fire can be explained as a purely internal development. See the references to "Fire" in the index to the *Bible of Jerusalem.* Nevertheless it must be recognized that in Jewish and

Let us only say that the development of the idea in Judaism paralleled Iranian ideas, thanks perhaps to a phenomenon of "induction" between the two eschatologies. There is indeed more resemblance between the Jewish fire and the Iranian fire than between the Stoic and the Christian fire because the Judaeo-Christian fire, exactly like the Zoroastrian, is the instrument of the justice of a God who transcends nature, while the Stoic fire is a moment of wholly immanent evolution in the cosmic forces. Since it is generally agreed that the Fathers of the Church did not disdain to adapt the Stoic fire to their own views, why should the Jews have shunned use of the Zoroastrian fire?

The *gatha* themselves established the figure of the Saoshyant, but he does not yet have the aspect of the apocalyptic figure we suggested above. The "saviors" — for the plural is customary in the *gatha* — are the princes

---

Christian apocalyptic literature this fire assumes an aspect that irresistibly evokes the theology of the *gatha* because the fire effects precisely an "ordeal." Certain details are interesting. Thus, according to E. Petersen, in *Vigiliae christianae,* 1955, 7, the *Sibylline books,* the *Apocalypse of Peter,* and the *Mandaean Ginza* share the idea of a purifying water, white like milk, that of the Jordan which must be crossed in order to enter Paradise, the same heavenly Jordan which is, moreover, generally thought of as a river of fire. But the Sassanian apocalypse tells us that the eschatological river of fire will be "as lukewarm milk" for the good. In addition, it has a purifying power for the wicked whom it tortures (on the river of fire, see Edsman, *Le Baptême de Feu,* Upsala). The Qumran psalm translated by Father Lambert (*Nouvelle Revue Théologique,* 1952, 285), with its fire which melts the base of the mountains and its eschatological level land, recalls the Sassanian apocalypses rather closely, but there the fire appears as the instrument of Belial while, more in Judaism than in Parseeism, fire connotes in general the divine power. The ascension of Moses, which closely recalls Essenian literature in many ways and includes the figure of Belial, causes the eschatological fire of the "Well-Beloved" himself to arise.

whom Zoroaster calls to assist in his reform and who serve him as a secular arm. Thus, they are "messianic" only in a terrestrial sense, analogous to that of the Jewish hopes that a descendant of David would come to re-establish Israel in justice here on earth.

Zoroaster surely envisaged a situation in which certain of the faithful would die before having seen the coming of the era of justice and happiness which would accompany the success of his reform on earth.[51] It is this that has caused some to doubt that there is question of a *last* judgment strictly speaking in the *gatha,* since they definitely indicate a *particular* judgment.

This opinion suits the type of scholar who thinks that any duplication of elements in a religious teaching originates as a clumsy collection of opinions from various sources. Yet the clarity of the teaching of the *gatha* on this particular judgment provides a striking contrast with the slow and obscure grasp of the same belief by the Judaeo-Christian tradition. This is not intended to imply a massive borrowing by Judaism from Iran in the realm of eschatological beliefs. Moreover, this fact does not lead us, either, to trace back to Zoroaster the doctrine of the resurrection of the dead. The rationalist critique generally agrees to separate as incompatible (in a doctrine which has not yet undergone corruption) a belief in a resurrection effecting a judgment of the whole man, body and soul, and one teaching the judgment of each soul, separated from its body — which would be immune from sanction in this type of eschatology — immediately after death.

<hr>

[51] Cf. Duchesne-Guillemin, *op. cit.,* p. 259.

According to this same critique the introduction of the doctrine of the particular judgment into Christianity is due to a Hellenistic influence contrary to the peculiarly Palestinian eschatology of the Gospels. The critique should logically conclude that since the particular judgment is well attested in Zoroaster this makes it highly improbable that he professed the resurrection of the body, and, thus, that this doctrine arose in Israel from an Iranian influence. But perhaps this is asking too much coherence in the attitude of men who deliberately accuse others of lacking such coherence.

What seems to us in the nature of a final argument is an examination of the attitude the reformer habitually took toward the body. We know that in the later development of the Iranian religions there was a strong tendency toward dualism which is manifested, among other ways, in a marked opposition between the world of bodies and that of spirits. This mentality is apparent in the Iranian Gnoses, Mandaism and Manicheism, but certain Mazdaean tendencies were not exempt and there are reasons to suspect the Magians of holding similar opinions. If a radical dualism opposing spirit and matter and condemning the latter could be traced back to Zoroaster, the case would be decided.[52] We would no more expect to find in him than in the Gnostics a doctrine of the resurrection of the body. But the dualism of the

[52] It is surely in the Indo-European origins of the Iranian religion that one must look to discover the root of its anthropological dualism. The common use of the root *men-, which gives to Iran terms as important as *manah, Vohu Manah,* involves a tendency to separate in man *that which thinks.* The manah of the just pass at death into the divine good thought (*Vohu Manah*) but with no implication of pantheistic beliefs. Even in India a certain dualism places body and soul in opposition, though we need not necessarily infer the soul's identity with the *Brahman*

(Cf. O. Lacombe, *Revue Thomiste,* 1956, 92). On the other hand, the spiritual world even though contrasted to the material world, is not, therefore, incorporeal. For instance the "fravarti," those celestial doubles of visible realities which are constituted of a stable essence inaccessible to accident and contingency cannot, however, be compared to the Platonic "ideas," but rather to the angels of rabbinic Judaism, corporeal, although invisible under ordinary conditions. The real is thus capable of more or less "subtlety." Under these conditions, an anthropological dualism will become radical only as the result of a depreciation of coarse corporeality corresponding to the discovery of the value of the spirit. In Iran one can say with certainty that this depreciation appeared, but in varied proportions, so that on this basis the great religious currents arising on the soil of Persia can be classified as Mandaism-Manicheism, Hellenized Magianism, Mithracism, Sassanian Mazdaism, Achaemenidaean Mazdaism, primitive Zoroastrianism. All those in Iran who affirm that a certain corporeality remains in the beatific state of the just surely conceive it under a "spiritualized" mode. For Zoroastrianism faithful to the spirit of the founder, one can say that if the material world were not included in some way in the final victory of Ahura Mazda, it would not be a total victory. Cf. *W. N.,* I, 31-32; *W. N.,* II, 76; Oepke, R. *A. C.,* art. "Auferstehung," col. 933.

". . . Present existence, the 'first existence,' begun by choice, will be terminated along the line of this choice. A 'second existence' will begin. The conception developed by Zoroaster could have varied — it must have varied according to circumstances. In particular, this conception is sometimes distinguished in the *gatha* from a doctrine that seems to be contradictory to it: that of the condition of men after death. But we should be mistaken to seek to form identical material into a coherent system, which doubtless never existed in Zoroaster himself" (Duchesne-Guillemin, *Zoroastre,* p. 155). This modest tone is surely praiseworthy, but we do not see incoherence in affirming both a particular and a general judgment in one doctrine—and here there is total agreement between Zoroaster and Israel — which is fully aware of the double dimension of salvation, individual and social. The resurrection of the body seems to us to accord well with Zoroastrian thought — without our necessarily believing it is found in the *gatha*—precisely because of the communal character of the prophet's religion, which naturally caused it to envisage the society of the elect in a concrete, slightly "millennial" fashion. Indo-Iranian anthropology by its learned character rather created an obstacle to the simplicity of these views, and it took its revenge by drawing the Iranian religions in a steady decline toward the Gnostic type of dualism which became an accomplished fact when corporeality and concupiscence were identified. But the moral health of the prophet of Ahura Mazda had opened the perspectives of his disciples to an eschatological kingdom more truly human.

gatha is *restrained* compared to that of later documents and it is so especially on the point of the opposition between the corporeal and spiritual worlds. This opposition, contrary to the general trend of Semitic anthropology, existed among the Indo-Iranians but from an early date did not permit condemnation of the body. In India, it would be the *Upanishads* which stressed the opposition, to the disadvantage of the corporeal world. In the *gatha* spiritual realities are highly valued, but salvation is nonetheless expected for both orders of reality:

> Give me, according to Justice, success in both worlds — the corporeal and that of thought —
> To sustain me by them and bring me into felicity (*Yasna*, 28, 2).
> And there came to these Devotion. . . .
> She has given the lasting quality of bodies and the breath of life
> So they will belong to you separated from those [i. e., the wicked],
> Like the first (?) through punishments by means of metal (*Y.* 30, 7).

This doctrine of the salvation of the body is also a doctrine of salvation by the body, and in the most expressly Zoroastrian manner, because the body appears as the means of the choice whose crucial importance we have noted:

> . . . in the beginning, O Wise One, you made for us the living, by your thought,
> Consciousness and the mental powers,
> . . . you endowed a body with the soul of life,
> . . . you created deeds and judgments so that decisions could freely be made (*Y.* 31, 11).

May we correctly conclude then that, because the punishments and rewards of Zoroaster are described in connection with corporeal things such as fire, food, or song, the eschatology of the *gatha* includes belief in the resurrection of the body? Such a conclusion would be premature because on the one hand these material notions could have been used metaphorically or analogically and because on the other hand it is very possible that the antithesis between the spiritual world and the corporeal world would not be such that *no* degree of corporeality would remain in the soul once separated from a visible body. Many indications point to this idea, beginning with the apparently very concrete conception of the bridge of the Chinvant which must be crossed by the soul the third day after death. In addition, neither the *gatha* nor the old *avesta* include the idea that death is a liberation of the soul from its bodily ties, and there is no evidence in Mazdaism of a metempsychosist mentality analogous to that of the Indian religions or of Pythagoreanism.[53]

If Zoroaster did not profess the resurrection of the body, or at least if we cannot be sure that he did, can we

[53] F. Cumont believes (*Lux Perpetua,* pp. 145-7) that the Pythagoreans had been influenced by the Magians. He emphasizes the fact that the Greeks always attributed revelations of the future to the Magians: the Er of Plato is one of them, as is the Gobrys of Axiochos. Pausanias claims to know that the Chaldeans and the Magians were the first to affirm that the human soul is immortal and so convinced the Hellenes, and Plato in particular (IV, 32, 4). In this respect, there were longstanding contacts between Greece and Iran, but the nature of the Zoroastrian reform separates it from the pantheistic Indo-European current from which Indian and Pythagorean metempsychosis seems to us to derive (perhaps, as has been suggested, by means of an ecstatic method of shamanistic type). The thesis according to which Zoroaster is a shaman, seems to us difficult to defend, unless one confuses shaman and prophet, which is unwarranted.

determine when this doctrine appears with certainty for the first time in the history of the Iranian religions? To Bousset, the evidence of Theopompus, who wrote in the third century before Christ and according to whom the Magians professed the doctrine of the resurrection of the body, is decisive. This evidence reaches us through two authors, Diogenes Laertius and Ennius of Gaza, the latter in a citation by Theophrastus. To give as much weight as possible to this evidence, Bousset minimizes the fact that Plutarch, citing the same passage of Theopompus, makes no mention of the resurrection. The text of Diogenes Laertius is as follows: "Theopompus, in the eighth book of the *Philippics* says that, according to the Magians, men will live again and will be immortal, and that the stability of things will come about through their prayers" (*Proem.* 9); and Ennius of Gaza clarifies further: "Zoroaster announced that there would come a time when the resurrection of all the dead would take place, Theopompus knows," (*Frag. hist. gr.* I, 289). Here in turn is the way Plutarch reports the eschatology of the Magians, according to the same Theopompus: "A time will come, and it is determined, when Ahriman, causing plague and famine, will necessarily perish and will disappear as a result of the ravages of the plagues. The earth will now be only a flat surface; there will be only one kind of life, one form of government; everyone will rejoice in perfect happiness and will speak the same language" (*De Is. et Os.* 47). It is obvious that each of these authors has read Theopompus from his own point of view. We have already seen that the legend of Osiris had undergone certain modifications in the Hellenistic period so that it would not contradict the anthropological ideas that Greek philosophy had popularized. Plutarch can be strongly suspected to have done the same with the Magian resurrection, transposing into the Platonic categories of the establishment of an ideal republic something that in reality was much less politically oriented and called for the transcendent intervention of a god into history. From this point of view, the terms used by Diogenes are interesting. He too retranslates Iranian thought into the usages of a Hellenistic mentality by introducing the familiar concept of immortality; but this immortality only follows a "resurrection" which brings the dead to life, a notion that would have sounded unusual to ears attuned to Greek classical thought. The silence of Plutarch and the evident embarrassment of Laertius taken together might seem to favor the substantial truth of the witness of Ennius, who strives to emphasize (for an apologetic end) the agreement between Zoroaster's doctrine and that of the Christians. It is true that Theopompus speaks of men's returning to life. Under what circumstances? Plutarch throws some light on the question: "Theopompus said, according to the Magians, that for three thousand years one or the other of these gods (Horomazes and Ahriman) was alternately ruler and ruled; that for the next three thousand years, they will fight and make war against each other, destroying each other's works. In the end, Hades will be defeated; men will be in possession of happiness; they will not need food and will cast no shadow"[54] (*op. cit.,* 47). Specifying that they do not cast a shadow is a way of stressing that they

---

[54] This lack of a shadow signifies that an essential "doubleness" joins one being of light to another being of light but never joins a being of light to a being of darkness. Salvation for the soul consists in rejoining

have no body at all, because having a body would not be unusual for pure spirits.

Among Iranists there is much discussion about the significance of the three-thousand-year periods which mark off the history of the world.[55] We will treat the matter only insofar as it is useful for our purpose. In the late apocalyptic of the Sassanian period, we are told that each of the periods of the world is in some way opened with the appearance of a savior; there are three thousand-year periods into which the three thousand years of conflict with which Theopompus ends the history of the world are divided. In this connection we are inevitably reminded of the Indian conceptions in which each great period of the world is marked by the appearance of a divine avatar. This doctrine had enough vitality to be introduced into Buddhism, where it was not originally found. Thus it seems that the same thing could be true of Zoroastrianism. Moreover, the saviors who appear at the outset of each period according to the *Bundahish* are very much like avatars of Zoroaster, as is also the golden seed preserved in the lake of Vourukasha that renders the virgin mother pregnant with Saoshyant and also proceeds from the prophet of Ahura Mazda. If one relates these considerations to the fact that the work of resurrection accomplished by Saoshyant begins with the first man, Gayomart, one is entitled to note in this

---

its *fravarti* or its angel counterpart and abandoning its accidental union with an angel of Ahriman, which caused the heaviness of its body and therefore its shadow. This doctrine of the two angels occurs in Christian patristic writing as well as in Gnosticism. See H. Corbin, *Eranos-Jahrbuch*, 1953, p. 106.

[55] H. Corbin, *op. cit.*, p. 153; Chantepie, *Handbuch*, II, 225.

conception of the world a distinct degradation of the
transcendentalism of the *gatha,* in the sense of a more
immanentist view of the rebirth of the universe. The difficulty of reconciling in detail the varied evidences we
obtain from Iranian eschatology demonstrates also that
these ideas retain a certain flexibility. For instance, the
fire of the cosmic ordeal that separates the good and the
wicked in the *gatha* becomes in turn a purifying fire in
Indian or Stoic thought, and the wicked who submit to
its rigor will pass into the realm of the good. Here again
there is the regression of a moral dualism, which was
certainly at the heart of Zoroaster's[56] preaching, to
cosmological monism. As a result it appears to us, as it
does to Widengren, that the eschatological figure of
Saoshyant is a later development of Zoroastrian eschatology produced under the influence of a return to Indo-

[56] This return to a cosmological monism is noted perhaps from the
time of the *gatha* — a proof that Zoroaster was not able to maintain a
perfectly pure transcendent conception of monotheism — in the role of
the *Vohu Manah,* the Zoroastrian Archangel who takes the place of
Mithra in the reformed heavenly court. He assumes the role which would
be played in the later Gnostic eon by the "Church above," receiving into
himself the *manah* of the just. In the Mandaean Gnosis, which is
Arameo-Iranian, it is Adakas-Mana who will represent the heavenly soul
descended into the first man, residing it would seem as a "power" in all
of humanity (Schmitt, *S. D. B.,* "Mandeisme," col. 777). This
version of things usually goes hand in hand with a vision of cosmic time which
unwinds in cycles, punctuated by the appearance of avatars of the first
man, with salvation proceeding as a continuous, permanent work. According to Schäder, *Religion in Geschichte u. Gegenwart,* art. "Perser,"
1086, precisely this conception of history was borrowed from Iran by the
late Judaism of the apocalypses. Adam and the true prophets of the
Pseudo-Clementine Homilies in fact recall homologous figures in Sassanian Mazdaism but since the latter is not definitely dated we can
conclude nothing with assurance. We believe, however, that the conception of the four periods of three thousand years implicitly contained in
the evidence from Theopompus and closely resembling the *kalpa* of India
is authentically Iranian but was borrowed by orthodox Judaism only as

Iranian cosmological conceptions. If these views are admissible, it follows that a collective resurrection had a less organic role in Mazdaism that in Judaism, where it was a response to a precise and peculiarly Jewish problem: to absolve the justice of God from all suspicion and to demonstrate His absolute fidelity to the promises made to the patriarchs.

If we compare our positions on this point with those of Bousset, we see that at the period of Theopompus there probably existed in Zoroastrian Mazdaism a collection of eschatological conceptions that called for a (periodic?) judgment by fire, accompanied by the re-establishment of men (or only the good?) amidst the good things of life on an earth purged of all evil. On this basis of comparison it is time now to turn to the evidence we have of Jewish eschatological conceptions at about the same period. As Father Lagrange noted, there is very little literary similarity between the *gatha* and the Bible, and we can say almost as much for the entire *avesta*. But we are not acquainted with all the Iranian literature of the epoch, and the Western Magians must have possessed writings which influenced the Sassanian apocalyptic. In this Sassanian apocalyptic we can find comparisons with the corresponding literature of Judaism, beginning with the Book of Daniel. The author of this book, who wrote

---

a convenient framework into which the peculiarly Israelite idea of God's sovereign interventions into history on behalf of the people of the covenant could be fitted. This was perhaps the case as early as Daniel. Only the authors whose orthodoxy was suspect on other grounds, like the Judeo-Christian writer of the *Homilies,* moved toward a vision in which the history of salvation is reduced to the reappearance of avatars of a primordial man. The Sassanian apocalypses themselves accepted this outline, as Mithraism had also done.

during the persecution of Antiochus Epiphanes must have looked with some nostalgia to the recent past of the Jewish people when they were still under only the comparatively mild law of the Persian monarchs. Now that the moral forces of the nation were fully mobilized to resist Hellenism, Iranianism would no longer seem so dangerous and could even be made an ally in the struggle being waged to preserve the nation's religious heritage. It is precisely in the Book of Daniel that there appears in all its clarity this vision of history, divided into periods and embraced in one glance by a Providence which determined "time" beforehand including the "time of the end" which completed it and wholly sanctioned it. These ideas can be fitted without difficulty into the tradition of the Day of Yahweh of ancient prophecy, but they have taken on a new cosmic breadth and are completed by the opening of the "books" during a universal judgment. Moral dualism is more strongly accentuated than before. It is in this context that we read the first unequivocal mention of the resurrection of the dead in the Jewish literary canon. Let us repeat the terms: "And many of those that sleep in the dust of the earth shall awake: some unto life everlasting, and others unto reproach, to see it always" (Dan. 12:2). Thus in the Book of Daniel are joined for the first time the three eschatological characteristics which would henceforward dominate all Jewish and Christian apocalyptic: judgment by fire (7: 9-10), the resurrection of the dead, and an ending to history. When this doctrine is traced throughout the Jewish writings it can be ascertained that they seem to mark out the distance which separates the eschatology of the *gatha* and that of the Sassanian apocalypses.[57] It is, however, very difficult to conclude from this that the development was uniformly affected by that of Iranian eschatology since we do not possess sufficiently explicit documentation. One may, therefore, just as well defend the opposite thesis: that there was a Judaic influence on the development of Mazdaean eschatology.

A close study of the recent condition of this latter thesis is instructive and affords some useful reflections. Those resurrected receive white haoma to drink from the fat of the mythic ox sacrificed by Saoshyant. This idea is certainly not Zoroastrian in origin because the reformer centered his preaching on the horror of the sacrifices of the old religion, respect for the ox and the outlawing of haoma drinking bouts. On the other hand, the central sacrament of the religion of Mithra is specifically the sacrifice of the ox, and we have every reason to believe that Mithra was the principal god of Zoroaster's enemies. But the figure of Mithra proved later to be too much alive to remain banished from the Zoroastrian pantheon. Saoshyant indeed seems to have been for his part only an avatar of Mithra. This leads us to relate the eschatology of late Zoroastrian Mazdaism to that of Mithraism. According to Cumont, the major part of whose works are devoted to a study of this religion, it competed very actively with Christianity in the Roman Empire of the third century, the resurrection of the dead forming part of its creed. Nevertheless Mithraism represents — and this characteristic seems contradictory — a type of particularly emphatic Iranian dualism and in this

[57] Cf. Oepke, *op. cit.*, p. 107, n. I.

resembles the Mandaean and Manichean Gnoses.[58] "After
death, the genie of corruption seizes the corpse, the dark
spirits and the heavenly envoys dispute the possession
of the soul separated from its corporeal prison. It is submitted to a Judgment presided over by Mithra, and if its
merits weigh more than its faults in the god's scales, he
defends it against the myrmidons of Ahriman who try
to carry it into the infernal depths, and he guides it
toward the ethereal spaces where Jupiter-Ormuzd sits enthroned in eternal light. [. . . .] the souls of the just go
to live in the infinite light, which extends beyond the
stars, and, stripped of all sensuality and all covetousness
in passing through the planetary spheres, become as pure
as the gods whose companions they will be. Yet, at the
end of the world, even their bodies will participate in
their beatitude because, like the Egyptians, the Persians
believed that the whole person should enjoy eternal life.
When time is completed, Mithra will redescend from
heaven to earth, and will resurrect all men and pour out
upon the good a marvelous beverage which will assure
them immortality, while the wicked will be annihilated
with Ahriman himself in the fire that consumes the universe."[59] Mithra, assimilated to Phaeton by the Greeks,
was thought of as the author of the final conflagration.

Insofar as the religion of Mithra is concerned, in the
form that it took in the Roman Empire at the beginning
of our era, one may indeed ask how far the presentation

[58] Mandaean eschatology, in Schmitt, *op. cit.*, 778. Manichean eschatology: Ch. H. Puech, *Le manichéisme,* p. 84. On the relations between
Zervanism, Mithraism and Manicheism, *W. N.,* II, pp. 101 ff.

[59] Cumont, *Rel. Orient.,* p. 147; see also Masson-Oursel, *Enc. Quillet,*
v. III, p. 40.

of its doctrine was influenced by the necessity of competing against the other oriental cults that were simultaneously spreading their message of hope in an afterlife. Thus it would not be very prudent to make use of the deliberate and yet hypothetical reconstruction of the Mithraist creed which Cumont has left us, in order to infer the doctrine of this religion in its Iranian habitat before our era. That it had been able to unify a dualism of spirit and matter (very similar to that of the Gnosis, in which death is a "liberation" of the soul) with belief in the resurrection of the body is already surprising and demands more solid proofs than those afforded by scattered documentation which is difficult to interpret.

If we return now to the eschatology of the *Bundahish,* in which, as we have said, Saoshyant plays a role exactly like that of Mithra and not very compatible with the authentic Zoroastrian spirit,[60] it may be questioned to what extent the fact of the resurrection in this late apocalypse is essentially tied to the person of the savior — Mithra or Saoshyant — who carries it out. In this case

[60] Saoshyant appears in the guise of the sacrificer who draws the elixir of immortality from the sacrifice of the bull. His deed, performed as part of the sacrificial action, gave birth to the cosmos in Mithraism. In late Zoroastrianism this initial act is attributed to Ahriman, a fact that is in one sense good Zoroastrian logic, since Zoroaster is the champion of the ox against his enemies, the henchmen of Ahriman, but leads to a serious contradiction by giving to the whole visible creation an Ahrimanian origin. This latter Zoroastrianism has already been taken over by the dualist spirit of the Gnosis. On the other hand, even the figure of Saoshyant as it appears in the late apocalyptic is not drawn from the teaching of the prophet but represents a recurrence of ancient Iranian conceptions connected with the cult of Mithra. Such is the thought of Lommel (Cf. the account in *La Religion de Zarathoustra, R. S. P. T.,* 1931, 527), who nevertheless persists in thinking that the resurrection formed a part of primitive Zoroastrianism. If one holds for an Iranian influence on Judaism, because resurrection and Messianism are indis-

the non-Zoroastrian character of belief in the resurrection of the dead would have to be accepted.

Another difficulty arises in connection with this same text. Haoma is obviously designed to procure immortality for the good after their bodies have been restored to them. This seems to imply a final destruction of the wicked, something very much in the spirit of the *gatha*[61] and found also in Iran, for instance in Manicheism. But the *Bundahish* forecast that the purification by fire which everyone would undergo but which would be as mild as lukewarm milk to the good would also restore the wicked to the innocence required for life in the new world definitively purged of all evil. There seems thus to have been a combination but not a co-ordination of two distinct eschatological trends. The fact is important for a comparison with Jewish eschatology.[62]

---

solubly united in the latter (Schürer, *Gesch. des. Jüd. Volkes,* II, 633, n. 60), one must admit that the Arian conception of periodic "saviors" was already combined with the properly Zoroastrian belief in the resurrection at the time when its influence was exercised. Bultmann is prepared to admit this: *Le Christianisme primitif,* p. 74. Cf. Nikolainen, *Der Augustchungsglauben, Annales Acad. Sc. Finn.,* v. XLIX, 100 and 143 ff.

[61] In the oldest portions are found such utterances as: "The creatures of Ahriman will be lost forever." Cf. Lommel, *op. cit.,* revised *R. S. P. T.,* 1931, 527.

[62] One of the arguments advanced against the thesis of Bousset is that Judaism conceived of a *general* resurrection only, and did this incidentally, at a late date. At first it professed only the resurrection of the good (for the sons of Abraham), sending others to destruction (Volz, p. 231 and *passim*). Judgment itself, the nature of which we believe conditioned by the nature of the resurrection, at first concerned only certain categories of men whose state was not automatically regulated by a general principle. Volz makes of the limited extent of the resurrection, attested in several ancient rabbis and in certain passages of the Jewish apocalypses, a proof or at least a strong presumption in favor of the originality of the Jewish belief. But to this opinion it must be answered that though the question of knowing who was resurrected was in effect disputed, among the opin-

The most convincing way to present the relationship between the two religions is to stress the fact that Judaism had in its own premises all that was needed to develop a doctrine of the resurrection, but that certain aspects of this doctrine, particularly those of the apocalyptics, assume cosmological ideas of a breadth new to Israel, which was not naturally gifted in this type of speculation.[63] The broadening of perspectives in which

ions coming down to us we find some which closely recall certain Iranian conceptions, notably the one in which the wicked are resurrected only to be again delivered to gehenna where fire completely destroys them at the end of a specified time. In a sense, the destruction of the wicked rather than their redemption, as it appears at a late date in the *Bundahish*, is more like Iranian dualism. Mandaism and Manicheism did include it, and it seems probable that this was the first form of Zoroastrian eschatology. Thus the notion of a "second death" that appears in the Sibylline texts and elsewhere, in the sense of a final destruction of the wicked (IV *Sib*. 180 ff.; IV *Esd*. 7, 75; *Targ. Jes*. 22, 14; *Bell. Jud*. II, 8, 14), favors rather a possible influence of Iranian dualism on Judaism. Volz's argument thus seems rather weak, and while it is difficult to deny that the Sassanian apocalypses underwent Jewish influence, it still has not been proved that Judaism was not itself first influenced by Iran in the development of its own apocalyptic.

[63] An element conditioning the Judaic conception of the resurrection, the idea of an awakening from the sleep of death, seems missing from the Iranian texts. According to Cumont, this conception was connected with sharing the condition of a god who slept and awoke in springtime and originated in Phrygia (*Symb. fun.*, pp. 361-362). Nilsson accepts the idea that in Phrygia funeral rites were closely connected with sacrificial worship in the temples, but he places the center of belief in the resurrection in Syria (II, 523). At the basis of the images Israel used to define its hopes there certainly is a foundation of beliefs (common to the Semites and to the other peoples of the Near East) in a god who underwent regular eclipses of his activity. This characteristic is not peculiarly Iranian, although the Western branches of the Iranian religions in contact with Asia Minor could have enriched themselves with such conceptions.

Bousset, *op. cit.*, pp. 579-582, and 582, n. 2; Michel, *D. T. C.* art. "Resurrection," col. 2508; Carnoy, *Histoire des Religions,* ed. Brillant and Aigrain, v. II, 246; Nikolainen, *op. cit.*, pp. 143 ff.

the Day of Yahweh occurs could have come about because of ideas introduced through foreign contacts. The chief eschatological event in Judaism and in Judaeo-Christianity is the judgment, and to it the resurrection is subordinated.[64]

While after Zoroaster the judgment in Iran appears chiefly as the final ratification of a choice, a freely adopted position,[65] in Israel the coming of Yahweh above all punished the enmity of the pagan nations which persecuted Israel, but also rewarded fidelity to the law in letter and spirit even within Israel; and this was increasingly true as the notion of the covenant and of fidelity were interiorized. The rabbinic debates clearly indicate that the process of interiorization had gone further with some teachers than others, for some held that merely being born an Israelite was a sufficient guarantee of salvation, while others moved toward judgment of souls such as the Sermon on the Mount assumes. For the Pharisee, however, the resurrection is required mainly so that the ancestors could participate in the Messianic joys.[66] Thus this is a tendency to limit the resurrection to those who are found faithful at the time of judgment.

[64] After St. Paul, Christian thought was to give more importance to the resurrection (for example *Act. Pauli* VII, v. 160), because of the close relationship between the resurrection of the dead and that of Christ. This change of stress is a corollary to the central place assumed by the Risen One in the Christian eschatological picture. The question of a possible Iranian influence on Christian ideas thus presents itself somewhat differently than the question of Iranian influence on pre-Christian Judaism. To measure this influence one would have to examine the view of the last judgment in both religions, even before comparing their conception of the resurrection.

[65] There is a similar conception in the Mandaean Gnosis; cf. Schmitt, *R. Sc. Rel.*, Strasbourg, 1956, p. 60.

[66] Cf. Schürer, *op. cit.*, II, 638, 641, 643; Bousset, *op. cit.*, 594.

Others are cast into gehenna, which corresponds to "perdition" although it is not clear whether this perdition involves a resurrection followed by destruction, or destruction of the soul without resurrection, or mere lack of activity by the spirit, preserved without individuality in a heavenly storehouse, which is needed to revivify the body.[67] Each of these different alternatives seem better to explain one or the other of the most explicit texts, but in reality these notions remain a rather confused collection.[68] This is easily understood in the context of Judaism, in which resurrection is usually connected with reward. Moreover, the existence of a current of pious Judaism even outside Alexandria should be pointed out, a belief not including a resurrection at all but cherishing the hope of an eternal life which would no longer be concerned with the body.

If the resurrection formed part of the teaching of the Zoroastrian Magians from the third century B. C., it seems that the internal logic of Zoroastrianism would require it to be general. And it is equally probable that it was anthropological considerations which led the Iranian religions to believe that the whole man, body and soul, would be present at the close of history so that all of him would be subject to the judgment. On the contrary, the reasons leading Judaism to profess the resurrection seem rather removed from anthropological notions.

The conceptions of man held in the rabbinical schools

[67] Volz, *op. cit.*, 250, on IV *Sib*. 180 ff.

[68] The reward of the good is postponed to the coming age, but the reward of the wicked for the good acts they perform is entirely consummated in this life; cf. Bonsirven, *Textes rabbiniques*, nos. 349 and 363.

varied widely, for some were willing to adopt modified Hellenistic categories while others strove to make use only of the traditional anthropology. Surely the most common reason in all Judaism for faith in the resurrection is as a consequence of God's faithfulness to the promises made to the patriarchs. It is impossible to imagine that those upon whom the promise had been personally bestowed would be deprived of its fulfillment. That this belief was at the heart of the authentic tradition of faithful Israel is proved by Christ's argument — at first glance unexpected in a discussion specifically related to the resurrection of the body: " 'I am the God of Abraham and the God of Isaac and the God of Jacob.' He is not the God of the dead, but of the living" (Matt. 22: 32). In other words, for Christ, assurance of the resurrection is founded on the indissoluble bond between God and the *verus israelitus,* created by fidelity to the covenant.

These views will be somewhat confused in the Fathers who, trying to develop an apologetic theology of the last things, would work with abstractions, and for this reason inclined toward more cosmological and anthropological views of Mazdaism or Hellenism. But in the Jewish tradition and in the teaching of Jesus it was a question of a concrete "filial" hope not resting upon abstract ethical considerations or anthropological fitness but directly upon faith in the covenant.[69] More or less poorly understood by certain Jews, the covenant led to some aberrant ideas of the resurrection. The "eschatological discourse" aimed to show that the judgment had been entrusted to the Son of Man and thus affected all

[69] Schürer, *op. cit.,* pp. 458-459.

men since all are called to take a position *vis-à-vis* the person of the Son. Men are judged by this choice itself. By the new criterion this judgment is universal, and St. John correctly drew the consequences of this universality in speaking of resurrection for life and resurrection for "Judgment," in other words for condemnation.[70] The introduction of the Son of Man into the history of the chosen people gave it, aside from all anthropological speculation, a universal character already grasped by the prophets who were aware of the universal and decisive value of the Word of God, and this fact resulted in removing doubts about the universal nature of the Judgment, placing all men *ex aequo,* in terms of a New Covenant. Thus, if the New Testament is more definite about the doctrine of a general resurrection than Judaism, this is due neither to the influence of a more highly developed eschatology nor to the introduction of anthropological categories of Hellenistic origin, but to an understanding of the universal meaning of salvation in Christ.

* * *

We have attempted to approach and clarify from various aspects this obscure question of the relations between the doctrine of the resurrection in Judaism and in the Iranian religions. We have no illusions about the compelling nature of our conclusions, modestly pronounced as they are. Closely studied, however, the striking similarity of structure between the two eschatologies, at first glance surprising, turns out to be more fallacious than it appears. There remain in Mazdaism important traces of an immanentism characteristic of the old Indo-

[70] John 5:29.

European heritage and more deeply marking the eschatological conceptions of India and Greece than those of Iran under Zoroaster's reform. This spirit is completely foreign to the Mosaic tradition. For Judaism found itself speculatively ill-prepared before the doctors of the great pagan religions, who were cosmologically and anthropologically better equipped. After the exile Judaism attempted, sometimes clumsily, to make up for lost time, rarely using borrowed notions in their primary meaning but bending them to its own monotheistic conceptions or using them to conceal Semitic ideas which were not equivalent.

For this reason, the doctrine of the resurrection, though it arises from exigencies proper to the fundamental principles of the Israelite religion, had not found clear and unanimous expression in the Judaism contemporary with Christ. The statements of Jesus, and His own resurrection, will completely affirm the teaching, but not until St. Paul was it inscribed, not in an anthropology nor a cosmology, but in a theological view of man which could serve as a basis for the efforts of the Fathers to develop their apologetic of the resurrection of the just. Meanwhile Jewish theology afforded them an essential heritage of undoubted originality: the resurrection of the dead is, in the last instance, founded only on God's omnipotence and the act of divine good pleasure which parallels the sovereign and inexplicable act of creation. In the authentic Mosaic tradition, each act God initiated in history has this abrupt character and the act which completes its course is equally sudden. To stress the sovereign liberty of the initiative of a transcendent God, the rabbis developed the conception of a reborn creation.[71] At first glance this notion tends toward the immanentist view of cyclic returns in the evolution of the cosmos, but in reality the meaning of the Jewish category of "re-creation" is diametrically opposite because it does not stress the autonomy of the cosmos as containing within itself the energies adequate for its rebirth, but emphasizes the inability of the creature to free himself from his sin and the death it entails, without the gratuitous intervention of the Creator. Along with this typically Jewish foundation for the Christian doctrine of the resurrection there is a second theme which we tend to call Pauline but which was probably general after the first Christian generation and perhaps even in the synagogue,[72] the idea of the seed which dies only to be reborn. St. Paul will give it such a place in his apologetic for the resurrection that it will remain a major theme throughout all patristic theology, especially the oriental and its interpretation will distinguish the various theologies of the "body of the resurrection."

[71] The rabbis were also aware of the parallel between God's intervention at birth and at the resurrection (thought to be less marvelous), a parallel found also in the Fathers. Cf. Bonsirven, *op. cit.*, 1902; *Methodius of Olympia, P. G.*, 18, 285. The idea exists in the apocalypse of the *Bundahish*.

[72] Bonsirven, no. 1901, *Sanh.* 90b: R. Meir (a rabbi whose pronouncements rather frequently show a certain sympathy toward Hellenistic categories) answers an adversary, acknowledging that the resurrection is affirmed. " 'They of the city shall flourish like the grass of the earth' (Ps. 71:16). But when they arise will they be naked or clothed?" The rabbi answers with an (a fortiori: "If the wheat which is buried naked rises reclothed in so many garments, how much more so the just, buried in their garments."

Oh, would that my words were written down! Would that they were inscribed in a record: That with an iron chisel and with lead they were cut in the rock forever! But as for me, I know that my Vindicator lives, and that he will at last stand forth upon the dust whom I myself shall see, and not another — and from my flesh I shall see God; my inmost being is consumed with longing.

Job 19:23-26

The hand of the Lord came upon me, and he led me out in the spirit of the Lord and set me in the center of the plain, which was now filled with bones. He made me walk among them in every direction so that I saw how many they were on the surface of the plain. How dry they were! He asked me: Son of man, can these bones come to life? "Lord God," I answered, "you alone know that." Then he said to me: Prophesy over these bones, and say to them: Dry bones, hear the word of the Lord! Thus says the Lord God to these bones: See! I will bring spirit into you, that you may come to life. I will put sinews upon you, make flesh grow over you, cover you with skin, and put spirit in you so that you may come to life and know that I am the Lord. I prophesied as I had been told, and even as I was prophesying I heard a noise; it was a rattling as the bones came together, bone joining bone. I saw the sinews and the flesh come upon them, and the skin cover them, but there was no spirit in them. Then he said to me: Prophesy to the spirit, prophesy, son of man, and say to the spirit: Thus says the Lord God: From the four winds come, O spirit, and breathe into these slain that they may come to life. I prophesied as he told me, and the spirit came into them; they came alive and stood upright, a vast army.

Ezechiel 37:1-10

Two

SCRIPTURAL SOURCES OF FAITH AND THE RESURRECTION OF THE BODY

Inquiry into the sources of the Christian dogma of the resurrection of the body is interesting in two ways. In the first place it helps us to define more exactly what this faith consists of, by clearly distinguishing it from certain more or less suspect forms of expectation of a hereafter. Secondly, such an inquiry will show us the influences under which this faith was born and affirmed. The movement which slowly led the Israelite people to affirm the resurrection and the new meaning this affirmation took on with the resurrection of Jesus are not haphazard affairs: they are found in the faith of all Christians and in the progress of all who come to this faith.[1]

I

Early ideas of life after death

It required centuries for Israel to arrive at the affirmation that the body of man was destined for resurrection. Even in the time of Christ, the Sadducees, who denied the resurrection, were certainly regarded as less fervent than the Pharisees, their rivals, but not as heretics. In their ranks were included great priestly families. Moreover, their denial had some arguments on its side. The great majority of biblical texts referring to life after death recognized only sheol, a kind of huge, common, under-

[1] It is impossible to treat the subject without referring to the article of R. P. Larcher, "La Résurrection dans l'Ancien Testament" in *Lumière et Vie,* no. 3, April, 1952, pp. 11-34.

ground cavern where the dead, regardless of their state or of their previous life, all led the unsubstantial life of shadows, without light, without joy, without relation to God (Ps. 87:7, 10, 13, 19; Ps. 48:18, Ps. 29:4, 10; Ps. 143:7). From this sad abode no one escaped. The death of man was final: "till the heavens be broken, he shall not awake, nor rise up out of his sleep" (Job 14:12). Moreover, no one tried to prolong relationships with those in sheol. Although a certain consciousness of solidarity with the dead was not lost because all awaited with a resigned abandonment the time of "reunion" with their people (Gen. 25:8, 17; 35:29) and hoped to find contact with the ancestors in some indistinct future, all that could be done for the most beloved of the dead was to assure them (Gen. 47:30) of honorable burial. This duty accomplished, there was nothing to do but live for one's own day of reckoning (Cf. 2 Sam. 12:22 ff.).

This resigned indifference sometimes surprises us. Compared to the care which certain highly civilized people — the ancient Egyptians, the Chinese — surrounded their dead, it seems the mark of an uncouth soul, of men too strongly attached to material and sensible impressions and reactions to suspect the possibility of another kind of existence, less dependent upon the body. Going further, one smugly blames, or tries uneasily to excuse, the grossness in which the Hebrew people lived for so long.

In reality this is a superficial point of view. Certainly the tribes of Israel always appeared barbarous in the eyes of the Egyptians, and they were unaware of the refinement of Egyptian culture and thought. But it is essential to appreciate the religious worth of their reactions to the mystery of the life after death. This value is perhaps other than one might believe. It is true that the Egyptians are always concerned about the state of their dead, and first of all about the state of the personage whose destiny governed that of all his people— the king. In life, the Egyptian king is god; in his person are concentrated the divine powers assuring the existence of his kingdom. Dead, he becomes, like all his ancestors, another god, Osiris. How can this coexistence of a succession of individuals under one unique personality be possible? Egyptian thought saw no impossibility there. Besides, this is not what is important for us. The important thing is the state of the god Osiris, an incarnation (if it may be called that, for the body is in a condition which is no longer precisely that of the flesh) of all the dead sovereigns, and then, after a certain period, of all the Egyptian dead. The dead god lives, but he lives as the dead do. His state is very different from the sad destiny of the shades in the Israelite sheol. He is drawn into the rhythm of the sun, the stars, the seasons, and becomes one with the blessed cycle without change or chance. Moreover, he becomes the power which causes the vegetation to be reborn each year and raises the dead waters of the Nile. He is the inexhaustible force of resurrection which animates nature.[2]

There is ambiguity in this resurrection. It seems to resolve into a natural occurrence. Undoubtedly there are in these phenomena, which so greatly exceed our meager individual powers and yet penetrate and dominate all our being so profoundly and organically, a

[2] On this resurrection, see H. Frankfort, *La royauté et les dieux*, trans. by Marty-Krieger, Paris, 1951, pp. 251-288, and especially p. 285.

breadth and a mystery capable of arousing a shiver of terror and astonishment. But to assure the afterlife of man by incorporating him into these impersonal cycles is to eliminate precisely what is important in man, to reduce him to a mere force, great as the universe, but blind and insensible. Imagination can multiply the most attractive creations in order to represent the existence of his divinized humanity. It will never extricate itself from the myth, it will never do more than give masks to the forces of nature or to social power. It is also undeniable that these hopes are often sustained by a very elevated moral sense. Man gains this immortality only by going through a rigorous judgment.[3] But how much of his real self can subsist in this perfect mechanism?

This consideration of Egypt leads us to appreciate the value of the silence of the Israelite texts on the world beyond. No speculation, but no illusion. What becomes of man after death? The Israelite did not seek to know. Firmly attached to concrete events, he is content to prolong endlessly what he sees of the dead that he buries: impotence, decay, shadows. This is not the whole truth. But it prevents errors and leaves the mystery intact. For God Himself can open a way to the depths and draw out, if He wishes, those who believe they can escape it (Amos 9:2 ff.; Is. 7:II; Job 38:17; Ps. 139:8).

Thus the resurrection, when its theory is developed, will appear as it really is: an extraordinary act of God, an intervention which overturns nature. It was a necessary preliminary that Israel be convinced that man's

[3] Cf. A. Barucq, *Religions de l'Égypte*. I. *L'Égypte pharonique*, Lille, 1947, pp. 112 and following.

normal destiny is death. An afterlife assured by the
natural development of the human person would have
no connection with the salvation that God reserves for
man, the only one which matters. For this salvation delivers us from sin, and sin is death. The long absence
in Israel of hopes for an afterlife is related to one of the
essential points of its religion, which remains the basis
of our faith: the consciousness of being subjected to a
slavery from which no human power can deliver us. Only
this radical disillusionment can give the divine initiative
its value.

II

Hopes for a resurrection of the nation

This divine initiative first manifests itself on the
national and collective plane. During these centuries the
Israelite did not suspect that he was destined for a personal resurrection. However, this time was not lost
for the faith which would be born. For Israel is steadfastly aware that its God is a God who can reanimate.
This resurrection is first that of the whole people, condemned to death for its sins. The message of the prophets
is to repeat endlessly to the people that its infidelities
lead it to catastrophe, that the anger of God has loosed
and will loose malediction. But it also repeats unwearying-
ly that this devastating anger is also purifying, that although it annihilates the sinner and his sins, the promises
of Yahweh remain unrevoked and that God can call forth
a just people even from the ruins of a guilty nation. This
is already the hope of Amos, Osee and Micheas (Amos
3:12; 5:4, 14 ff.; 9:8 ff.; Osee 2:20-25; 14:6-8; Mich. 4:6-8
and 9-13) who express it especially by the image of
remains sifted through a sieve. Isaia takes up the idea

again (4:2 f.; 7:3; 10:20 ff.; 28:5; 30:17), and with the intuition of his prophetic gaze, sees the salvation of Jerusalem born of its trials and its death. Jerusalem, the once faithful city, now prostituted, must pass through fire. Yahweh will defeat all His adversaries. But the fire will cause the rebirth of the city, purified and transformed:

> I will turn my hand against you, and refine your dross in the furnace, removing all your alloy.
> After that you shall be called city of justice, faithful city (Is. 1:25-26).
> He who remains in Sion and he that is left in Jerusalem
> Will be called holy: everyone marked down for life in Jerusalem (Is. 4:3).

These images are not unimportant. Not by chance does the prophet see death in the power which triumphs over all human grandeur and identify the work of God with life:

> Because you say, "We have made a covenant with death, and with the nether world we have made a pact . . ."
> Hail shall sweep away the refuge of lies, and waters shall flood the hiding place.
> Your covenant with death shall be cancelled and your pact with the nether world shall not stand (Is. 28:15 ff.).

But the life Yahweh gives to the regenerated city will not be an ordinary existence. The new Jerusalem certainly remains for Isaia the Sion whose houses and streets he knew. But he sees it transformed, penetrated by a new spirit, filled with the justice and the glory of Yahweh who sits enthroned on its summit (Is. 2:2-5; 33:5). To explain this renewal, the prophet uses the image of building. Yahweh Himself will rebuild the ruined city. But

He will build it in His own way:

> See, I am laying a stone in Sion, a stone that has been tested,
> A precious cornerstone as a sure foundation; he who puts
> his faith in it shall not be shaken (Is. 28:16).

These threats and hopes do not remain unfulfilled. The destruction of Jerusalem in 587 B.C. and the exile showed that the people of Yahweh could die. But the promise remained. At the height of siege Jeremia says: "Houses and fields and vineyards shall again be bought in this land" (Jer. 32:15). For God shall take up His work again, and His work will be a work of life. He will sow "the house of Israel and the house of Juda with the seed of man"; He will watch over them "to build and to plant" (Jer. 31:27 ff.).

In a more imposing tableau, Ezechiel sees this resurrection in the dry bones which cover the plain and return to life by the breath of the spirit of Yahweh (Ezech. 37). As concrete as it is, to the degree that, for centuries of Christian art, it remained the most suggestive illustration of faith in the resurrection of the dead, this resurrection still did not affirm the resurrection of individuals. It prophesied the resurrection of the people of Israel. But it is not a matter of indifference that this rebirth was expressed in such a striking vision. Such a tableau would never be forgotten. Who can know what obscure workings it set in motion in hearts and imaginations? It upheld the conviction that nothing is impossible to God and that even death gives way before Him. It showed the divine breath penetrating the scattered skeletons one by one, giving them a new life. It spontaneously moved toward an individual hope. Yet it also gave this hope, when it would be affirmed, a collective context. The resurrection of the individual coincided with the resurrection of all his people. This characteristic, which was to mark so strongly the Christian expectation of the resurrection, a reunion of redeemed humanity with Christ, surely found one of its sources in Ezechiel's vision.

III

The resurrection of individuals

It seems that the same atmosphere of collective and total resurrection distinguishes all the texts in which the Old Testament hints at an awakening after death. It is difficult to determine the exact significance of the texts in which the "Apocalypse of Isaia" sings the triumph of Yahweh over death, to know whether it is a matter of a resurrection of individuals or simply, in an audacious poetic vision, of a re-establishment of the nation including all the children of Israel who have died but are recalled to life in such a way as to participate in their way in this triumph. Is it the poet or the believer who is expressing himself here?

> But your dead shall live, their corpses shall rise; awake and sing, you who lie in the dust.
> For your dew is a dew of light, and the land of shades gives birth (Is. 26:19).

Similarly, in the tableau describing the universal reconciliation:

> [The LORD of hosts] will destroy the veil that veils all peoples,
> The web that is woven over all nations; he will destroy death forever.
> The Lord GOD will wipe away the tears from all faces
>
> (Is. 25:7-8).

One does not know exactly what meaning to give these details. Are they images or statements of fact? But even if we reduce their value to a minimum, seeing in these perspectives only the description, transformed by poetic spirit, of events pertaining to the history of our world, it is still a step forward when this event is described as a resurrection, as an opening of tombs, with these concrete details of the dead who will rise out of their shrouds, of sheol which opens to give up its prey, of these faces over which God leans. Images like these are unforgettable. If they still do not express a belief, they at least attest that this theme of the real resurrection is developing in men's minds (cf. Larcher, *Lumière et Vie,* 3, April, 1952, p. 19). They also give evidence that this theme involved the whole people and humanity itself. The victory of God over death and suffering would seal the union of all people reconciled together. If the dead were to receive back their bodies and all that they had been, it was in order to participate fully in the joy of all.

Perhaps this collective insight throws the most light on a passage that is certainly the most celebrated (in any case the most obscure) of all those in the Old Testament concerning the resurrection of the flesh—Job's great act of faith.

> I myself know that my vindicator is living,
> That He will be the last to rise up on the earth.
> My skin once destroyed, I shall see Him;
> Out of my flesh, I shall see God.
> He whom I see shall be for me,
> To my eyes, He will no longer appear indifferent
>
> (Job 19:25-27).[4]

[4] The text itself is uncertain. This translation follows that of R. P. Larcher in the *Bible of Jerusalem.*

One surely cannot give to this text the meaning St. Jerome gave it: "I know that my Redeemer is living and that I will be resurrected on the last day." Although widespread in the ancient Church, this interpretation is not universally accepted. St. John Chrysostom held that Job was speaking of his cure. Such certainty of rising would take away any point in Job's anguish. If he were certain of obtaining justice in another world, why would he persist in wanting his rights in this world?

The best qualified exegetes hesitate before a text as obscure as this one. Recent studies, however, do agree on the orientation of the text. They reject the "minimizing" interpretation which became widespread as a reaction against the Vulgate translation and according to which Job awaits only the restoration of his happiness. Verse 26 is then translated: "Beneath my skin I shall perceive him, with my flesh I shall see God." Such a translation relates to the end of the account, but it hardly agrees with the whole of the poem. The poem pushes the tragic to its limits. Job feels himself to be dying. He sees this end as the only issue of all the afflictions that strike him. He is convinced that his state is irrevocably decided (30:16-23; 23:13-17). He accepts it, but there is one thing, only one, to which he desperately clings: that God, who seems to overwhelm him, will make his innocence known publicly, that He Himself will come to take the side of the creature whom He has made to suffer so much. At what moment does Job expect this intervention? We cannot say. R. P. Lefèvre (*Supplément au Dictionnaire de la Bible,* IV, 1090 ff.) thinks that it is the instant of death: "God will have the last word, and through his ulcered skin, and eyes burned by tears, Job will see his justification" (1091). Father Larcher in his introduction to the *Bible of Jerusalem* leans toward a divine intervention after death.[5] Death will not change Job's condition of being reduced to the common state of shades under the earth, but it will allow him to be present on the great day when God will finally come to earth to order all things, to destroy the impious and make justice triumph. Job "thus, in a flash of faith and confidence, has applied to his own situation the tenet of general eschatology" (Larcher, *op. cit.*, p. 30). He accepts death, he renounces happiness, but he cannot admit that God would be the accessory of injustice, and he knows that someday He will re-establish justice.

It seems impossible to elucidate in this definitive fashion a text which will always remain obscure. But these analyses are not without value. They agree in demonstrating that the emphasis of the passage does not rest primarily upon Job's material condition. On the contrary this condition seems miserable. The major affirmation is that God, at the time He has determined, will make good triumph over evil. Thus understood, this famous text retains a place of prime importance in the preparations for the dogma of the resurrection of the body, a more important place perhaps than that given it by the old interpretation. It does not include a representation of the resurrection. It does not have the perspective of Ezechiel: it does not show the flesh in the process of flowering again. But it affirms, without being able to say when or how, that God, even when He seems to permit injustice and to reject His servants, remains

[5] In his article in *Lumière et Vie*, August, 1952, p. 20, he seems to return rather to the first hypothesis.

the just God, and that at the very time when they sink into death they can depend upon this justice. How this will be done, Job does not know. He believes. Against all hope he is faithful to hope, with a feeling surely like that of Abraham raising the knife over his son. In this way, Job gives a new value to a fundamental feature of the dogma of the resurrection. It is not the natural prolongation of existence. It is the victory of God over death. When Jesus rises He will demonstrate to His own that this law dominates the whole of Scripture. It explains the destiny of the patriarchs. It is constantly verified in the history of Israel; the major example is the exile and the return. Job's faith assumes this God who is stronger than death.

Definitive affirmations about the resurrection appear only in the last periods of the history of Israel. They are clear and unequivocal (Dan. 12:2-3; 2 Mach. 7:8). It is obvious that they did not develop all at once. They express a faith already well established, perhaps for a long time. They do not give the impression of a discovery.

It is understandable, however, that circumstances gave an object to these hopes, which might have remained vague. There was the question of the martyr, and of bodies maltreated by torture. Nothing was better suited to give a concrete content to the images of the prophets. What scene could do more than the vision of Ezechiel to nourish the faith of these men whose limbs the torturer tore away one by one? The God who had given life back to an unfaithful people could not fail to restore to His servants the body they had sacrificed to Him. The God to whom a mother offered her sons tortured before her was well able to return them to her.

The martyr thus succeeded in giving due importance to the expectation of the resurrection in the Old Testament. This accomplishment worked, one might say, on two levels. At the level of representation, the sacrifice and the destruction of the immolated body sanctified the vision, made ready by the ever-concrete understanding of Hebrew thought and nourished by the prophetic images, of an awakening of this same body to a new life in a world transformed. At the level of certitude, the anguish which weighed upon a Job conscious of his innocence but unable to provide men with indisputable proof and of sharing the secret with a God who eludes him—this tragic anguish has disappeared. Job is willing to die in the dark, knowing that God is for him, but not knowing how he will find Him again. The martyr who delivers his body to torment dies in the light; he knows that he dies to serve his God, he knows that he dies with his God.

The feature so marked in the earliest hopes persists up to the Old Testament's supreme expressions of faith in the resurrection. The individual will rise to be incorporated with his entire people. Men who brave persecution do so to remain faithful to the Law of their people (2 Mach. 7:2, 24, 30, 37), conscious of its sins (7:18, 32, 38) and hoping for its return to God (6:16, 33, 37).

IV

The New Testament

Not only does the New Testament announce the fact of the resurrection of the body with complete certainty and unhesitating precision, it does much more. It places us in the presence of the risen Body of the Lord Jesus.

Certainly the contemplation of this Body is more fruitful for us than the care to obtain—in texts some of which, like the episode of Lazarus and the rich man, are parables, while some are more definite—those certainties which our imagination craves. St. Paul writing to the Corinthians indeed means to recall that we are dealing with a mystery which is beyond mortal man (1 Cor. 15:35-44).

But one fact is clear. The risen Body of Jesus is surely the one He had before He died, the Body which suffered. Doubtless it is now in a new state, capable of movement as He wills, not bound by extension or weight. Nevertheless it is not the body of a phantom, and in a mysterious fashion there is a continuity between its present and former state, in particular a continuity with the suffering it underwent.

This very consistency has not failed to arouse doubts. Some find in the setting of the apparitions the still crude expression of a faith naive and not very spiritual, which has degraded to the sensible level experiences on a much higher plane.

We need not vindicate the accounts of the apparition here. Yet loyally accepting them we can only observe that this Christian faith, which we have thought naive and subject to debasement, has given proof of an extraordinary spiritual penetration. For the most important Christian assertion is that Jesus is God, seated at the right hand of the Father (Acts 2:33-36). The natural way of imagining Jesus' spirit is that it would appear in divine glory, radiant with light too bright for human eyes. It is true that this glory was manifested at the resurrection of Jesus. The earth trembles, celestial personages appear in a supernatural light which spreads terror. But all this glory is, if one may so speak, only a husk. Its heart is Jesus, and Jesus Himself remains the same. In none of the apparitions is He unrecognizable. Undoubtedly He can change His appearance and bearing. However, He continues to show Himself in the simplest lineaments, in the most familiar attitudes. If He conceals Himself, it is under the appearance of a traveler, a gardener, a passer-by on the lake shore. He tries to show that He is not changed, that He not only has a tangible Body but also one which uses the familiar gestures by which He was known. He appeared so ordinary that no one knew Him, as He busied Himself to give His own a meal when they returned from fishing; He even ate what they left. The continuity of His Body now assumes its full significance. Everything is quite natural, from the moment that Jesus appears the man that He was, more simple, more accessible than ever. Glory has changed nothing of His physiognomy, His heart, His person. He remains a man, spontaneously at ease among men. One cannot imagine angels sitting down at table with the disciples. Jesus is happy with His own.

Thus the Evangelist reveals to us the secret of the resurrection of the body that we await. It will be a mysterious transformation of the entire man, bringing to flower a reality as different from his earthly body as the flower is from the seed; it will also be the flowering of all that he has been, of his familiar gestures, the habits ingrained in his body, all the details of his appearance. It is mysterious, yet the body will appear at its most authentic.

This resurrection will also be a gathering together, a

meeting. This is a further revelation of the Evangelists' accounts. The resurrection of Jesus brings together people who have already begun to disperse. The message of the angels to the women, the meeting at Emmaus, accomplish this. And it is not by chance that eating at meals held such a place during these hours. Jesus wished to lay the foundations of the Church-to-be-born upon indestructible ties, those of His Spirit. He wished those bodily present at a common table to be unified in heart. But neither hearts nor bodies would remain united if they were not gathered around His risen Body. Thus the meals eaten by the risen Lord accomplished the promises that the Old Testament always associated with the expectation of a resurrection: the vision of a reunion of Israel, of a reconciliation of a divided humanity.

Doubtless the apparitions of Jesus do not tell us everything about the condition of the risen body. He Himself, after a few meetings, disappeared from sight, lost in the heavenly glory which absorbed Him. To Mary Magdalen who tried to touch Him He said it was necessary that she leave Him and that He leave her. He must enter into a glory that no human glance can attain, He must escape all earthly embrace. The transfiguration was for the purpose of revealing the unaccessible nature of this glory. As a prolongation of the theophanies of the Old Testament it made Him appear in the very center of a radiating brightness which dazzled the Apostles, in a uniquely intimate relationship with the invisible God. But the originality of the accounts of the apparitions after the resurrection is rightly different from that of the transfiguration. The former share, certainly, the world of the transfiguration, the dazzling light, the clouds, the sleep which overwhelms the witnesses. And one finds them at the tomb on Easter morning; one finds them at the Mount of Olives, at the ascension. They are there to convince us that Jesus has really entered into the glory of God. This is how He was at the transfiguration. But He is at the same time, and this is the point He wishes to underline, such as He was among them; such as He had been known, such He remains for eternity. This persistence, in a totally spiritual world free of all terrestrial chains, of a man of flesh and blood is the mystery of what faith makes us call the "glorified body"; it is the immediate testimony of the Gospel texts.

When we wish to contemplate our Lord, we do not have to put aside these images. They are the last He wished to leave of Himself. They are the ones which should feed our expectation. Yes, when He returns to judge risen mankind, we shall see Him come as the Apostles saw Him go away (Acts 1:11), with the human features that are His for eternity. As He will be, so we also shall be, since our hope is to be "always with him" (1 Thess. 4:17; 2 Cor. 5:8; Phil. 1:23). If we wish to form an idea of resurrected humanity, the surest way is to contemplate the face of the resurrected Christ. We too readily imagine heaven as a luxurious setting of stately solemnity, gleaming with gold, shining and immobile, and all this éclat creates for us today the effect of a "very boring marvel" (D. Dubarle, "Resurrection et Science," Lumière et Vie, April, 1952, p. 97). The Gospel parables, and still more the accounts of the resurrection of Jesus, give us a very different image of God's glory, full of simplicity and humanity, of easy familiarity transfiguring the most ordinary gestures, without anything to cause them to lose their authentic density. And how would the Beatitudes be verified otherwise, if the glory of the omnipotent God, in order to transfigure men's tears and suffering, did not begin by jealously respecting all that have paid the price, all that have borne the daily effort of courage and devotion?

Perhaps this Biblical perspective on the resurrection of the body will help us adhere with more faith to the dogma of the assumption of the Blessed Virgin. The immediate resurrection of the Virgin Mary could not be different from that of her Son, announced by the Old Testament. It is a unique privilege, but it is also one of the actions by which God gathers mankind together. Mary did not undergo the corruption which will overtake our bodies. This was not in order to bypass our condition, but to be intimately present and united with the long travail of maturation by which all creation is prepared for its redemption. How this nearness is accomplished is God's secret; but Christian piety invoking its Queen never doubts it, and the reading of Scripture can only confirm this certainty.

An essential aspect of the Christian veneration of the Virgin is, justly, the stress it always places upon her nearness, upon the unerring intuition with which this woman, this mother, bends over the most miserable. The more suffering there is, the more despair threatens, the nearer is the Blessed Virgin. She continues to be the one we invoke when we have tried everything and there is nothing more to do. This faith is not born of a naive or puerile sentimentality. It expresses the most authentically Christian meaning of the resurrection. It places Mary exactly where she belongs, following the apparitions of the risen Christ. The Queen of the Church and of sinners is not a *grande dame,* distant and majestic. She remains in the impenetrable radiance of her glory what she was on earth, what she was all her life: a simple woman, accustomed to work, to rebuffs, concerned with care for all, one whom people were not ashamed to turn out of doors but who kept her own door open to all.

But someone will say, "How do the dead arise? Or with what kind of body do they come?" Senseless man, what thou thyself sowest is not brought to life, unless it dies. And when thou sowest, thou dost not sow the body that shall be, but a bare grain, perhaps of wheat or something else. But God gives it a body even as he has willed, and to each of the seeds a body of its own. All flesh is not the same flesh, but there is one flesh of men, another of beasts, another of birds, another of fishes. There are also heavenly bodies and earthly bodies, but of one kind is the glory of the heavenly, of another kind the glory of the earthly. There is one glory of the sun, and another glory of the moon, and another of the stars; for star differs from star in glory. So also with the resurrection of the dead. What is sown in corruption rises in incorruption; what is sown in dishonor rises in glory; what is sown in weakness rises in power; what is sown a natural body rises a spiritual body.

If there is a natural body, there is also a spiritual body. So also it is written, "The first man, Adam, became a living soul"; the last Adam became a life-giving spirit. But it is not the spiritual that comes first, but the physical, and then the spiritual. The first man was of the earth, earthy; the second man is from heaven, heavenly. As was the earthy man, such also are the earthy; and as is the heavenly man, such also are the heavenly. Therefore, even as we have borne the likeness of the earthy, let us bear also the likeness of the heavenly.

Now this I say, brethren, that flesh and blood can obtain no part in the Kingdom of God, neither shall corruption have any part in incorruption. Behold, I tell you a mystery: we shall all indeed rise, but we shall not all be changed—in a moment, in the twinkling of an eye, at the last trumpet. For the trumpet shall sound, and the dead shall rise incorruptible and we shall be changed. For this corruptible body must put on incorruption, and this mortal body must put on immortality. . . .

(1 Cor. 15:35-54.)

Three

THE TEACHING OF THE FATHERS

Discussion about the resurrection of the body occupies an important place in the Christianity of the first centuries. The reason for this should be sought mainly in the fact that few Christian dogmas were so offensive to the mentality of the Hellenistic world, scene of the first Christian conquests. Indeed the debate had begun even before the coming of Christ. The diversity of conceptions of the afterlife in Judaism is best explained as hesitancy concerning, not so much the nature of religious hopes, as the composite structure of man. These hesitancies are for the most part the result of a penetration into the Jewish world of ideas spread by popular philosophy throughout the entire Hellenistic world. Historians have not always agreed on the degree of Hellenism which Palestinian Judaism had willy-nilly absorbed at the time of Christ,[1] but since this absorption continued to exert its pressure on the patristic milieu we may conveniently recall the main characteristics of the anthropology and eschatology of Greco-Roman paganism under the Empire.[2]

---

[1] Cf. R. Meyer, *Hellenistisches in der Rabbinischen Anthropologie.* He is sure that body-soul dualism had already penetrated Palestinian Judaism at an early date, but he is no less sure that conceptions like metempsychosis jostled constantly with the Jewish sense of God's decisive intervention, under the form of a judgment without appeal, cf. Wolfson, *Philo,* 407. On other points, the degree of Hellenization in rabbinic thought could vary a great deal from one teacher to another.

[2] Cf. the great works of Cumont, *Symbolisme funéraire, After-life, Lux Perpetua.* The résumé which follows is based on these findings and on the critiques of Nilsson, *Gesch. d. gr. Rel.*

The idea of the body as the soul's prison and of death as a liberation dominated the imagination more and more and found expression in funerary monuments. This practical dualism did not always involve the conception of a spiritual soul. Stoicism, while remaining fundamentally materialist, deliberately adjusted to common, popular conceptions, distinguishing subtle states and more gross states, or better, states more or less "dynamic," more or less animated by the *pneuma,* the fiery breath endowed with understanding which organizes the universe. The Stoa popularized the philosophical conception of correspondences and "sympathy" between the parts of the universe and the parts of men. The best in man is thus related to the best in the universe, that is, to the heavenly bodies—the disciplined throngs which move in an orderly path across the vault of heaven. From on high they rule the great rhythms of our lowly existence on earth. But their ordered influence can come to us only after having traversed the atmospheric zone, troubled by the capricious activity of the spirits of the air.[3] This intermediate region corresponds with the passionate and imaginative soul in man which intervenes between the domain of reason and corporeal life. Serenity of soul is thus the condition of happiness and the reward of virtue. After death the soul spontaneously looks for its "natural place." The soul of the wise man will proceed towards the higher regions where a purer and calmer air receives with less delay the influx from on high, while the souls

[3] In Philo, the air is the abode of souls awaiting incarnation (Wolfson, *op., cit.,* 413). In Plutarch it is the dwelling of "lost" souls, and it is from the air that "appearing" souls borrow their phantomlike bodies, according to a consistent tradition beginning with the Phaedo and continued by Origen, Gregory of Nyssa, etc.

of "carnal" men will seek low places where memories draw them and where passions agitate them. If to this is added belief in a *daimon,* which may have been the integrating part of the individual or a pre-existing tutelary spirit but which in any case plays a capital role in imaginations striving to penetrate the mysteries of the world beyond, we obtain a succinct but adequate picture of the common pagan basis of funerary representations. We cannot overlook this simple outline when we seek a meeting ground with those whose particular philosophical system coincides with that of cultivated paganism. The basis of resistance to the Judaeo-Christian dogma of the resurrection and the point of departure for an accommodation between the two mentalities should not be looked for elsewhere.

Moreover, the popular mentality remained suffused with archaic conceptions resembling those we have met in the East. The relationships between life and death are envisioned on the model of the return of the seasons.[4] The traditional celebrations marking the change of seasons had the purpose of freeing, for the advantage of the living, the forces accumulated in the common reserve where death consigned them. The actions of sowing and harvesting were simultaneously acts of life and of death since the seed "died" in order to be reborn and the sickle "sacrificed" the sheaf so that life could be nourished by it. Death is therefore the gate where the two domains of life and death meet, a place of barter and of trade, in the image of the market held at the city gates. This archaic conception continued active beneath the more

---

[4] Cf. Jeanmaire, *Dionysos,* 54.

learned conception of the correspondence between microcosm and macrocosm, permeated by astrology. The archaic conception was nourished by oriental contributions
for which it had a real affinity. Under one of these aspects,
the idea of the resurrection finds a ready-made basis, but
it is especially belief in metempsychosis which exploits
this foundation of pantheistic attraction. This attraction
to pantheism can easily unite the archaic tendency to
conceive life as a sum of homogeneous and interchangeable energies and the later trend toward anthropological
dualism. Life is borne by a certain number of transmigratory spirits whose number remains constant but
whose continual circulation through the various parts of
the cosmos maintains the rhythm of natural phenomena.[5]

Yet the Pythagorean "system of life" consists essentially in "accompanying the divine," that is to say, conforming to those natural rhythms, while keeping free
of all that could disturb their course. Here there is the
basis not only of a morality but also of an eschatology,
of which metempsychosis is the natural form. The wise
man who by ascesis and virtue achieved in his soul
and his body a well-ordered universe is the equal of the
gods and will share their joys in the celestial heights.
Men of passion, according to whether their passions are
noble or base, will rejoin their celestial types, wandering

[5] Opinions on the origin of the idea of metempsychosis in Hellenism
are divided. Cumont turns to the Orient, more particularly to the
India of the *Upanishad*, but Nilsson, basing his critique of Cumont
on only one point, the predominant role of the moon in the thought
of the Brahmans, believes he finds in the archaic Greek religious
foundations all the elements for the elaboration of a theory of the
transmigration of souls. Cf. Nilsson, *op. cit.*, I, 694-5, and the note
in loco.

stars, or else will enter into the bodies of animals, characterized by blind submission to a particular passionate temperament.[6]

A final idea, doubtless originating in a popularized Platonism, colors the pagan mentality on these matters: the notion of *fall* and *return*. There is in man a "divine" element which feels its earthly life as an exile and proves itself of divine origin by the sense of reminiscence that often accompanies man's acquisition of knowledge. Fallen from the heavens, man tends to return there. But this Platonism is charged with Stoicism and, in the world conceived as a great living being, the dynamism of constant exchanges prevents a conception of total stability even in the most elevated positions. While the abode of the wise in the heavenly places, where they contemplate divine realities stripped of the gross covering of corruptible matter, can extend for long periods, there will nevertheless come a day — for instance the day of the conflagration which according to the Stoa periodically renews the face of the universe — when things will begin again. Thus arose the widespread idea of seeking blessedness *above* the cosmos. Of course on such a point of detail, each philosophical school had its own dogmas. The Peripatetics, for instance, believed in the perenniality of the astral gods. But the main features present in all imaginations when they ventured into the world beyond are those we have described, as the patient labors of Cumont have definitively established.

The idea of eternal return did not arouse in Greece the basic repugnance which the *samsara* inspired in the sages

[6] Cf. The eschatology of the Gnostic Basilides, in Clem. Alex., *Strom.,* II, XX, 112.

of India. Nevertheless, toward the Christian era there appeared in certain Hellenistic milieux an evident aspiration to put aside forever the ceaseless play of life's fluctuations. This brought a renewal of interest in cosmological speculations as to what lay beyond the vault of the firmament.[7] There perhaps exists a region — would it be accessible to the spirits of mortals? — where happiness is eternal. Beyond all death, all corruption, beyond all conditioning by time and space, beyond — who knows? — all distinct thought, could there not be an infinite and indefinable God whom reason approaches only by the formidable power of an absolute negation? This is the thought of certain audacious spirits, unfaithful in reality to the traditional inspiration of Hellenic thought, which venerates the beauty of the cosmos and has only contempt or horror for the madmen whose *hybris* extends to the point of wishing to colonize the ἄπειρον.

To think of an eschatology dependent upon a cosmology is so natural to the ancient mentality that certain Fathers, reacting with good reason against what the Hellenistic framework held that was unacceptable to the Christian, will justify their doctrine on the basis of other cosmological arguments, drawn from Scripture.[8] The history of eschatological doctrines in early Christianity is thus profoundly involved with the confrontation of two more or

[7] It was a matter of re-entering a perfectly stable place where one escaped the necessary fluctuations of the parts because there one "comprehended" the whole. The place was somehow God Himself who comprehends all without being comprehended by anything. Cf. Wolfson, *op. cit.* 304; *Corpus Hermeticum,* XI, 20; Philo, *de Fuga,* 75. Cf. Rohde, E., *Psyche,* French translation, 400.

[8] A good example: the framework within which the eschatology of the apocalypse of St. Paul moved.

less irreconcilable conceptions of the world.[9] But while pagan eschatology was based essentially upon a cosmological pivot, the living equilibrium of the All or the stability of thought equivalent to the All, Christian eschatology rested on the fact of the resurrection of Christ, a fact that can be described in cosmological language but which in itself transcends a conception of the world. Thus when pagan funerary symbolism is adopted and adapted into the Christian climate, as in the catacombs, reading it requires a transposition equivalent to a real conversion as far as its religious content is concerned.[10]

The theme of repose may be given as an example. The formulas are often identical, and the *requies aeterna* is found on pagan tombs before it appears on Christian ones, but while in a Christian context the idea of sleep irresistibly evokes the "awakening" of the resurrection, it is not the same in a pagan context. Here, sleep has value in itself.[11] It is a state of happiness, prelude to complete freeing of the soul from corporeal ties. Death is the perfect sleep because it guarantees a state of prolonged dream without the risk of a sorrowful awakening. Death in the pagan context is an evasion.

The idea of the relations between soul and body found in the academic philosophy of the Hellenistic period is no longer the same as the thought of the Platonists or Aristotelians. The notion of the soul has been influenced

---

[9] From Judaism on, Cf. *Th. W., N. T.*, art. παράδεισος (Jeremias), the confrontation had taken place and adaptation had begun.

[10] Cf. Basanoff, in his review of Cumont, *R. H. R.*, v. 129, 156 ff.

[11] Cumont, *Symb. fun.*, 363-4. There is, however, in Plotinus a distinctly disparaging idea of sleep and repose, *Enn.*, I, VIII, 9.

by popular fancies along the way. The soul is thought of as a mold giving form to the body, clothing it as with an adornment (κόσμησις). The mold subdues the matter it envelops by the "quality" it confers upon it. Thus a transformation of the soul must have consequences for the body. If the soul, liberated from a first body, begins to be uneasy for a new instrument, it will choose it in harmony with its own dispositions. These mutations were thought of like the physical transformations that alchemy investigates. The vocabulary of spiritual direction was borrowed from that of the goldsmith and vice versa. Does not Hermes' caduceus rule over both domains? Gnostics and Hermetics tended to multiply physical entities of a more and more "spiritual" quality, which are superimposed as tunics one upon another, and, beginning with the most gross, are shed gradually as one ascends. Anthropology acquired the imaginative attraction it still holds for our theosophists and contemporary spiritualists who have also gone to ancient and oriental sources. While death restores to the four elements what the visible body has borrowed from them, the subtle outer envelopes have their own *place* and the most "divine" element alone, according to certain Gnostic conceptions, migrates beyond the limits of the cosmos.[12] Through logical extension of the "macrocosm-microcosm" theme the cosmos becomes a vast prison filled with shadows into which the Gnostic "revelation" has thrown a ray of light, the only thing capable of conveying those who are worthy of it into a motionless universe freed from the curse of time.

These ideas, which are combined and shaded in in-

---

[12] *Exc. Theod.*, 27; cf. Festugière, *Hermes Trism.*, III, Ch. IV, I.

numerable ways according to the whim of each founder of a sect or school, seem able to afford some interesting points of connection for the Christian apologists of the resurrection. Nevertheless they offer a great many snares, sometimes subtle ones, to which the most intelligent are perhaps most exposed. The most apparent obstacle is that the body, as the doctrine of metempsychosis best illustrates, is for the Greeks merely the transitory and interchangeable instrument of a soul, which is the only bearer of the individuating quality. Insofar as it remained faithful to Semitic anthropology, Judaism on the contrary saw in the body the real center of the person, to the extent that the words used to designate it refer also to the whole human being.[13] As to the vital breath, it is an impersonal power that God gives or takes back as He wills. To a Greek, this conception could only seem barbarous. For him, on the contrary, matter, fitted to receive all qualities, had none of its own. The soul united to matter finds itself willy-nilly carried along in an incessant becoming. Yet the rational soul aspires naturally to an order without vicissitudes. The union of soul and body thus pre-

[13] Tresmontant, *Essai sur la Pensée hébraique*, pp. 106-107: "The idea of a dichotomy between body and soul does not exist, and the term 'body' itself is missing. The resurrection of the dead is the resurrection of men." It is well to temper these statements somewhat by the remarks of Rust, *Nature and Man in Biblical Thought*, p. 96: "Flesh is not the only constituent of human personality, however. It is, in a sense, the dead stuff out of which man is individualized, and he needs the animating *nephesh* if he is to be vitalized." And it must be noted finally that the most extreme dualism is introduced into certain Jewish circles toward the beginning of our era; Philo is an example, and not an absolutely isolated one. In Palestine, however, relations between body and soul were not thought of as so unsubstantial, the salvation of both elements being considered as dependent upon the divine will and the fulfillment, both corporal and spiritual, of the Law. Cf. R. Meyer, *op. cit.* pp. 30-32.

sents a problem to the Greek mind, and each philosopher takes up the task of finding an explanation for it. Philo, the Gnostics, the Hermetics, Origen and the neo-Platonists in turn concerned themselves with this question. All do not take the Gnostic way, according to which union with nature is the only evil, and Iamblichus, for example, will admit that the descent of the soul into the body is not in every case an evil.[14] According to a solution already developed by Philo, the soul could have come to earth to consume, purify and perfect terrestrial things, but a solution—advocated by Origen and certain neo-Platonists—can also be envisioned in which the soul submits to the coarser body as a trial which purges it of its own previous errors and thus gives it the opportunity to win back purified, a more suitable place. Since it seemed to several Fathers that the conception of the soul's "descent" into the body could scarcely be reconciled with the dignity the Judaeo-Christian tradition bestowed on the body and that it made the dogma of the resurrection superfluous, they tended to reject it, despite the support that it seemed to receive from the inbreathing by Yahweh of the *spiraculum vitae* into the clay from which Adam was formed.[15] If the personal and responsible element in man is wholly bound to the soul, how can one explain that judgment is delayed until after the resurrection? From ancient rabbinical teaching onward there

[14] Iamblichus, *Stobaeus,* 40, I, analyzes the main solutions proposed to the classic problem of the reason for the soul's fall, and its consequences. Cf. Festugière, *op. cit.,* III, 69-71, 93-96. For the extreme dualism of Mani, the body is the soul's hell; cf. Kroll, *Gott. u. Hölle,* 310; Origen is not very far from the same conception.

[15] Irenaeus, V, 6, 1, and Tertullian, *de res. carn.,* VI, both attach the quality of image of God even to the body, sprung from earth.

had been a tendency to admit a kind of particular judgment. But such a revolution in the conception of man could not be completed without a crisis. Here Philo is, as so often, in the extreme avant-garde, but his position must have seemed utterly untenable to many. With regard to the popular Christian apocalyptic, the Fathers of the Church are true pioneers who strove to make the Christian dogma acceptable to the Hellenic mind. Their boldness did not, however, lead them all as far as Origen on the path of the assimilation of Greek categories. As to the pagans, when they condescended to turn as philosophers to Jewish or Christian eschatological conceptions, they tended to see in them a plagiarizing from Stoic ideas of the destruction of the world by fire, and the regular recurrence of events experienced by the same individuals in successive cosmic periods.[16] The religious value in the Pharisees' hope of resurrection, brought about by a holy life passed in the service of God in an endless liturgy and free of all fear of falling into legal impurity by contamination, was to escape even the cultivated pagan.

The central fact of the resurrection of Christ slightly shifted the focus of Christian hope without, however, upsetting the major features of Jewish eschatology. If the Son invited His disciples to know His Father as He knows Him, this knowledge cannot be confused with the contemplation of the order of the world which the Stoic sage practices. On the contrary it is as a type of perfect

[16] Cf. Nemesius, *de nat. hom.*, 38; Tatian, *adv. Gr.* 6, and Origen's frequent allusions in the *Contra Celsum* where he, however, does not hesitate to make rather free use of conceptual material afforded by the Stoa, for example VIII, 72.

worship offered eternally by the risen Christ surrounded by His own that it must be understood, for to a Jew, perfect knowledge involves the exercise of corporeal life in its entirety and, more precisely, of the integral dynamism of life. In a word, "eternal life" is not the result of a sloughing off of all the "corruptible" in order to free and "sublimate"—to use the language of alchemy—the incorruptible element, but, on the contrary, according to St. Paul, "this corruptible body must put on incorruption" (1 Cor. 15:53). It is very true that the Johannine ideal of the knowledge of the Father through the Son awakens echoes in the Hellenistic mystique and particularly in Hermeticism,[17] and it is no less true that the "pneumatic" characteristics of the risen Lord's Body in the synoptics, privileges that Paul extends to all the risen at the time of the Parousia, transposes us into a mode of hope at first glance very different from Judaizing millenarianism. Some of the Fathers interpreted this difference when introducing certain elements of pagan religious mystique into their own interpretation of the resurrection. The risk they took was thus comparable to the ones taken by those who, being careful to "integrate" and preserve a certain traditional Jewish aspect of the Messianic hopes, laid stress upon the weight of the grape clusters in the vineyards of paradise. In fact the two trends, which had been in opposition even within Judaism, continued into the work of the Fathers, but instead of diverging, they converged in proportion to the progress made in the development of the dogma, thanks to the ever greater faithfulness to Scripture,

[17] Cf. the works of R. P. Braun in the *Revue thomiste*, 1954-1956, on Essenism, Hermeticism and Johannism.

which was taken up integrally, in the totality of its affirmations, and read in the light of the traditional meaning of the Savior's resurrection, lived in the liturgical and mystical life of the Churches.

Christ Himself had in a way encouraged His disciples to walk the borderline between two possible areas of a theology of the resurrection when He compared the life of the risen to that of the angels. He did not in this way empty the resurrection of its physical reality, as the thought of certain Fathers tended to do, but in reality He decided in favor of *one* rabbinic trend as opposed to another. All the rabbis understood the resurrection of the body in a completely realistic sense, but while some believed that the risen would begin to procreate in the millenarian kingdom, others, comparing the resurrection to the simultaneous and definitive creation of the angelic hosts, suspended the application of the Genesis precept, "Increase and multiply." In choosing this latter solution, Jesus eliminated with the same stroke a certain type of coarse millenarianism, but He did not compromise with the excessively "etherealized" visions of the world of the risen.[18] Having lost contact with the rabbinic way of posing problems, the Fathers disagreed on the question of this comparison with the angels because they took it too generally to mean total identity of physical characteristics. They sometimes tried to bring about agreement by distinguishing two resurrections, the first providing access to the millenarian kingdom while the second assimilated the just to the angels. Such solutions are at the origin of those complete but complex accounts

[18] Thus Kümmel, *Verheizung, u. Erfüllung,* 82, following Baumgartner.

which try to integrate and reconcile everything believed
to be traditional. They keep irreconcilable elements from
mutual destruction by spreading them out in space or in
time. Separate stages, various tiers of the cosmos, successive eons,[19] are the indispensable framework for a
coherent redistribution of basically contradictory fac-
tors. Here we must point out one of the major defects
of patristic exegesis: its arbitrarily analytic character.
It tries to interpret every word and image, without taking into consideration that these expressions often represent different approaches to and images of the same
mysterious reality. Only a fully tested sense of tradition
saved the syntheses thus erected from the diffuse and
the fantastic. To this, the apocrypha did succumb.

As we have said, those Jews who, like Philo, gave
an enthusiastic reception to Hellenistic anthropology did
not find much room in their eschatology for the resurrection. It is worth while to mention the example provided by the *Psalms of Solomon*. In spirit this work is
undoubtedly Pharisaic, but it was hospitable to the doctrine of the survival of the soul. Whether it also professes the resurrection is debatable.[20] The traditional

[19] Separate stages: the two resurrections of the millenarians, as in
Ambrose and Lactantius; tiers of the cosmos, in most of the Fathers,
who distinguish paradise from the kingdom of heaven, with (in the
apocryphal apocalypses) a multiplication of specialized heavens, for
example, *Apoc. of Paul;* successive eons, in Origen. See Stolz, *Théol.
myst.,* 25-27.

[20] Martin, editor of the *Ps. Sal.* believes it professes the resurrection,
but Molitor, in *Die Auferstehung der Christen u. Nicht-Christen,* hesi-
tates. In any case, if there is a resurrection, it is in an extremely
spiritualized form. The eschatology of the *Jubilés,* which about 140
B. C. knew only a survival of the soul without the body and whose
trend was also pre-Pharisaic, is similar. The pseudo-Phocylides unites
the notion of a survival of the soul to the idea of a resurrection conceived in a very "etherealized" manner, according to Schärer, III, 618.

expressions which allude to it are not decisive. Some wish to interpret the ambiguous character of the text on a point which appears essential to the Pharisaism of the time of Christ, by the fact that the Psalms were pre-Pharisaic. This hypothesis obliges one to admit that at such an early epoch Palestinian Judaism already had pious groups which accepted the Greek idea of the soul's survival. At any rate, no bodily punishment awaits sinners, whose perdition does not mean annihilation but being consigned to pangs of conscience. No mention is made of a general judgment, but the "visit" of God seems to concern only the living. It leads the just to joy and surrenders sinners to their lot. The just will be taken into the final place God has prepared for them. In 4 Esd., which probably adopts a threefold anthropology—body, soul, spirit—the *pneuma* rejoined God, who had lent it to the body at the same time as life, while the soul went into the heavenly "warehouse" also mentioned in other texts and apparently used as reservoirs of impersonal life. Rabbi Meir places in the seventh heaven, the nearest to God, the spirits and soul of the just, which to him seem distinct from the "dew" which gives life to the remains of the dead on the day of the resurrection. These conceptions are comparable to the idea of a provisory "return" of souls to the place where they had been held in reserve before birth. In 4 Esd., the body is qualified as a "corruptible vessel,"[21] which recalls St. Paul and perhaps implies that the content of the vase is itself incorruptible. This was a feature unique in the Jewish literature of the time. The word "vessel" is a Hebraism,

[21] Cf. Volz. *op. cit.*, 252.

whose meaning, extremely vague, is best translated as "thing," but read by a Greek it could evoke the anthropological dualism familiar to Hellenism. The most remarkable attempt to interpret the resurrection with a view to reconciling the two anthropologies is found in 2 Bar.[22] It is to such mixtures of Hellenism and Judaism that we owe the idea that the "new land" where the risen will dwell will be "heavenly." This idea will very naturally find a warm reception in Alexandria, where it was customary to transpose terrestrial into ideal realities. In the book of the *Parables of Enoch* such a transformation of the "earth" accompanies the "angelization" of the just.[23]

Among the elements of rabbinism playing an important role in the patristic development of the dogma of the resurrection, the metaphorical use of such terms as "seed" and "garment" must be mentioned. The two are combined in the saying of Rabbi Meir referred to above and reveal a sensitivity to Hellenistic categories.[24] The discussion centers on whether the just when risen will be naked or clothed.[25] From the time of the attempts to Hellenize the Jews under the Seleucidae, the horror of nudity— common among Semites— had become a symbol of resistance to idolaters. But one may suspect a deeper level in the rabbi's response. To arise could only mean that one succeeded to a life without need of a body, a life such as a Philo or other Hellenized Jews could conceive it, while to arise clothed implied the acceptance of the

[22] 2 Bar., 5:1-13 and Charles's note in his edition of the *Apocryphes de l'A. T.*, II, 508. The Christian *Apoc. of Thomas* resembles it.

[23] Cf. *S. D. B.*, art. "Judaïsme," col. 1251; *Lagrange, 257.*

[24] Lagrange, *Messianisme*, 181; cf. p. 132, n. 2.

[25] *Sifré sur les Nombres* 31, Bonsirven, section 112.

usual Pharisaic views. What inclines us to accept the possibility of such an explanation is the use that St. Paul himself makes of the comparison of clothing and seed.

There is a connection between the image of the "dew" of the spirit, which vivifies the bones of the just, and the image of clothing, through the intermediate image of the anointing.[26] The spiritual dew works a vivifying anointing upon the members of the elect which "clothes" them in the glory of the resurrection. The connecting of these images, certainly attested from the time of the oldest baptismal homilies, could already have existed in Judaism before becoming a patristic leitmotiv. The metaphorical treatment of images was not exclusive with Alexandrian Judaism, which elevated it to the level of theological method. It is also found in Palestine even in the most formalistic rabbinic casuistry. Seed, dew, anointing, clothing were perhaps the earliest features of a theology of the mode of the resurrection.

There exists some early evidence of a conflict within Judaism on the nature of the resurrection, evidence which until recently has not perhaps been understood. It is a question of the Zadokite sect which fell into schism on the resurrection. The Sadducees have been said to have rejected the resurrection but if we think of the discovery of the Qumran documents and recollect Josephus' account of the eschatology of the Essenes, there arises the hy-

[26] Bousset, *Religion des Judentums,* 1906 edition, 319; *Apoc. Th.,* edited by James, 561. There is probably also a relation between the dew and the cloud of glory which descends upon the elect and gives them the power then to ascend into the heavens, carried by the angels. The liturgical and even baptismal character of these representations is apparent.

pothesis that the Zadokites in question could be the authors of the Damascus document.[27]

From the place St. Ephrem gives them, it is a question of the "just" who are separated from others by a concern for purity which accords with the ideas of the pre-Gnostics of Qumran but which does not apply to the Sadducees of the Gospel. Moreover, the schism, according to the account of pseudo-Clement, occurred among the followers of the Baptist, and the motive of schism finally led to a different conception of merit. Those who strive hoping for a reward—owing to the resurrection of the body—are accused by the Zadokites of a mercenary spirit. It could be that we have here the trace of two opposing trends within the baptist communities of the Jordan and the Dead Sea. They are found again in the Gnostic distinction between "psychics" and "pneumatics," the first striving in the hope of a paradise of pleasure, the second aspiring only to "spiritual" rewards. Josephus' account presents Essene eschatology in a wholly "Pythagorean" light. Even taking into account the philosophical travesty which Josephus uses to present the Jewish sects in such

[27] Father de Vaux in his communication to the Academy on the Qumran discoveries cites Ps. Clem., I, 53-54; Ephrem, *Evang. concord.*, ed. Vienna 1877, p. 288; *Abot R. Natan*, V, 13 c. Josephus, *Bell. Jud.*, II, says of the Essenes: "They firmly believe that, as our bodies are mortal and corruptible, our souls are immortal and incorruptible, that they are of a very subtle aerial substance, and that being enclosed in our bodies as in a prison, where a certain natural bent draws them and holds them, they are no sooner freed from these carnal ties which bind them as in a long servitude, than they arise into the air and fly with joy. In this they agree with the Greeks . . . " (VIII, II). There is no doubt that Josephus has stretched the point into a meaning that agrees with Greek eschatology, but he could not have done so without a real basis in the differences between Essenian teachings and common Jewish belief.

a way that the differences are understandable to a mind formed by Hellenism, we see clearly that the Essenes held an especially "spiritualizing" conception of the state of the just. Some of them renounced marriage, leading an "angelic" life, and the allusion to Pythagorean doctrines almost certainly implies a horror of the body and a quest for complete purity confirmed by frequent bathing. Thus the atmosphere within the sect is eminently favorable to a resurrection of the soul alone, or at the very least to a deeply "angelicized" resurrection. Moreover the sect possessed an extensive angelology. The presence of such a tendency in the immediate neighborhood of a nascent Christianity explains the place assumed by the problem in the communities from the time of St. Paul.

To profess slightly "realist" opinions about the resurrection led to schism in Palestine, but this does not seem to have been the case in the *diaspora,* since Philo was able to teach a completely spiritual "palingenesis" without arousing any opposition in his milieu. The case of Philo is an extreme example of concurrence with Hellenism. It is all the more interesting to note the points on which his Judaism is not compromised. His eschatological conceptions are based on Jewish moralism: αδανἀσιἀ is conferred only upon the just.[28] The soul of the wicked man "dies," while the virtues of the just man allow him to be reborn to an immortal life in the company of the angelic powers. With Plato, if there is a kind of death for the soul, it consists of descending into the body of brute beasts. Thus the soul, deprived for a time of the

[28] Nikolainen, *op. cit.,* 170-173.

exercise of reason, is "dead." But Philo, like several representatives of middle-Platonism, rejects the passage of a rational soul into the body of a beast.[29] If he holds that the soul is mortal, it is because he believes it created. It can, however, be raised to incorruptibility by perfect observance of the Law and by contemplation of its transcendent Principle. The soul of the just is moved to rejoin the divine Logos, whose image it is, by purifying itself of all corporeality, source of corruption. It dwells in heaven, first with the immortal stars and then with the invisible powers, to penetrate the immaterial world, finally to rejoin the Logos, First-born of God, Idea and Law of all the cosmos. In this strictly individual eschatology there is no place for either the judgment or the resurrection. The Gnostic eschatology outlined in a note taken by Clement of Alexandria from Theodotus, disciple of Valentinus, is very similar to that of Philo.[30]

Josephus attempts a harmonization of the beliefs springing from Philo, and the more traditional conceptions.[31] The terms he uses can be better applied to trans-

[29] Wolfson, *op. cit.*, 407.

[30] *Exc. Theod.* 27. The notion of a "hypercosmic" place occurs in Hippolytus, *Comm. Dan.*, Sources Chrétiennes edition, p. 173; Origen, *Contra Celsum*, VI, 59; it could arise from the Epicurean idea of a habitation of the gods located in an intermediate space between various simultaneously existent universes.

[31] Cf. Volz, *op. cit.*, 269. Josephus, who includes himself among the Pharisees, presents their belief in the resurrection like this: "They hold that souls are immortal, that those of the just pass after this life into *other* bodies, and that those of the wicked suffer torments which last forever" (*Bell. Jud.*, II, 13). *Other* bodies can very well designate the same body but in a glorified state, for a Greek spirit must be eliminated from a completely spontaneous critique (Cf. Cumont, *Symb. fun.*, 363-4), a spirit which considered the state of the just reincorporated into the same body (in other words enduring the same ills as those on earth) as more of a punishment than a reward.

migration than to resurrection, but this must be due to the care he took to explain Jewish ideas in terms comprehensible to the Greeks. The body the soul repossessed was not the same as the one it had left. Nevertheless, nothing in the text indicates that this occurrence should happen more than once. Since Josephus' beliefs are expressed in terms approximately equivalent to the Pharisees' and he declares himself a Pharisee, without, however, concealing his Essene sympathies, one may believe that in reality he does speak of the resurrection of the body. But he does so in terms that reverse the traditional relation between soul and body and personality, giving to the soul—conformably to Essenianism such as he himself describes it—that which defines the person, while depriving the body of all real individuating value.

One can (as we have) categorize the various Jewish trends concerning the resurrection in relation to their nearness to or distance from Hellenism or, what comes to the same thing, by the nature of their anthropological basis, but it would be correct, following Volz,[32] to relate them also to the properly Jewish religious motif animating each one. Those who stress corporeal identity wish thus to give to the persecuted Jews the assurance that they will recognize their persecutors, crushed under divine punishment, while they imagine themselves and their coreligionists enjoying the Jewish religious and community life of which persecution had deprived them. Those who insist upon the incorruptibility of the soul and in the resurrection give it a new body, more or less subtle and luminous, wish to reduce the distance between the

[32] *Op. cit.,* 254.

divine holiness and the too evident impurity of our present state.[33] Since the angels draw near God's throne, the elect are imagined as transformed into the image of the angels, who are not pure spirits but possess a refined body. The majority of the Pharisees certainly hold the first view, although some of them, like Josephus, more or less tainted by Hellenism, made rather important concessions to the other side. The latter surely include the Essenes.

The variety of Jewish conceptions reappears in the Christian writings,[34] and one can understand why the

[33] Jehuda I, interrogated by Emperor Antoninus on the presence of the body at the judgment turns the course of the conversation toward the judgment of the soul, which he says, is "pure," while the body is "impure." Obviously he is looking for a common meeting ground of Jewish and Greek conceptions exactly as did Josephus (p. 187, or. 1), and finds it in a common horror of the corpse and a common esteem of the soul, capable of appearing before God. We can see how far this concurrence could lead; cf. R. Meyer, *op. cit.,* 30. Without doubt we must consider the statements of the rabbis, which had prepared Antoninus' mind and which specified that body and soul, united in moral acts, are also united in the judgment, a reaction against the consequences of a body-soul dualism which endangered the dogma of the resurrection (*Mekhilta sur Ex.,* XV, I; *Sanh.* 91 b; Bonsirven, no. 86 and 1902).

[34] *Apoc. Thomas*: "Then each spirit will return to its own vessel and the bodies of the saints who are asleep will arise. Their bodies will then be changed to the image, the resemblance, and the glory of the holy angels and in the power of the image of my holy Father" (James' edition, p. 56). The *Apoc. of Paul* is a real compilation of all the eschatological conceptions of Judaism and early Christianity, essentially centered, however, on the journey of the soul after death and giving only a small place to the resurrection. In its present form it is probably contemporaneous with St. Jerome, but it brings together much older material. It undoubtedly had great popularity and shows by its mere existence the replacement of interest in the judgment and the resurrection by a concern with death, the trials of the soul in the course of its ascension, the suffrages of the Church, the washing away of venial sins. The elect seem to lack no joys even now: they are described as grouped around David in the heavenly Jerusalem in a truly corporeal manner. There is a particular judgment for each

Jew confronted by Celsus[35] in his work against the Christians could affirm that the eschatological doctrine of the new sect contained nothing original. Originality does exist, however: it is the fact, now central, of the resurrection of Christ. It is surprising that in answering the argument of Celsus, Origen does not stress the resurrection but rejects Jewish hopes as originating in fable; lacking understanding of the Scriptures, the Jews look to earth as the happy habitation of the risen, while he places the risen in heaven. It is the Alexandrian principle of the spiritual interpretation of the promises which seems to Origen to assure the superiority of Christian hopes to Jewish hopes. Deluded by his method, this assiduous and attentive reader of St. Paul remains blind to the essential point.

The contemporary Hellenistic[36] milieu in which Christianity began was suffused by a religious current in which a savior-god played a role often compared to that of Christ, the Son of God. The Fathers related their conceptions to this idea and perhaps borrowed some technical terms to express their own conceptions more effectively to the Greeks. What were the eschatological notions of these religious groups and how did they agree or dis-

---

individual, after which the wicked are sent into prison to await the "great day of Judgment." The fact that the compiler found an abundance of already traditional material to embody his subject shows that the current of an immediate and individual eschatology was already strong in his time.

[35] *Contra Celsum,* II, 5.

[36] We use this word in a broad sense to designate the cultural milieu of Greco-Roman paganism, including the Hellenistic period, strictly speaking, under the Diodochi, as well as under the Roman Empire to Constantine and even after him, and including the last philosophers of paganism.

agree with the dogma of the resurrection? In the not very esoteric circles of the Hermetics,[37] for instance, Hermes was invoked in these words: ". . . You reign over the elements . . . for you are the pilot of the whole universe. At will you make souls descend into Hades, and again awaken them to life. For you are the adornment of the world, you cure the ills of mortals. . . .[38]

What is to be understood by this mastery of Hermes over death and life, invoked in terms recalling the powers of Yahweh? In the *Corpus Hermeticum,* more radical than Plotinus himself in this respect, the death of the soul is its descent into matter, while its perfect life coincides with its perfect liberation.[39] Thus the soul's regeneration here has a meaning comparable to that in Philo of Alexandria. The mystery religions and the various Gnostic sects shared analogous convictions, each, however, with important nuances of its own. Hermeticism itself was far from homogeneous. Thus, according to treatise IX of the *Corpus,* man is a complex of hierarchized elements in which the lower serves as a vehicle and outer covering of the higher. Body and breath are material, rational soul and intellect are spiritual. Death is the separation of those diverse elements. Sometimes it seems to be said that the soul withdraws into the breath, sometime the opposite. The pious soul becomes wholly intellect but the soul of the wicked person is condemned to return to a human body, where it will be tor-

[37] Our material on Hermeticism will be derived from the works of Father Festugière, including his edition of the texts in collaboration with Nock, and the four volumes of his *Hermes Trismégiste.* Our citations will be from his *Corpus Hermeticum* referred to as *C. H.*

[38] Festugière, *H. T.,* I. 295.

[39] Cf. for example *Asclepius* 11; *Th. W. N. T.,* art. θάνατος (Bultmann).

tured by its own passions. In the same treatise, intellect (νοῦς) sometimes takes on the attractiveness of a distinct spiritual entity of the type of a "daimon." The ambiguity of this notion is perhaps related to that of the "pneuma" in Philo or even in St. Paul; sometimes it is an element transcending the individual human being, sometimes an integral part. Like the Gnostic, the Hermetic does not make the body an integral part of the "real man." Thus the elect one who climbs the degrees of mystical ascension successively abandons his outer coverings to become fully himself. The Gnosis understands the mystique of the cross, which it derives from Plato rather than St. Paul, in such a way that the real cross to which every man in the world is nailed is his own flesh. As to victory over death, won by our Savior, it consists of flight from the world which crucifies us to matter and through it determines our destiny. Once free of the wall of our material prison, having penetrated into the Pleroma, welcomed by the songs of angelic powers, the soul will finally enjoy perfect spiritual liberty. Interpreted like this, the cross is no longer "foolishness to the Greeks." It can easily be seen how the Greeks' rejection of the resurrection was consistent with their rejection of the true Christian meaning of the cross. How could these Gnostic sects pretend to be Christian when they rejected the common belief on such essential points? Doubtless because their founders lived the Christian life from the very beginning only in an ambiguous manner, even from their Baptism. Formed in the school of pagan mysteries, and "spiritualized" by consistently Platonizing philosophical exegesis, they very naturally interpreted Baptism as a present and total divinization which needed no more to manifest itself than the putting off of the coarse garments of the flesh; in short, the Gnostic, like Hymeneus and Philetus (2 Tim. 2:18), assumed that "the resurrection has already occurred."

It would seem a priori that the Hermeticism of the alchemists should have less radically attacked existence in its corporeal mode. But when the current of Hellenistic mystique took possession of the techniques of the goldsmith-magicians to transmute it into a theoretic schema of transforming ascesis, it (as in the case of Christian Baptism) transposed the symbols into another mode.[40] This transposition is not fortuitous, because alchemy performed its transmutations by means of "baptisms." The goal of this art was always to change base metal into precious metal, and the principle at the bottom of the alchemic edifice is the universal convertibility of matter, totally devoid of quality of its own and thus capable of receiving all qualities. Transposed into mystic terms, this alchemic truth means that the vile human dough is capable of divinization. The alchemist who wishes to work is limited by one condition: he must introduce into the mass a particle of the noble metal he wishes to produce, because "one can only reap what one has sowed."

Zosimus, in whom these images are found, distinguishes two areas where the art can be practiced: on the body and on the incorporeal. The mystical transposition is therefore consciously proposed. We may note in passing that Zosimus undoubtedly came under Jewish influence. In particular he was acquainted with the interpretation

[40] Festugière, I, 220, 235-236, 253, 263.

of the beginning of Genesis which held that the magic arts were the price paid by the "sons of god" for fornication with the "daughters of men." But in radically separating the two areas of the body and the incorporeal, Zosimus demonstrates a purely Greek and even Platonizing mentality and does not even (like Philo) attempt a union between Greek spiritualism and Jewish "somatism," because of the introduction of a certain mixture of materialistic stoicism.

The agent of the alchemic transformations, along with "bathings," is "fire." The "artisan" or "intelligent" fire is interpreted according to the popularized ideas of the Stoa. It purifies and divinizes what passes through it without being destroyed. The image of the purifying fire is Biblical but with the Fathers it received a contribution from Hellenistic theory. According to the interpretation of the three children in the furnace abundantly represented in the iconography of the catacombs, those who enter the fire accompanied by the "angel"—that is, the guardian angel or more probably the Logos—leave it glorified, and Hippolytus here derives an argument for the integrity of their "clothing" against those who deny the resurrection:[41] How then will the corruptible body

[41] According to Steinmann, *Daniel*, 70, the account of the three children in the furnace itself has the value of an eschatological allegory. Cf. Hipp., *Comm. Dan.* on IV, 37, where the flaming appearance of the Angel-Logos signifies his κριτικὸν, power, by which he separates (like the fire of the Zoroastrian ordeal) the just and the unjust. In the *Adv. Gr.* 2, it is the earth itself to which the body descends that acts as the "foundry" for the purification and remolding of the corporeal "vessels." The Gnostics frequently use the symbolism of clothing. Thus their "saved savior" has several garments, of which one is outer, one is psychic, and one is pneumatic. The psychic garment does not penetrate into the Pleroma but is kept in the Ogdoad, the intermediate and fiery region corresponding to the empyrean, which cannot be entered by

which a holy soul inhabits not itself also be sanctified
and transformed into incorruptibility? (*Comm. Dan.* II,
28). The Gnostics allowed a place in their schema for
the eschatological fire. They placed it in the "Intermediate" where the God of the Old Testament, the God
of the "psychics," rules. At the end of time, fire will have
as its mission the destruction of the material content of
the universe and with it all the "hylics." The "pneumatics" pass through it in the course of their ascent to
the Pleroma. Here one can easily recognize the "empyrean" heaven with its role in pagan eschatology. The
fire is found also in the Fathers, where it keeps the
wicked from entering paradise, assimilated both to the
flaming sword which closed it to Adam and Eve and to
a celestial Jordan which had to be crossed to gain access
to the Promised Land, itself transposed into heaven.
Fire[42] functions like the Zoroastrian ordeal to separate
the good and the wicked. Generally it will try those who

---

those, lacking Gnosis, who remain simple believers. Although the coarse
matter, destroyed by fire descended from this part of the cosmos at the
moment of the *ekpurôsis,* does not rise, the psychics in the Ogdoad
maintain a kind of "psychic" body whose analogue we shall meet again in
Origen. The "pneumatics" put off all "clothing" and enter naked — that
is with the *voûs* alone — into the Pleroma; cf. *Exc. Theod.* 28; Sagnard,
introduction to the *Adv. Haer.,* III, *Sources Chrétiennes* ed., p. 57. The
empyrean fire is the agent of apotheosis in pagan eschatology. St.
Augustine demonstrates a curious recollection when he compares Christ's
resurrection to an apotheosis by the fire of the eschatological conflagration: *Quaest. in Num.,* 19; cf. *Mél. Casel,* p. 19.

[42] On the relation of fire to the resurrected body, see especially:
Anrich, *Clemens u. Origenes als Begründer der Lehre vom Fegefeuer,*
Festgabe Holtzmann; Edsman, *Ignis divinus,* and by the same author,
Le Baptême de Feu. In particular, the idea of the "recasting" of the
body through the vivifying action of fire is found in *Mart. Polyc.* 15;
Act. Pionius; Cl. Alex., *Ped.,* I, 6, 46; Greg. Nys., *Cat.* 25, 13-15;
Theodore of Mopsuestia, 11, 496-7.

have already been resurrected. But as the fire can be more or less "spiritualized," so will it be with the risen body. Its presence does not necessarily imply a realist conception of the resurrection. The schema originating with the Gnostic sect of the Ophites described in the *Contra Celsum*[43] includes a φραγμός which distinguishes the invisible heaven of the angels of Elohim and the transcendent heaven where the Father, the Son and the Agape exist, but also includes the "sword of fire" which divides the visible heaven of the "angels of Eden" from that of the "angels of Elohim." The latter corresponds to the "intermediate" of other systems. The popularity of this conception arises from the fact that it provided a point of contact between Hellenism, Iranianism and Judaism, between eschatology based on cosmology and eschatology based on ethics, between "horizontal" eschatology with an "end of the world" and "vertical eschatology" with its passage through celestial spheres. Fire thus had remarkable "reductionist" properties which were exploited in order to Hellenize the presentation of Jewish eschatology, including the resurrection of the body. The numerous representations of the three children in the furnace in Christian cemeteries suffice to show that this vogue was present in the most orthodox milieux. They are an indication in favor of a "heavenly" conception of the resurrection in these same milieux.

The feverish speculation engaged in in the Gnostic "chapels" did not have the same importance in the true

---

[43] The schema in reconstituted by Th. Hopfner, *Charisteria Alois Rzach dargenacht,* pp. 86-98 and in H. Chadwick's translation of the *Contra Celsum,* pp. 338-339; see note 3, p. 346 in this edition.

Church. In tranquil possession of the faith, it did not devote its attention primarily to parallels with pagan thought or esoteric systems, in order to explain the world. When such preoccupations endangered large numbers of the faithful, the Church very naturally turned to Tradition. Christian orthodoxy had always believed in the perfect continuity—though not the complete homogeneity—of the two Testaments. Since the Bible is very restrained on the question, the inquiry was enlarged to include Jewish writings which, though noncanonical, were nevertheless strongly credited in certain communities, for instance 4 Esdras. Good weapons against the exaggerated spiritualism of the Gnosis were found here. But some also drew from the suspect sources of millenarian hopes, as did the Jew Celsus rightly accused by Origen. St. Irenaeus did not completely escape either. We then see the anti-Gnostic doctors give their support to views which had doubtless always been widespread among the "popular" Christian groups, though it is immediately necessary to point out that the iconography of the catacombs does not really favor the popularity of gross millenarianism. Two trends stand out among the apologists of the resurrection of the body, one which stresses courageously whatever in the Christian expectations shocks the pagan mentality, and another which tries to soften the contrasts and facilitate access to the dogma by making concessions in presenting it.

The appeal to divine omnipotence to explain how completely disintegrated mortals can be brought back to life, even after this dust has been scattered to the four winds, relates rather to the first trend, because such an appeal offers no help to reason or imagination in suggesting how the act will be accomplished.[44] According to the Greek spirit the gods' government of the world is not exercised by decrees based solely on the arbitrary divine will. Such an exception to the laws of the cosmos as occurs in an intervention like this, though acceptable in a universe created *ex nihilo* and completely dependent upon the free will of the Creator, becomes unthinkable to those who conceive the divine as immanent in the cosmos and who find in the very regularity of physical laws proof of the divinity of the universe. This opposition in the Greek mind resembles the objections to the proof of the existence of God by miracles which still persist. On the other hand, the parallel between the creative act and the resurrection was perfectly harmonious with rabbinic theology, accustomed to consider Yahweh's solemn interventions in human history as "renewals" of the creation. This creation-resurrection parallel will continue throughout the entire patristic period as a leitmotiv of resurrection apologetic: the resurrection introduces a new humanity into the "new land" in the train of the "new Adam." The new eon, markedly contrasted to the old one beginning with rabbinic theology, is a pure world which replaces a corrupt one. Such a corruption, envisaged in cosmic dimensions, has been compared to the periodic aging of the Stoic universe which ends in disaster to bring about a rebirth from ashes. It is understandable that the Fathers who had looked for a point of contact between Judaeo-Christian eschatology and Hellenism believed they

[44] Justin, *Apol.*, 18-19, goes back to the rabbinic argument from the creative action of God upon the drop of sperm, which a fortiori proves possible for the remains of the body. Tertullian, *de res. carnis* 11, and Tatian *adv. gr.* 6 start directly from creation *ex nihilo*. On the position of the rabbis see R. Meyer, *op. cit.*, 81.

found it here.[45] The rapprochement was not in every respect fortunate because the new eon of the Stoics' view was no improvement over the preceding one, and because it could give the impression that the Christians preached a kind of metempsychosis, which justified the Gnostic interpretation of the Christian message: by fleeing beyond the cosmos, the Gnostic escapes the hellish cycle of rebirths. The entire treatise of Plotinus against the Gnostics refutes this crime of outrage against the cosmos. Did the orthodox Christian who on the contrary believed the whole universe shared in the effects of the redemptive act find favor with Plotinus? Perhaps. It seems in any case that the Fathers who professed the "apocatastasis," or the return of the entire cosmos to its original state of perfection, whether in the strict sense of Origen or in a broader sense more compatible with orthodoxy, as in Gregory of Nyssa and others, tried to satisfy this demand of the Greek mind to found its repose only upon an *integrally* recovered cosmic order.

Hippolytus possessed a deep grasp of the distance between the Greek and the Judaeo-Christian ideas of the "law of life." Taking up again the argument of the intervention of divine omnipotence to explain the resurrection, he says: "How can he who became mortal only through an act of disobedience be incapable of being resurrected by divine omnipotence?"[46] One cannot do more to begin

[45] The tradition goes back at least to 2 Pet. 3:10.

[46] *Comm. Dan., Sources Chr. ed.,* p. 171. The idea was already present in Irenaeus, II, 34, 3: "For life did not originate with us nor our own nature but was bestowed according to the grace of God. And this is why he who sustains the life that has been given him and returns thanks to Him who gave it will receive life eternal. But he who sets it at naught and shows himself ungrateful to his Creator because, being

to discover the true source of life eternal, which flows out as it were naturally from omnipotence to obedience and which derives from a friendship between two liberties, one sovereign, the other subordinate. Thus our resurrection appears precisely in the line of that of the Crucified who atoned for the sin of Adam by obeying the Father even to death on the Cross. In this light it is easier to understand why Hippolytus and the majority of the Fathers before the fourth century hesitate to such a degree to declare the soul immortal.[47] They seem in this way to free it from its relation of essential dependence upon divine omnipotence. To the Greek, the affir-

---

created he does not acknowledge Him who gave him existence, will lose eternal life."

[47] See Nygren, *Eros et Agapé*, II, 61-64. The tie between cosmology and anthropology brought it about that the opposition of the Fathers to the eternal world of the Greeks is reflected back in their opposition to the immortality of the soul, understood as the Greeks understood it. From this point of view it is strange that Justin did not perceive the possibilities opened up by the branch of Platonism to which he was won over, in which a created world could still obtain the status of eternity. Cf. Andresen, *Zeits. N. T. W.*, 1952-3, p. 163. A more careful study of the notion of the soul's mortality held by the Fathers (cf. *Irenaeus*, II, 34, 2) would in our opinion show that it coincides in large part with the rejection of an uncreated and impeccable soul, appearing before the face of God or sharing by nature in the divine privilege of incorruptibility, and thus that Protestants like Althaus (*Die Letzte Dinge*) or van der Leeuw (*Onsterferlijkheid of Opstanding*) are wrong to present immortality and resurrection as two horns of a perfect dilemma. Nevertheless their arguments, as well as those drawn from Semitic anthropology, should incite Catholic theologians to return to the question of the status of the separated soul, the ties it has with the past and future body, and the kind of duration in which it subsists. To turn to the documents on the "corruptible" soul the texts of Clement of Alexandria, *Adum. in I Pet.:* "Hinc apparet quoniam non est naturaliter anima incorruptibilis, sed gratia Dei, per fidem et justitiam et per intellectum [gnose] perficitur incorruptibilis"; "corruptibilis igitur est anima, quae cum corpore simul profunditur, ut quidam putant" (*P. G.* 8, 729-730) ; cf. Tatian, *Disc. aux gr.*, 13, 1-4.

mation of immortality was in effect equivalent to that of necessary existence, freed from all dependence upon an efficient cause and impossible of birth in time. Now the redemption lost its realistic meaning and continued only under the guise of a rescue. This was the line followed by Gnostic Docetism.

It remained to Tertullian to push to its extreme point the trend which had recourse to divine omnipotence to provide a foundation for faith in the resurrection. It was in connection with Christ's resurrection[48] that he initiated his famous *credo quia absurdum,* thus exaggerating to the point of fideism the legitimate and necessary attitude of submission to the First Truth which adherence to dogma demands of the intelligence. In the treatise on the resurrection, his vindication of the body rests absolutely upon the omnipotent Creator since this corruptible body in the end possesses dignity for no other reason than that God wills or at least permits it. This is enough to preserve it from the note of absolute evil disqualifying it to the Gnostics. They had tried to draw an a fortiori argument from the words of St. Paul: "the figure of this world passes"; thus the flesh also passes since it is a part of the world. But, retorts Tertullian, cannot God restore what has been destroyed? And even if the universe is destined to perish totally and finally can it be concluded from this that the same will be true for all parts of the universe, for instance, the risen body?[49]

But when it is a question of explaining how the resurrection will be brought about, the distance between the

---

[48] Tert., *de Carne Chr.* 5.

[49] *De. res. carnis,* 5; cf. also 6-8 and the beautiful expression *"caro salutis est cardo."*

various theologies stands out more. On this point the interpretation of the dogma depends upon anthropology. It will only progress slowly toward a certain unanimity. On one point, though, there was unanimity from the beginning in reaction against the Gnostics: the resurrection affects *the whole man*.[50] Pseudo-Clement, in his second epistle to the Corinthians, in an image which retains some ambiguity and allows some room for a Gnostic interpretation, honors our flesh as the temple of God.[51] Tatian fortunately specifies that it is the very unity of the body and the soul and thus the whole man who through the presence of the spirit is the *naos theou*. The same Spirit who vivifies us in Baptism will complete His work in us when we are resurrected. This interesting conception presents two drawbacks, the first arising from the ambiguity which continues to surround the notion of the *pneuma:* is it a question of what Yahweh breathed into the nostrils of Adam, or of the Holy Spirit? The second difficulty is that the conception leaves obscure the resurrection of the wicked. Justin Martyr shows a considerable advance in the anthropological precision of his argumentation. He tries to steer a middle course between an excessively Platonized view of man and a too rudimentary Semitic anthropology. Departing from the Aristotelian definition of man as a reasonable animal, he argues successfully: "Is the soul alone man? Not at all, but it is the soul of man. Is the body therefore man? Not at all, but we call it the body of man; . . . if then God called man to the life and to the resurrection, it was not a part but the whole of him, in other words body

[50] Strongly argued by *Irenaeus*, II, 29, 3.
[51] 2 Cor. 9.

and soul, that He called."[52] The spirit is not included here in the enumeration of the parts of man. Elsewhere, however, Justin's argument assumes a threefold division: the spirit in the soul and the soul in the body, all three of which must be saved in order for the whole man to gain salvation. There cannot be a question here of the Holy Spirit, but perhaps of shared divine grace. Such impressions will continue to appear in certain Doctors for centuries to come. Justin's argumentation is also found in Athenagoras:[53] the animal is an integral whole, and both the soul's activity and the body depend in man on the judgment of sense and of reason. All these elements must thus be brought back to one and the same unique end.[54]

In his great work against the Gnostics, Irenaeus very judiciously connects the reality of the resurrection of the body to Christ's resurrection.[55] Tertullian had done it in a roundabout way: the dignity of the body arises from the fact that the slime of the earth was made to the "image of God," that is, to the Man-God, Jesus.[56]

[52] *De resurr.* 8.

[53] *De resurr. mort.* 15.

[54] Tertullian goes back to the argument from the moral solidarity of the soul and the body that we met in the rabbis (p. 144, n. 33). Justin has another argument (*De resurr.* 10) which occurs in Theodoret and John Damascene (*Ench. Patr.*, nos. 2153 and 2375): Only that can rise which has descended, but the spirit does not descend; it is therefore the flesh which rises. If, nevertheless, Philo and the Gnostics were able to term the stripping of all the soul's hylic and psychic envelopes "palingenesis," it is because "man" for Philo and the Gnostics is the pre-existent *νοῦς* and not the soul united to a body. The resurrection is thus the act of a man who gets up and washes himself after having been buried in a slough.

[55] V, 14, 1: "Si enim non haberet caro salvari, nequaquam Verbum Dei caro factum esset." The idea is illuminated in *in Act Pauli* 7 (line 160).

[56] *De res. carn.* 6. A similar idea is in Irenaeus, V. 6, 1: "If the spirit is lacking to the soul, one who as such is by nature animal, and, remain-

Thus it is not only the work of God but the pledge of immortality. This interpretation of the "image of God" will remain unusual, but the solidarity of our flesh with that of God even in the resurrection is clearly affirmed in the face of Gnostic Docetism. In a famous text,[57] Irenaeus will make this solidarity in some way sensible by arguing from the reception of the Eucharist to prove that our flesh is destined for incorruptibility. The Pauline theme of the seed is curiously mixed into the argument, in a manner which inevitably recalls the archaic formula used for the Eucharist in the *Didache*. If the grain that decays in the earth can germinate and provide matter for the eucharistic Body of Christ, our bodies, which will decay in the earth after having been nourished by this bread, have the right to hope in the resurrection which will integrate them with the glorious Body of Christ. This theme of the seed follows the general line of Irenaeus' theology, according to which man is involved in a process of growth which leads him from the state of

---

ing carnal, becomes an imperfect being which indeed possesses the image of God by reason of its formation but has not received the likeness by the spirit, and thus this being is imperfect." As far as the indecisive anthropology of Irenaeus can be clarified, the true resurrection consists in living the life of the spirit, but even without the spirit, by reason of the presence of the image in the "animal" man, a resurrection also awaits those who have not received the spirit or have been unfaithful to it. The spirit, in effect, is conceived, as in Tatian, as the agent of the true resurrection.

[57] V, 2, 3; see also IV, 18, 5. This text emphasizes how conscious Irenaeus is of the fact that the sacramental economy of salvation is by its very nature opposed to Gnostic Docetism. Certain Gnostics were not at all conscious of it. They multiply the sacraments, while emptying the sacramental act itself of meaning because they refuse to give any value to the world of the senses.

The apologetic for the flesh by Tertullian in his *de res. carnis* 5 is based on the same sacramental economy of salvation.

infancy of the first Adam to the full-grown age of Christ.

The anthropology of Irenaeus is tripartite. Depending upon whether the soul—intermediate between flesh and spirit—is "sowed" in one or the other, it will reap corruption or incorruptibility. The state of the damned is not thus conceived to be "incorruptible." Without the spirit, man remains in effect "carnal." He indeed possesses the "image" in his flesh but has lost the "likeness" of God. But what is only "flesh and blood" does not inherit the kingdom, remaining without form and without unity.[58]

St. Irenaeus combats metempsychosis as much from the anthropological argument of the bond between the soul and its own body as by affirming the absence of all true recollection of a previous life.[59]

Finally, on the faith of the presbyters of Asia, Irenaeus believed it necessary to integrate into the economy of a millenarian period,[60] despite the lack of agreement between these grossly material conceptions and the spiritualization of the life of the just that he steadfastly professes. These material conceptions evidently provide a weapon against Gnostic Docetism; still he would not have welcomed them with so much eagerness if they had not seemed to him strongly supported by tradition. Certainly Asia was herself the heir of Judaeo-Christian currents which, in all the early years after the fall of Jerusalem when the imminent expectation of the Parousia gave a renewed favor to dreams of the old millenarian

[58] V, 6, 1; V, 9, 1; see, however, 3, 22, 1, where the spirit does not seem an integral part of man.
[59] II, 23, 5.
[60] V, 33, 3-4.

messianism, were weighed down with useless Jewish impediments. The Churches were to find themselves divided on this question, some—those who also accepted the canonicity of the Apocalypse—thought that the "kingdom" should be accepted, while others, with Alexandria at their head, rejected it absolutely. The voices raised against the canonicity of the Apocalypse came from the East. In the West the book was accepted and interpreted generally as teaching millenarianism. Not until St. Augustine was another interpretation forthcoming. In the East, Origen was to throw all the weight of his authority against millenarianism, and, generally, against every gross, material conception of Christian beliefs. His influence would determine a particular *tone* for the eschatology of the Eastern Church, even though many of his personal opinions would one day be actively criticized there and even officially condemned.

We do not possess very much information about the eschatology of Clement of Alexandria,[61] Origen's predecessor at the head of the catechetical school, and those which we do have do not seem to be an adequate preparation for the brilliant synthesis of the *Peri Archon*. In effect, Clement seems to see the soul as perishable,[62] while Origen certainly considers it to be immortal, going so far as to accept what he thinks to be the binding corollary of this doctrine, knowledge of its eternal pre-existence. Clement also rejects metempsychosis,[63] and he does this in terms which seem to leave no place to

[61] Almost all is found in the *Adumb. in I Pet., P. G.,* 8, 729.

[62] Cf. p. 155, n. 47 in *calce,* which does not contradict the fragment *de an. P. G.,* 9, 751. In effect, immortality remains with him accidental to the nature of the soul. On the other hand, see Origen, *C. C.,* VII, 32.

[63] *In I Pet.* 1, 3.

the form of this doctrine that Origen would attempt to advocate in the "superior" teaching of Christianity. In the resurrection, soul and body will reunite according to a proper mode (*juxta genus proprium*), each adapting itself to the other by a kind of congruence.[64] Certainly Clement meant by this to exclude the possibility that the soul could take up a body other than its own or, at the very least, that a rational soul could be reincarnated in the body of an animal. The general view of Clement on the course of salvation, conceived as continuous, an ascension with no retrogression, probably excludes any idea of a "recirculation" of souls such as is found in the Stoics or Origen. Though Clement sometimes employs the word ἀποκατάστασις, used as a token of infamy, a word abhorred in Origen's system, Clement's usage does not literally involve any Origenist tendency.[65]

Origen's doctrine of the resurrection arises from an attempt to reconcile traditional views, especially those of St. Paul, Platonic anthropocosmology and the Hellenistic mystique particularly as it appeared in Hermeticism, neo-Pythagoreanism and the Gnosis. Origen's teaching,

[64] *Id*. Cf. *Strom.*, IV, 159, 3 where its tabernacle (σκηνή) is said to be returned to the soul for its happy use. This passage is noteworthy in that it (in other respects) provides a striking parallel with the Gnostic conception of the return of the perfect into the Pleroma, afer they have been stripped of all vesture. Clement even cites Job 1, 21: "Naked came I out of my mother's womb and, naked shall I return thither." He explains: naked of all vice and sin and of the shapeless specter which accompanies those who do not live justly. This ghost or ξ"δωλον takes its pleasure in the lower regions and appears around tombs (cf. p. 124, n. 3). Though we do not have here a very sure allusion to the resurrection of the body, we naturally tend to interpret the passage in the sense of Philo or of the *Exc. Theod.* 27. Cf. *Strom.*, V, 32: Philo, *De vita Mosis,* II, 108-1332.

[65] Cf. Karpp, *Probleme altchristlicher Anthropologie,* 117.

while extremely stable and coherent, is often difficult to grasp, because as a teacher he presents to each hearer the aspect of his system which is most accessible, striving to show only familiar things to the simple while suggesting profound things to the learned. Every word used by the *Didascalia* should be carefully sounded and every possible meaning systematically tried out, before certifying that when Origen uses ordinary language, he is expressing what is ordinarily meant.

At the beginning of the *Peri Archon,* Origen makes a profession of faith in the ecclesiastical kerygma. There will be a time for the resurrection of the dead, when the body which was "sown in corruption rises in incorruption, and what was sown in dishonor rises in glory." Surely it is not by chance that Origen has chosen to give witness to his fidelity to the teaching of the Church by citing these words from Corinthians. It is in this chapter, and especially in this verse, that he always looked for the best weapons against ideas he believed too crude. All his effort at an anthropological elaboration of the dogma consists in defining the ontological preparation for the existence in incorruption, glory, and contemplation.[66]

---

[66] Origen gives evidence of his faith in the resurrection in many other places and often does so in very strong terms, apparently not susceptible to equivocation. See for instance *Peri Archon,* III, VI, 6: "We must hold that it is not one body of which we are now making use . . . and another which we shall use in incorruption, power, and glory." Cf. *hom. in Num.,* XVIII, 4. Origen describes the resurrection: "The dead rise when the soul (is) with the body. Not that the soul disappears during the interval, it remains inactive and without the properties that go with the body. What is common to both is in effect something of each one ($\xi\nu\ \tau\iota$): a man, and it is by means of both that life is sustained beyond death" (*Hom. XXXIX in Luc.*). It is really astonishing that the same author also writes: "The dead are praised more than the living, for they have at least reached the point where

The flesh of earth is "sinful flesh" (*Comm. in Rom.* V, 9; *P. G.* 14, 1045). Not that Origen uses these words in the Gnostic sense, with the idea that the *engagement* of the spirit with the flesh is sin itself. But the soul takes on this coarser vesture only as a consequence of a cooling of its first spiritual fervor; at the beginning it followed the impulsion of the divine Logos without inertia. Everything that exists is divided into two natures, spiritual and material. Matter, however, was not created for itself but by virtue of being the accompaniment of spiritual nature. It is only a shadow, attached to certain created spirits when they wander from the spiritual "equator" of the Logos, which is their real "natural place." But this shadow, essentially mobile, exactly indicates the distance between the ideal and the real state of each created spirit. To each spiritual "climate" correspond shadows of a certain length or, in other words, a more or less heavy body. Movement from one state to another should always be possible, for Origen's system is based essentially on the opposition between astrological determinism and the fixed predestinationism of the Gnosis, according to which one is by essence elect or damned.[67]

---

they are no longer attired in flesh and skin nor framed with bones and nerves; . . . behold thus that all is vanity, and also every man living, let us despise this vain life and let us hasten toward the holy life, the blessed and true one, and let us tend toward it, all 'vanity' cast off" (*Hom. I in Ps. 38,* par. 10). There is no contradiction, however, thanks to the doctrine of the εῖδος.

[67] This point is important and Origen often returns to it: *Peri Archon,* III, VI, 6; IV, 33; *C. C.,* III, 41; IV, 56, etc. The central thesis of free will would seem to him to be compromised if matter were not suited to receive all the qualities; cf. the strict parallel between corporal and spiritual qualities: *Comm. in Rom.,* VIII, II (*P. G.,* 14, 1191). See p. 15, the same principle serves as a basic for alchemic prac-

Origen also raises several objections to Aristotle's doctrine of the "quintessence," by which the matter of heavenly bodies is of an incorruptible nature, essentially different from the matter of common elements. If this were so, how could "corruption" put on "incorruption"? In order to protect the truth of the Apostle's words, it is thus necessary to hold firmly the Stoic position in which matter is of itself ἄποιον, that is, free of all quality but able to receive all.

Corporeality is not directly tied to evil, not even because it is flesh of sin (σάρξ) but because of its diversity.[68] Under these various aspects, it "characterizes" the variety of moral dispositions.[69] Certainly, bodily modification does not immediately accompany every modification of the state of consciousness, but the body

---

tice and mystique. On the question of the place of matter in Origen's system, see Urs von Balthasar, *Rec. Sc. Rel.*, 1936, *Le Mystérion d'Origène*, pp. 537 ff., reprinted in *Parole et Mystère chez Origène*, Edit. Cerf, 1957, pp. 42 ff. and our article in *R. S. P. T.* 1959.

[68] *C. C.*, III, 42; *Peri Archon*, II, 1, 4. While it is determined that the sinful flesh will disappear, it is not certain that the same will be true of all corporeality. Père Daniélou, *Origène*, 215, believes the final state will be purely spiritual, but this conflicts with the proper function of corporeality, which is to assure diversity. To do away with the body completely is to fall into a pantheism of which Origen has not been accused. There must thus remain what is necessary of the body so that one's own "name" does not disappear (*De Or.* 242), for if it is true that at the end all beings endowed with reason will again become perfectly equal (III, VI, 4), they will, however, be distinct from one another. Daniélou's opinion (also that of Hal Koch, (*Pronoia und Paideusis*, 37), should be compared to that of U. v. Balthasar, *op. cit.*: "This basic nonidentity is the materiality of every creature, pure as it may be. God alone is truly incorporeal." The flesh is only the fallen state of corporeality, which of itself is not "visible," but no more than the "earth" or the "heavens," which were created even before the firmament and the "dry land" appeared. It is in that earth, the "land of the living," that the elect dwell.

[69] *De. Orat.*, 2; *Comm. in Rom.*, VIII, 1; *Hom. in Num.*, II, 2.

nevertheless tends to adapt itself to it. This adaptation perfectly effected is the resurrection of the body. To arrive at this definition of the resurrection, Origen bases his argument on a Pauline comparison which had already been exploited by Hippolytus of Rome and Theophilus of Antioch and taken over by the Gnosis, the comparison between vessels of honor and dishonor.[70] The catastrophe ending each period of the world involves the remolding of the vessels in the eschatological furnaces. The redistribution of bodies is in some manner the very promulgation of God's judgment.[71] This redistribution will probably not be made once for all because spiritual beings will retain the use of free will in their new situation. The new eon will also end in disaster, and the face of the world will be renewed once more. Let us see briefly how these things are to happen.

[70] *Hom. in Jer.*, XVIII, 1. See also p. 149, n. 41, above. The reshaping of vessels explains their "hardening," which lasts a whole eon. This problem of the "induration" is absolutely central for Origen who devotes to it the whole third book of the *Peri Archon*. It is the problem of free will itself. *Hom. in Num.*, XIV, 2, demonstrates in detail the application of the principle. In the coming eon, those, for example, who have inhabited animals will be transformed, not into beasts (contrary to those who have accused Origen of a doctrine that he and a number of pagan thinkers held in horror) but rather with angels appointed to the beasts. Punishment justly consists in having to remain burdened with care for this "vanity" of "shadows" of *visible* corporeality. It is indeed to this position that Jerome replies: ep. 84, 8; *P. L.* 22, 750.

[71] God bestows bodies according to His will (*C. C.* V, 22); this principle recalls the general position of the Fathers on the role of divine omnipotence in the act of the resurrection. Yet at the same time, the utterances of God are rendered according to an immanent justice (*id.*, 23) for God does not will anything that would be contrary to nature. But this law of nature is that there is a proportion between the nature of the resurrected body and merit. This is what is shown by the comparison with the seed, which contains the *raison séminale* of the future state. These "reasons" (λόγοι) are the "words" (λόγοι) which will not pass away (Matt. 24:35),

At first glance, Origen's statements on the soul could seem contradictory. Sometimes the soul appears completely incorporeal, sometimes on the other hand, it seems inseparable from a certain subtle materiality.[72]

While professing a spirituality of the soul that he does not hesitate to put on the same plane as that of the Persons of the Trinity, Origen sees all created spirits, even those of the angels, as involved by essence in a certain relation with matter. Compared to the divine substance,

---

[72] What the soul has in common with matter is its essential mobility, as is already shown by Origen's taking over the Aristotelian definition: οὐσια φανταστικὴ κάι ὁρμητική. This mobility is the condition for the exercise of free will but also causes the soul to be able to die and to decay, not, however, to the point of complete dissolution but to the point of being unable to continue to "contain" the mobility of the matter it animates, a fact which makes it a corruptible and mortal body. When the soul is thus buried in a corruptible body it has "descended into the tomb," because of a previous sin which caused it to "die." Exactly as matter, essentially mobile, can still receive more or less stable form depending on the quality of the soul which controls it, so also can the soul itself attain to incorruptibility for a longer or shorter time if the great cosmic and incorruptible soul of Christ takes it up and encloses it (II, III, 2). Cf. p. 171 and n. 1; *C. H.*, X, 14. This is, according to 2 Cor. 5:1, to possess *domum non manufactum aeternam in coelis* and to have exchanged his "vessel of dishonor"—sinful flesh—for a "vessel of honor"—the divine Logos in its function of κόσμος νοητός containing in itself the perfect exemplars of all beings and playing the role of the Gnostic Pleroma. The doctrine of "vessels" occurs in the *Gospel of Truth,* a Gnostic document; cf. *Vigiliae christianae,* 1954, 36. The best synthesis of this doctrine is found in the *Peri Archon,* III, VI, but it should be clarified and completed by several other passages: *C. C.* III, 41; VII, 32: *Comm. in Rom.,* VIII, 11. All of this could not be openly exposed to the eyes of the simple, for fear of unsettling their faith in the reality of the resurrection, but Origen did not believe it possible to concede less to the principal argument of the Docetist Gnostics than to know that "flesh and blood do not inherit the Kingdom of God" (*C. C.* V, 19). But if it is not necessary thus to scandalize simple Christians, it is no more necessary to impose Jewish "fables" upon well-informed minds, e.g., hopes of sensual happiness in a land of milk and honey. Cf. *C. C.,* V, 15 and 18.

the soul is thus in some way material while, compared to the world of the body, it is, on the contrary, spiritual. Thus, as we have said, each soul by reason of its moral disposition seeks in the universe a place adapted to its merits or demerits.[73] Because of the requirements proper to this natural milieu the soul assumes a particular body, for example the burning and subtle body which is suitable for the souls of stars, or the bodies, also subtle but cold and ill-smelling, of the demons of the atmosphere. Here again, the basis of Origen's conviction is a Pauline text: "All flesh is not the same flesh, but there is one flesh of men, another of beasts, another of birds, another of fishes. There are also heavenly bodies and earthly bodies, but of one kind is the glory of the heavenly, of another kind the glory of the earthly" (1 Cor. 15:39-40). Though the heavenly bodies endure during the whole intervening time between two total destructions of the cosmos, the earthly do not. Nevertheless, even dispossessed of their bodies, the souls of men do retain at least a certain relation to the matter which distinguishes them and appropriately "characterizes" them. On reading the texts in which Origen discusses this *eidos*[74] one may ask whether

[73] Each type of corporeality possesses its own duration (*Comm. in Rom.*, VIII, 11) and the duration passed by the soul in "vanity" corresponds to the sum of the punishment due the wicked acts perpetrated in the preceding eon (frg. *de. Res.*, II, *P. G.*, 11, 94). Only those who have found their "place" in the Logos can live on more than one eon.

[74] Cf. *Comm. in Ps.*, I, 5, *P. G.* 12, 1097; frg. *de Res.*, II, *P. G.* 11, 93; Origen, as Chadwick shows in the *Harvard Theological Review,* 1948, 87 ff., takes up in this passage the classical arguments of the Academy against the Epicurean conception of the gods, arguments based chiefly on a *topos* of the philosophy of the time: matter is always in flux (ῥευστα). Since Origen does not accept the Aristotelian solution, to which Philo and others subscribe, of a special matter for incorruptible celestial bodies, he must seek elsewhere the principle of the permanence

it is a question simply of traits characteristic of physical individuality or if on the contrary it is a matter of moral character. In reality, the two are related. The traits of the physical character are in this cosmic period the materialization of moral traits that a clearly defined practice of free will imprinted upon the soul in the course of the preceding cosmic ($\alpha\iota\acute{\omega}\nu$) period. The separated soul after death bears both moral and physical traits, the physical traits remaining from its earlier existence, which explains why ghostly ($\check{\epsilon}\iota\delta\omega\lambda o\nu$) apparitions present the exterior aspect and attraction of the dead person.[75] The $\epsilon\check{\iota}\delta o\varsigma$ suffices to assure the permanence of the personality in the course of its transformation from one eon to another. It also explains the persistence of the individual

---

of individuals. Each possesses his "sign," and must progress according to his proper sign. However, it is possible without losing the "proper" sign of a name to obtain better signs by the practice of virtues, to the point of attaining the totality of signs, and thus escaping to the realm of the specialized "angels," in order to take one's place under the banner of the Logos, Pleroma of all virtues (*Hom. in Num.*, II, 2; XI, 5; cf. *C. H.*, XIII, 7-14). Earthly corporeality rewards those who marched under the banner of the prince of this world, whose goad is death (*Hom., in Num.*, XVIII, 4); the various heavenly corporealities reward those who have practiced various virtues (*Hom. in Ps.*, 36, V, 7); the "pneumatic" body those who have been "one spirit alone" with God and have observed the Law in its entirety. The soul, become again a *pneuma*, possesses the body so that the latter "becomes soul" (*in Eph.*, 5, 28-29), repeated by Jerome, *P. L.* 14, 1289.

[75] Some (Bonwetsch, *op. cit.*, 113) believe that Origen rejects all reasoning *a pari*, beginning with the resurrection of Christ and concluding with the mode of His apparitions and that of the resurrected body. This is true only in the measure to which the retribution for sin maintains a certain difference among these resurrections, for in several instances he argues, on the contrary, conforming with tradition, from the resurrection of Christ to ours. See for example *Scholies in I Cor.*, 15:20-23, *J. T. S.*, 1909, 30 ff. Cf. *Comm. in Rom.*, I. *P. G.* 14, 852.

identity in the corruptible world in spite of the flux incessantly renewing the matter of living bodies.

"All men are liars": in Origen's system this expression of the Psalmist is pregnant with meaning. It indicates that no one's exterior appearance here on earth ever corresponds exactly with his moral worth. At the end of the eon, the resurrection will re-establish each thing in its place by giving to each the appearance and the mode of life which corresponds to his moral worth. Equipped with a body made to live in such a natural milieu, the rational being (λογικός) must assume its duty of living according to the rule or particular λόγος proper to this milieu. For this it is more or less gifted, according to its earlier life. Thus, for example, the physical difference between Esau and Jacob can be explained, and also all the variety of races and hereditary dispositions. The laws "natural" to various milieux must give place to the pure and simple law of reason, of which the Logos was the perfect revelation. In other words the end of the education of rational beings that is carried out by God in the world is to free them from all "provincialism" which confines them to some particular part of the earthly world or even the cosmos and lead them to the "liberty of the children of God," who feel at home everywhere and who share the privileges of the risen Christ, whose Body adapts itself to all situations without being constrained by any. If we conceive the resurrection in traditional terms as a new birth, the "mendacious" body with which we are now clothed, which serves us "provisionally" in a given milieu and violently restrains the natural aspirations of the λόνικος to the totally free life of the universal Logos, can well be called the "after-

birth" which we shall discard following rebirth in the new
eon. The resurrection of the dead delivers them from
the terrestrial world, this "matrix," narrow as a prison,
where the new man is formed.

If we knew in more detail the cosmic "vitalism" that
the Stoic Posidonius of Apamea professed, it is probable
that we would discover in him the origin of several
characteristics of Origen's system insofar as the resurrection is concerned.[76] His system is characterized by
a perfect "symbiosis" between the unfolding of physical
phenomena and of biological rhythms. What should be
accounted proper to Origen or to his unknown source[77]
who previously had adapted the Posidonian system to
this end, is the new and strictly established correspondence between the vicissitudes of the moral life and the
conditions for the reincarnation of souls.[78] This correspondence inevitably recalls the doctrine of Indian *samsara;* for the human relations existing at the beginning
of our era between India and the Roman Empire do not
eliminate a possible influence. It is rather difficult to
admit that only the doctrine of metempsychosis as it
existed in the Hellenistic milieu had given Origen the

[76] The εἶδος plays exactly the role of the λόγος απερματικός in the con-
stitution of the new personality and in its adaptation to its new environ-
ment: cf. Jerome, *ep.* 61 *ad Pammachium*; Bonwetsch, *Die Theologie des
Methodius,* 1903, 112 ff.

[77] Perhaps Ammonuis Sacca, as we shall see later.

[78] E. Rohde, *Psyche,* French translation p. 397 and n. 5, points out
that the Pythagoreans held the idea of a strict compensatory justice,
and he deduces from this that their doctrine of successive reincarnations
had for its end the re-establishing of an equilibrium between actions
and their compensations. Even if we admit that these ideas are old,
nevertheless the precise mechanism of this retribution, such as Origen
conceives it, has no parallel in Greece but has very definite ones in
Indian speculation.

idea of his system. Not only did Origen, according to the consistent practice of the Christian apologists of the resurrection, reject and refute Platonic metempsychosis,[79] but the essential part of his own system of reincarnation, which tends to unite the mystique of the ascension of souls with the dogma of the resurrection of the body, is in neither the Greek nor the Christian tradition. On the contrary, the Indian notion of retributive reincarnation, linked to the mystique of the ultimate identity of the law of the individual with the law of the whole cosmos, a fundamental dogma of the *Upanishad* (*atman-brahman* identity), provides a middle term between Hellenistic mystique and the judicial "somatism" of the Judaic tradition. These connections find a certain basis in the person and doctrine of Ammonius Sacca, whose pupil Origen was but who had also taught Plotinus. Sacca, according to E. Benz,[80] could have been a *Sakki-muni*, that is, another monk of the tribe of the Sakya from whom the illustrious Buddha had arisen. Even without going to the length of such a definite relation, it is certain that the word *Sakka* is best understood as an ethnic

[79] The *ep. ad Mennam* and Jerome in the *ep. ad Avitum* (*P. G.* 11, 140, n. 44) accuse Origen of having professed the return of the soul even into the bodies of animals. Certain sinful souls, pursued by the fire of remorse, had preferred to lose the consciousness of their dignity as rational beings and chose to descend into the waters and become fish. But the contrary affirmations of the Alexandrian didascalia are so numerous and so formal that one should ask whether the lost passage of the *Peri Archon* thus summarized was well understood by its critics. Life in the "lower waters" could well mean all life—even human—completely ruled by the senses, before the rise of reason, like the child before it comes of age. The allusion to fish refers to 1 Cor. 15:39.

[80] The thesis is defended by E. Benz, *Indische Einflüsse auf die frühchrisliche Theologie,* Abh. Geistes-und Sozialwiss. Kl. Akad. Mainz, 1951, 197-202. On the relations between Ammonius and Origen, see R. Cadiou, *La Jeunesse d'Origène,* 196-200.

designation, which leads us towards the frontiers of Iran and India and the neighborhood of the "silk route" whose importance in the cultural exchanges between the Mediterranean and the Far East Groussel has shown.

Origen discusses a system of metempsychosis which seems to excel in power of organization anything that the Western philosophers had developed so far in this field. He had indeed seen the major objection that the Christian would oppose to these conceptions: the fact that an indefinite returning of souls into different bodies emptied moral decision of its absolute character, in this case always subject to appeal. The quality of eschatological Judge acknowledged in Christ by the whole of tradition would be emptied of meaning. In spite of this critique, Origen believed it possible to turn to his account the idea of retributive reincarnation, by means of modifications he could bring to it in order to make it assimilable by Christianity. If it is really a doctrine of Indian origin he was dealing with, he found there the notion of periodic destruction of the cosmos, with the *karman* of individual souls not yet completely freed from the obligations of the cycle of reincarnation maintained by the "power" of a supreme God. Relating this idea to that of the judgment and the Greek notion of an "ideal" world contained within the Idea of the All, Origen imagined the judgment as a divine Thought, demanding a decision to make a new world, projected into matter by a Logos-Demiurge containing in itself, as seeds, all the "reasons" ($\lambda \acute{o} \gamma o \iota$) for things and therefore the executor of the sublime works of the Father (*C. C.* IV, 57; V, 40). Was there a new redemption for each of these successive worlds? Doubtless Origen did not settle the question. In any case he declared formally that sins against the Holy Spirit which are remitted neither "in this world nor in the other" would be remitted in the third eon, that is, after a new eschatological fire had destroyed the lasting results of such a sin, capable of determining the destiny of a soul for a whole eon. This idea permitted the notion (exactly as with the Gnostics) that certain souls were dedicated to evil by an absolute predestination,[81] though there was no falling into the absurdities of Manichean ontological dualism. At the end of each eon, there was a return of the Kingdom to the Father; then those of the just who had followed Christ up to His ascension left the vicissitudes of the changing world to enter the "promised land," which was located beyond the fiery river—the spiritual Jordan—of the Milky Way.[82] These latter escape from the cataclysm at the end of the eon. Whether they are finally freed from all matter or have with it the relation perfectly free from all constraint which Christ's glorious Body manifests, it is difficult to decide. The texts of Origen

[81] Cf. above, p. 166, n. 70.

[82] It is certain that Origen envisages the happiness of the elect after the model of the blessedness of souls who contemplate suprasensible realities in the myth of the Phaedra (247 c-248 a). We shall thus grasp more clearly the outcome of Origen's eschatology if we can define the properties that he attributes to the "supercelestial" region. A primary principle is that only invisible things are eternal, while the visible "firmament" disappears in the conflagration at the end of the eon (I, VI, 4; C. C., VI, 59). This other heaven, invisible to us, is present in Theophilus of Antioch, a heaven completing the octave of the seven visible heavens (Strom., IV, 159, 3). This heaven is inhabited by the archetypes and the "back" of the firmament it uses as earth (Hom. in Ps., 36, V). Origen transfers to this world the generally recognized property of the visible world envisaged as one whole, immortality (II, III, 6). Like the "invisible" soul of the world, the "eighth" heaven serves as the "body" of the Logos.

coming down to us lean toward the latter idea,[83] but they are under suspicion of having been subjected to the softening revision of Rufinus or are "rudimentary" instructions, true on their level but capable of further development. The internal logic of the system seems to support those who accuse Origen of having professed the final return of souls to a total spirituality, as well as complete disappearance of all matter in the interval between the destruction of one age and the birth of the next.[84] During the interval, only the memory of the divine Logos preserves the trace of the merits of the individual whose morally imperfect state will bring about a new creation. Sentences of judgment on souls will become the "seminal reasons" of the new world.

Origen always took the greatest care to integrate into his views all the elements of the tradition, and though he is very careful to distinguish between what seems to him strictly *de fide* and what leaves room for discussion,

[83] One of the least suspect and also very beautiful ones envisages the return into "the house" as a cohabitation of the soul with the Logos in the same bed, which is the body (*Hom. in Cant.*, II, 4). For a contrary meaning one may cite *C. C.*, VII, 33: "We need a body for various uses while we find ourselves in a material place and it is therefore necessary to divide the nature of this place whatever else it may be; and when we need a body we put it on over the 'tabernacle' [that is, the εἶδος, a conjunction of qualities that are in themselves incorporeal]. But to know God, we do not need a body." Cf. Asclepius 11: "But it is necessary to hold all earthly things as foreign to all that in man which is related to the divine . . . even the body: in this way we should have contempt not only for the objects of our appetite but for the source from which the vice of appetite springs in us. For, according to rigorous reasoning, man would be man only to the extent that by contemplation of the divinity, he holds in contempt and disdain the mortal part which has been united to him by the necessity in which he finds himself in taking care of the inferior world."

[84] For a more finely developed opinion, cf. our articles in *R. S. P. T.* (1959) and below, p. 180, n. 91.

he does not make this a pretext for neglecting apparently secondary details that the tradition transmits to him. But he does reserve the right to interpret them in the light of his own principles. So it is, for example, with the role of the Spirit (*pneuma*) in the revivification of the body. Origen gave it a place in his system but one rather far from the meaning it had in the great scene described by Ezechiel. As for Philo, the *pneuma* is the vital power (δύναμις ξοτική) of souls. Our sanctification is accomplished under the direction of the Spirit, who leads us into the "land of the living." The Spirit acts through contact with our spirit, which is itself the guiding spirit of our moral action (ἡγεμονικόν). When our spirit unites with the Lord by becoming "only one Spirit" with Him, our soul ceases to be drawn toward the body in order itself to adhere to the Spirit.[85] This state is achieved in the resurrection of the just, which gives back to them not the carnal body they had on earth but a "spiritual" body. The body is as docile to our spirit as is the entire cosmos under the impulse of Providence. The liberty of the "sons of the resurrection" rightly originates from this absence of all inertia on the part of matter. They go where they will, for they have become "spirit" and the spirit breathes where it wills. Having become "sons" in the "household," they move about there with the ease fitting to those animated by the Spirit of the Father.

[85] "Idem corpus, quod nunc pro ministerio animae nuncupatum est animale, per profectum quemdam cum anima adjuncta Deo unus cum eo spiritus fuerit effecta, jam tunc corpus, quasi spiritui ministrum, in statum qualitatemque proficiat spiritalem, maxime cum, sicut saepe ostendimus, talis a Creatore facta sit natura corporea, ut in quamcumque voluerit, vel res poposcerit, qualitatem, facile subsequatur" (*Peri Archon,* III, VI, 6).

Moreover, to be "as the angels of heaven" is not taken by Origen as a simple comparison. The "sons of the resurrection" really become angels who see the face of the Father and serve Him.[86] The angel possesses a pneumatic body. He defines it: a λογικός who enjoys a life coextensive with an entire eon. The "wicked angels" possess the same privilege but to their unhappiness, since for them it postpones to the third eon the possibility of reaching the happy state of the good angels. But one can also say with Origen himself that only the angels, "sons of resurrection," are *truly* men. In this sinful flesh, man is no more than a "shadow" of himself, and it is only in the pneumatic body that Origen truly finds his definition of "men": to be "in the image of God."

As can be seen, the notions of "man" or of "angel" do not constitute true specific differences from the notion of the "rational being" or λογικός. That is why the relation of the λογικοί to matter is so loosely conceived in the Alexandrian system. Many of the Fathers experienced a certain uneasiness in the exposition and defense of the doctrine of the resurrection because of a comparable deficiency in their anthropology, but none had the intellectual audacity of Origen in pushing to its extreme consequences the Platonic view of the world of the spirits that, for the most part, they shared as he did with contemporary philosophy. Those who, like Tertullian, reacted the most resolutely against this trend did not do so with any satisfaction, believing they had to accept instead

---

[86] All the angels do not have this privilege, which is the sign of perfection in contemplation. The other angels must be contented with the contemplation of the cosmos, which, moreover, they busy themselves in governing (*Hom. in Ps.* 36, V, 6).

very materialistic Stoic views which made of the soul another body. Aristotle's *De Anima,* the foundation of St. Thomas' anthropology, was read during this period, but in the perspective of the time, and in addition Aristotle, was suspect to the early Christians.

Nevertheless, the first and the most penetrating opponent of Origen whose work has come down to us, Methodius of Olympia, author of a treatise on the resurrection entirely devoted to the refutation of Origen's and his disciples' extravagances, perceived very clearly that the dogma would receive a correct interpretation only through an anthropology that respected the specificity of human nature. And since the period had no doubt about the close ties between anthropology and cosmology, it was on this ground that Methodius undertook his refutation. Upon examination it appears that Methodius, seeking to demonstrate that the body is an integral part of man, sometimes overshot his mark, or did he indeed wish to bring down Origen and certain Gnostics at one blow? He assumes in any case that the doctrine he is combating makes the flesh not only the consequence but also the cause of sin, but this is only an approximation of the Origenist position, in which the body does not appear as a true cause. It is indeed the occasion of sin but can also become its remedy.[87] It is true that Origen conceives the body as a source of almost irresistible temptations while Methodius, following the ever deepening current of anti-Gnostic reaction in the East, tends to be more optimistic. But it must be added that Origen's

[87] Origen accepts in effect the Gnostic conception of the soul nailed to the flesh as to its cross, for punishment, but also—and this is not Gnostic—for its redemption.

pessimism (though less extreme than that of Augustine, who did not have to the same extent the sense of a medicinal role that the body could play, as soon as the soul turned resolutely toward the spirit) suffered the body as a burden.

Methodius is more fortunate in his critique when, starting from the specific differences among the various classes of blessed angels, he deduces that men retain their own specific differences even into beatitude. He thus foreshadows St. Thomas' refutation of the Alexandrian Doctor.[88] It was on the basis of the principle of a diversity of nature willed by God from the beginning for the beauty of the cosmos that the Angelic Doctor was to argue when he demonstrated against Origen that the return of natures to their primary goodness brought about by the resurrection does not require that beings who have free will put off all differences (for Origen these were accidental because contracted as a result of sin) in order to lose their identity in one sole essence. Another equally weighty argument of Methodius (cf. p. 157, n. 50) showed that one cannot really speak of a *resurrection* if there is not question of the body that has decayed in the grave. However, Origen is an adversary hard to refute because of the frequent ambiguity in his discourses. It can be ascertained that he himself used against the Gnostics the argument that Methodius opposes against him.[89] Origen's loophole here consists in distinguishing between σάρξ and σῶμα. Methodius saw this

---

[88] Bonwetsch, *op. cit.,* 115; cf. *de Pot.,* 3, 16 *in corp.,* II *C. G.* 44; St. Thomas was preceded here by Maximus the Confessor. Cf. Urs v. Balthasar, *Liturgie cosmique,* 26.

[89] Bonwetsch, 116.

and tried to do away with the distinction. We shall not examine whether he was right as an exegete, but he certainly was not wrong when he denounced the abuse Origen made of the distinction.[90] He was also correct in refusing to interpret the "outer" man of 2 Cor. 4:16 as the clothing of flesh flung by God over the true man who was the heavenly Adam.

Methodius goes to the heart of the question when he seeks to correct the interpretation of the words of St. Paul which Origen constantly used in discussing the resurrection and which served to define for him the "ecclesiastic kerygma" on this point of doctrine: "What is sown in corruption ($\phi\delta o\rho\acute{a}$) will rise in incorruption" (1 Cor. 15:42).[91]

The passage is really an embarrassment for one seeking to define the subject of the verb "sow," and Father Allo in his commentary prefers the imprecision of the impersonal verb. But Methodius is surely nearer than Origen to the thought of the Apostle when he thinks of $\phi\delta o\rho\acute{a}$ as above all the corruption of the grave, the characteristic state of impurity (and thus for the Jew a state of separation from God), rather than of the "state of

---

[90] Origen protested many times that he believed in the resurrection of the same body which lived on earth; he does not say so of the flesh of sin. But it is indeed this body, and not the $\epsilon\tilde{\iota}\delta os$ that is going to decay in the grave. He thus turns the meaning of the word "resurrection," just as his Gnostic adversaries did, into the "raising" of a pre-existing element that had undergone a fall.

[91] Methodius pointed out that $\phi\delta o\rho\acute{a}$ is not $\phi\delta\epsilon\iota\rho o\mu\acute{\epsilon}\nu o\nu$, a corruptible thing, but on the contrary the thing corrupting ($\phi\delta\epsilon\iota\rho\acute{o}\nu$). Origen interpreted $\phi\delta o\rho\acute{a}$ as the perishable $\sigma\acute{a}\rho\xi$, and the subject sown by the pre-existing soul. Methodius replies that it is not possible that the soul was sown, since it is what is sown that is subject to corruptive action. Cf. Bonwetsch, 118.

corruption" understood as the law of all corporeal life.[92] This idea is too formally associated with Greek philosophy to have been at the center of Pauline thought. Thus Origen was wrong to base on this passage his gnosticizing views of the descent into this world of pre-existing souls which one day would have to return to their proper status disengaged from the perpetual fluctuations of matter.

Nevertheless, Methodius's refutation again leaves an opening for his adversary. It is not the soul that Origen conceives to be the subject of the verb "to sow," but the εἶδος, true "seminal reason" of future existence. By so doing, Origen obviously avoids the logic (surely less subtle) of St. Paul's reflections, but he nevertheless escapes the reproach of having given contradictory interpretations to different elements of the disputed passage. The εἶδος, as we have said, is capable, according to the "earth" in which it is sown, of being clothed again, in corruptible flesh or in incorruptibility. Moreover, Methodius understood that this εἶδος was the stronghold of Origen's position, from which he believed it possible to face any attack, regardless of where it came from. He thus proposes to destroy it down to its foundations. According to Origen, the εἶδος provides the soul with a "tent," that is, a provisional dwelling for the interval between two reincarnations. This εἶδος is not really material,[93] but is formed from a conjunction of qualities.

---

[92] According to the Greek idea that the whole sublunary world is the domain of *generatio et corruptio*.

[93] The fragment of the commentary on the sixth Psalm which was preserved for us by Pamphilus in his *Apology* does not contradict the immateriality of the εἶδος; while it tells in effect of the hypersensibility of the subtle body after it will have been stripped of the gross vesture

To put its existence in question, it is enough to deny to
the qualities the possibility of existing outside a material
substratum. This time Origen is really hard pressed,
because the subsisting εἶδος is the mainspring of the
whole system. It is what permits the transition from
the moral to the ontological plane where, in other words,
it is the transforming agent metamorphosing the totally
spiritual activity of free will into the physical conditions
of retributive existence. It is through the εἶδος that
sanction is immanent and we are automatically punished
where we have sinned. On account of the εἶδος, the resurrection is not so much a new creation as it is the result of
a maturation; it is less an intervention of divine omnipotence than the final step of a quasi-natural ascent.[94]
The whole weight of the system is thrown upon the
comparison with the seed, but the idea of the new creation received only "honorary" treatment. Hellenic im-
manence has triumphed over Judaic transcendence. Having found the weak points of Origen's doctrine, how does
Methodius build up his own conception? He shows himself most commendable in not overreacting to the point
of again falling into a coarse millenarianism, and on many
points we feel that he accepts the views of his great
antagonist with very little change. To begin with, he
returns to the classic argument that divine omnipotence

---

of this flesh, it must not be forgotten that the εἶδος only puts off one
vesture in order to put on another. It must be held that the pneumatic
body is a true body but not that the εἶδος is anything other than the
complex of qualities which characterize the individual.

[94] Origen seems, moreover, to evade the possibility of real miracles,
which would do violence to the laws of nature. He considered them
as contrary to a just notion of Providence (C. C., V, 23), while firmly
maintaining the existence of a properly supernatural order which would
however respect the order of nature.

is able to remake what it had created from nothing, or
rather, to a form of the argument that the rabbis and
Justin had used, that omnipotence is able to remake what
it had made in the first place from a tiny droplet on the
day of conception.[95]

Methodius uses another traditional comparison, that
of the remolding of vessels by the artisan who had made
them, in order to bring them again into conformity with
his first idea.[96] Origen had known and used this idea, but
Methodius gives his exposition a polemical turn when he
insists on the fact that the remolding required that the
material be the same as in the original. We need not conclude from this that Methodius did not conceive the
resurrected body as having undergone a profound trans-
formation. For Origen, the preservation of the $\epsilon i\delta o\varsigma$ from
the conflagration at the end of the eon was consistent
with the destruction of the old $\sigma\chi\hat{\eta}\mu\alpha$ because of the
saying of St. Paul that the figure ($\sigma\chi\hat{\eta}\mu\alpha$) of this world
passes. Methodius maintains the identity of the $\sigma\chi\hat{\eta}\mu\alpha$
and the resurrection, and he understands it to relate to
the exterior aspect of the body. This seems to him necessary in order to identify individuals and thus guarantee
that the judgment they receive will be public. We know
that this trend was shown earlier in the Jewish doctrine
of the resurrection. But the survival of the $\sigma\chi\hat{\eta}\mu\alpha$ is not
definitive. Methodius thus leaves room for the glorified
body. He imagines the entrance into the promised land
as occurring in two stages (a trace of millenarianism?),
and, taking as a type of the reassumption of bodies under

[95] *Sanh.* 90 b; Justin, *Apol.* I, 18 ff.; cf. R. Meyer, *op. cit.*, 34-37.
[96] Cf. Theoph. of Antioch, *Ad. Aut.*, II, 26; Methodius of Olympia,
De Res., I, 607, *P. G.* 18, 272; cf. above, pp. 174, n. 82 and 167, n. 72.

their first appearance the dwelling in "leafy bowers" (Lev. 23:42-43), he makes the day of resurrection a homologue with the feast of "tabernacles."[97] The just follow only Jesus (the true Josue) into the promised land and they then abandon human form (ἀνδροπινόν ὀχῆμα) in order to put on the majesty of the angels (ἀνγγελικόν μέγεδος). Here Methodius' ideas are strikingly similar to Origen's, for the latter acknowledges the resurrection to be a stage in the gradual ascension towards the angelic life and the complete abandonment of matter. Was Methodius the advocate of a neomillenarianism for whom only the "first resurrection" was understood in a "realist" manner? In any case Methodius is thus witness to a trend one finds in Justin, in Irenaeus, and in Origen himself— to mention only the greatest names—a tendency to make of the resurrection only the beginning of a training period for the elect to prepare them to approach God and contemplate Him face to face. Moreover, it is not certain that when Methodius speaks of passing out of human form to "angelic grandeur" he means, like Origen, putting off what makes us essentially different from the angels. But the mere fact that the terms he uses leave room for doubt shows how spontaneously the idea of the "angelic" life of the blessed was taken literally in the Eastern Church.

Particularly interesting are the ideas of Gregory of Nyssa, as later those of Maximus the Confessor, for while Gregory was a disciple of Origen, he still remained on guard against certain speculative excesses of the Alexandrian Doctor. It can be said that his eschatological

---

[97] Bonwetsch, *op. cit.*, 124-125.

views follow Origen's step by step but that his adoption of modified ontological principles changes them. In the area of principles, the boldness of Gregory of Nyssa's thought yields nothing to that of Origen. Gregory is also determined not to admit to Origen any material veil interposed between man and God. Yet, aware of the difficulties raised by Origen's key notion of the εἶδος, an entity made of qualities but playing the role of a quasi-corporeal vesture for the spiritual soul, Gregory (like the neo-Platonists) defines corporeality itself as a simple conjunction of qualities. The difficulty is thus settled boldly but with finesse.[98] As Gregory conceives it, the εἶδος is strangely reminiscent of the Buddhist *samskara,* completely empty of ultimate substance, pure conglomerate of moral and physical dispositions. It is composed of the relations of the soul with place and space which situate it in the temporal flux. This εἶδος has no separate existence. It disappears with death, which rightly undoes this relation of the soul and its milieu of relativity. Nevertheless, though really dissolved, it leaves a remembrance in the soul, and it is this which guarantees the identity of the risen body.[99] The persistence of the remembrance in itself explains the classic ghost stories which had been passed down since Plato and which Origen explained by the persistence of the εἶδος. In opposition to Origen, Gregory does not attribute quasi-physical action to the persisting εἶδος, acting as a λόγος σπερματός, the reconstitution of a body in the new eon. He returns on the contrary to the classic theme of creation renewed, divine omnipotence bringing together the

[98] Urs von Balthasar, *Présence et Pensée,* 21, 36 and 148.
[99] Daniélou, *Vigiliae Christianae,* 1953, 156; *de hom. op.* 27.

dispersed elements to reconstitute what death had dissolved. The remembrance preserved by the soul allows it to retrieve the particles of its body in the same way that Christ brings souls together, that is, in the way the shepherd reassembles his flock.[100] As Father Daniélou notes, the version of the εἶδος proposed by Gregory of Nyssa assumes that it is the body that impresses its marks upon the soul, and not the other way around, as was natural in the Platonic atmosphere of the Fathers' philosophy. Gregory thus appealed to the Aristotelian principle of the *tabula rasa* despite Aristotle's bad reputation in Christian circles.

The condition of resurrected bodies is "angelic" precisely because they have ceased to have any connection with the things of sex.[101] Sexual generation is considered by Gregory to be the specific consequence of the fall of our first parents, and return to the lost paradise abolishes it. By his virginal birth, Jesus anticipated the new creation, taking His role as the second Adam. The eschatological unity of men in the Body of Christ is founded upon the physical unity of men in a common humanity. Moreover, the glorious Body of the risen Christ is in the most formal sense the virginal "type" of the body of the resurrection. In Christ, divinity has undergone a "kenosis," so that in exchange Christ, "elevated in His humanity to the true Father, makes us ascend in our turn by Him, all of us who are of the same race."[102] There is a blending (κρᾶσις) of humanity and divinity.

It seems indeed that Gregory, like Origen, groups all

---

[100] Daniélou, *op. cit.,* 164-5.

[101] *De hom. op.,* 17.

[102] Quoted by Urs von Balthasar, *op. cit.,* 148.

rational beings into one species. He does so in any case with the angels, thus differing from Methodius on this point. As also for Origen, the resurrection is only the beginning of an upward progression which is to follow our assimilation to angelic and divine natures. The entire cosmos is involved in this ascent, since corporeality, which is ultimately only a concourse of qualities, is to find its unique completion in Christ's glory extended to all his members. The whole creation will become again the paradise it was in the beginning.[103] This cosmic apotheosis seems to allow no place for hell. This is doubtless because souls are only temporarily excluded from beatitude (apocatastasis). Gregory does not specify very precisely the place where they dwell while awaiting their full amendment. A dark dungeon, a prison, are only the traditional images. It seems that in reality it was the conception of an atmospheric Hades popularized since the triumph of Ptolemy's astronomy that was favored by our Christian philosopher. Gregory's attention, completely taken up by the ascent toward beatitude, does not delay over those left behind.[104] We may note the distance between Gregory and the Jewish or Christian apocalyptics, whose descriptions of the torments of sinners constitute the clearest of their insights on the life beyond. It appears that the general movement of Origen's eschatology is preserved, but the system is relieved of its indefensible repeated eons and of the ambiguous role of the εἶδος, Origen's half-moral, half-physical entity which in Gregory is a simple complex of qualities always able

---

[103] Cf. Urs von Balthasar, *op. cit.*, 52, n. 5; 59.
[104] Daniélou, *op. cit.*, 159.

to guarantee the individuality of the resurrected body and perhaps also its degree of glory.

The Syrian Fathers were in general the most faithful to the line of the first Judaeo-Christian theology. We need not be surprised that Aphraates believed the resurrection could be given its full meaning by making the waiting period a time of deep sleep for souls, undergoing at the most some anticipatory dream which serves them as an aperitif for the feasts to come.[105] Aphraates has no need either of a "heavenly" body for the resurrected and he argues from the basis of the theme of the seed to demonstrate the identity in appearance between what sprouts and what is sown. The theme of creative omnipotence also appears, with a fortiori the existence of a seed for the resurrection, making the divine action easier than the first creation.

Western theology did not experience the temptation to build brilliant syntheses of the exposition of the dogma and profane science and philosophy. Although Ambrose and Hilary were assiduous readers of the Eastern Fathers, particularly Origen and the Cappadocians, they assimilated their views only by detaching them from their philosophical background. They were satisfied to take over the solutions they found to be good ones, but without sacrificing common sense or the meaning of Scripture to the system's requirements for internal cohesion. In the West, what always restrained any tendency toward a system was the more simple, more "naive" reading of Scripture. This docility to the text, sometimes too materialistic, is the general rule, although all analogic interpretation is not outlawed.

[105] *P. O.*, I, 366.

St. Hilary[106] demonstrates the universality of the resurrection on the basis of the universality of the redemption. However, the wicked are resurrected only to their eternal confusion, and their bodies have only the consistency of dust or water. Hilary's description of the glorified body is as splendid as that of the most "angelist" Greek Fathers. The elect will be as gods, corruptible flesh being absorbed in the *forma Dei*. Doubtless, as with Origen, it is a question of a celestial quality which takes the place of the earthly qualities of matter. But Hilary is careful to affirm that it is truly the same matter that formed a part of the earthly body that is now glorified. The Doctor of Poitiers is thus in accord with the moderate Origenism of the Cappadocian Fathers. St. Jerome, who at first was an enthusiastic admirer of Origen, later devoted a share of his acerbity to refuting him. He affirmed the identity between the matter of our present body and the resurrected one, while recognizing that the latter will have qualities which will make the elect "in some way similar" to the angels. In addition, he fixes the age of the resurrected at the age of Christ when He died.

Origen's influence has not eliminated all traces of millenarianism from Ambrose. The "first resurrection" seems, however, to be general, but, as in Methodius, it inaugurates a series of transformations and purifications for the elect which are also called resurrections. The reunion of soul and body is justified by Ambrose according to the traditional theme of the moral solidarity of the two components of the human being.

[106] Cf. *D. T. C.*, art. "Resurrection" (Michel), 13, 2539-40.

Cumont has been able to recognize in the seventh book of the *Divinae Institutiones* of Lactantius the remains of an apocalypse of Iranian origin, the *Oracles of Vishtaspa*.[107] This influence perhaps affected the special form of Lactantius's millenarianism, but it has not been proved that the influence extended to his conception of the resurrection. It appears that for Lactantius death should some day *naturally* lose its domain over the living, for "just as this life is temporary and possessed of determined limits because it is corporeal, so death is equally temporary and possesses a definite end because it attacks the body. Once the time fixed by God for death has been completed, death itself will come to an end. And since a temporary death follows a temporary life, the result is that souls will arise to a perpetual life, because temporary death has reached its end. And thus also, just as the soul's life is everlasting, during which it enjoys the divine and ineffable fruits of immortality, so its death must necessarily be perpetual, during which there await it punishments without end and the infinite torments which its sins deserve" (VII, 10-11). Also, Lactantius refuses to give any reason whatever for rejecting metempsychosis, for he would seem to fear that there were still some people who believed in it. Here we find evidence of a certain reversal of the situation since the time of the first Christian opponents of metempsychosis, who did not take this doctrine lightly. Lactantius's contacts with the Sibyl and with Iranian eschatology could only have strengthened his Christian convictions about the eternity of the state of the damned and ruled out

[107] *R. H. R.*, 1931-1, 29-96.

all inclination to profess the apocatastasis in the sense of Origen or Gregory of Nyssa. "It is therefore necessary that the resurrection take place only once," he concludes, "when evil will be destroyed, because it is not fitting that those who are resurrected should again have to die or submit to the least violence, so that they can lead a happy life" (VII, 22). If the poets have introduced the myth of successive rebirths it is because, observing the excessive evils of the age, they conceived the idea of a river of forgetfulness which led them to make mortals be reborn from the maternal womb.[108] But Christians believe that God, who has created man, will know how to resurrect the same person who has lived (the implication is, with consciousness of his past).

St. Augustine[109] does not bring anything really new to the question, but he supports moderation with his authority and also stays as close as he can to the Scriptural texts. He began by meeting the obstacle of millenarianism, which seemed to have strong support in the

[108] Cf. above, p. 171, n. 78.
[109] St. Augustine has laid down clearly a valuable theological principle: Christian psychology and anthropology should accept the norms of soteriology, and not the other way around: cf. *ep. 190 ad Optat.* written in 418 at the end of the great Doctor's career. In the same text, the other major methodological principle, the primacy of revelation over a systematic elaboration, is clearly recorded. Augustine immediately applies it to reject the doctrine of the soul's pre-existence, although some years earlier in a letter to Jerome (*ep.* 166) he had still held it to be a plausible solution. As a matter of fact, despite the clarity of his principles, Augustine remains under the influence of Platonic and Manichean dualism, which obstruct his wish to do justice to the frankly somatic character of Biblical anthropology, which contains not a physical but a moral dualism. Consequently there is in him a certain ontological aspect to the opposition of "flesh of sin—body docile to spirit," which the doctrine of concupiscence seeks to clarify, but without forcing it into a rigid system, as Origen had done.

Apocalypse. The Fathers of Alexandrian sympathy had suspected the canonicity of this book, or had used analogical methods in interpreting it which enabled them to make all the transpositions they thought necessary. In the circumstances, given the general character of the book, this solution was not inadequate, and Augustine deserves the merit (rare in the West) of turning it to his account. Thus was eliminated the distinction between two resurrections, which had caused considerable difficulty in the development of the eschatology of the Latin Fathers. All the weight of the authority of the Bishop of Hippo would not be too great to restrain the strong millenarian current established in the West. Even into the high Middle Ages, penetrated by Augustinism, recurrent outbreaks of millenarian hopes would occur. The birth of Protestantism itself is linked to a resurgence of adventism fed by the literal reading of the Apocalypse.

It is exactly the same flesh which has undergone the test of this earthly life that will receive eternal reward in an "angelic" life. But Augustine does not believe that the angels have bodies. How then can the risen have been said by the Lord to be like angels? Because mortal bodies will then have put on incorruptibility.[110] This is granted even to the resurrected bodies of the damned. Thus at one stroke the problem of eternal torment inflicted upon perishable flesh is resolved. Lactantius had come to grips with the same question and had attributed the durability of the bodies of the damned to a property of the infernal fire, which was able to re-create the body to the extent that it destroyed it, not to a special property

[110] *Serm.*, 264, 6; 256, 2; *Ench.*, 89 and 92.

of the flesh itself.[111] Augustine's solution led him to deal with the resurrection of the wicked according to the same principles he used to explain the resurrection of the just. Earlier, St. Hilary's idea of basing the universality of the resurrection on the universality of the redemption had pointed this way, and from this had begun the attribution of a new property of the flesh (incorruptible for the just as well as for the damned) to the fact that the resurrection is the result—valid for all of mankind—of Christ's victory over death, which in Adam had involved the whole human race.

Like all the Fathers, Augustine makes the resurrection the special work of divine omnipotence, able to bring together from everywhere the elements which made up the body. To the objection that the matter which passes through living bodies is in constant flux, he answers indirectly by taking up the comparison already used by St. Methodius: the statue must submit to remolding; it is of small importance in this case that the old elements receive a new disposition at the interior of the renovated work, provided that this new disposition removes every defect and proves suitable for the artist's purpose. Thus the sense organs and the genital organs will remain, because they are fitting to human nature. Still, the way in which Augustine envisages this reshaping allows room for very profound transformation and is in short situated in the line of the $\mu\epsilon\tau\alpha\sigma\chi\eta\mu\alpha\sigma\tau\iota\mu\acute{o}\varsigma$ assumed by St. Paul and strongly emphasized by Origen.[112]

So that this rapid survey of the Fathers' opinions will not be completed without bringing the debate about

[111] *Div. Ins.*, VII, 21.
[112] *Ench.*, 89; cf. Jerome, *ep.* 61 *ad Pamm.*

Origen's[113] work—which to us occupies a central position —to conclusion, a word remains to be said about the doctrine of an attentive and critical disciple and that of a final adversary of the Alexandrian, namely Maximus the Confessor and Antipater of Bostra.

One of the last champions of the reality of the resurrection against Origenist spiritualism was Antipater of Bostra, Bishop of Arabia, where Origen had come to correct the Semitic opinions of the prelates of his time who could not imagine that the soul was not contained materially in the blood[114] and did not go down into the grave with the body. It is doubtful that all the theses Antipater contends with were really drawn from Origen's work, because it does not appear that Origen ascribed geometric forms to the resurrected body. There did exist in middle-Platonism a notion of ὀχήματα or vehicles of the soul which could be related to geometric forms, but it does not seem that Origen accepted it. However, Antipater refuted Origen well when he criticized the survival of only the εἶδος, and not of the σχῆμα, in the resurrected body. The main argument follows exactly the line whose traces we have pointed out in one of the Jewish notions about the resurrected body: in order for the body to be recognizable when leaving the grave, it must be as it was when it entered.

[113] The quarrel about Origenism spread far beyond the limits we have traced; it was related mainly to pre-existence and the apocatastasis and only indirectly concerned the resurrection. It was Antipater who brought the argument closest to the subject we are concerned with.

[114] Kretschmar, Z. f. Th. u. K., 1953, 268 ff.; the fragment in which Antipater combats Origenism has been preserved among the works of John Damascene. P. G., 96, 498. Chadwick, J. T. S., 1947, 42 and H. T. R., 1948, 95 has treated exhaustively the discussion of "spherical bodies" in Origen.

Maximus was the greatest theologian of the seventh century. As his authoritative interpreter, Urs von Balthasar says: "Instead of the provisional world of Origen and even Denys, the neo-Platonic effusion and return, diastole and systole of the divinity, there is established a definitive world, instrument of a supernatural one, which while elevating it, leaves to it its integral form. It is very significant that the dignity of the natural world would be the essential argument of Maximus against Origen."[115] Soul and body, matter and spirit unite to form a unique man, and neither of the elements whose growth occurs in the union suppresses or repudiates the other. This is why Maximus absolutely refuses to admit the least priority in time either of the soul in relation in the body or of the body in relation to the soul.[116] The interdependence of the parts is so fundamental that it constitutes for him both, the "nature" (φύσις) of man and the *raison d'être* of the individual (ὑπόστασις). Thus the center of the Platonic infection, which always threatens to contaminate the whole Origenist eschatology with heresy, is finally cauterized.

Maximus professes the total immateriality of the highest angels.[117] Thus a clear metaphysical frontier between angelic nature and human nature is traced, and this can serve to confirm the meaning of those propositions which provide man with a proper ontological status.

In this rapid review of the patristic theology of the resurrection, certain ideas stand out. To begin with, the importance of the intervention of divine omnipotence in

[115] Urs von Balthasar, *Liturgie Cosmique,* 17.
[116] *Ibid.,* 122 f.
[117] *Ibid.,* 89, n. 3.

the act of the resurrection will be seen nearly everywhere. The Old Testament had stressed Yahweh's rights over death and life according to His good pleasure. Judaism's attitude toward the resurrection already included this idea, making the resurrection a new creation, and St. Paul had given his authority to this development by adopting it under the form of a theology of the two Adams and of a renewal of all creation at the end of the work of the redemption. "For we know that all creation groans and travails in pain until now. And not only it, but we ourselves also who have the first-fruits of the spirit—we ourselves groan within ourselves, waiting for the adoption as sons, the redemption of our body" (Rom. 8:22-23). This theme is found throughout the patristic period, and even the Fathers whose individual syntheses least require it, such as Origen, cannot neglect it, for all of tradition, and their own Christian conviction besides, strongly impose it. The relation between the universality of the redemption and the universality of the resurrection emerges more slowly. In the beginning its development is obstructed by the influence of Jewish views denying any parallel between the states of the just and of the wicked, whether the wicked were thought not to be transformed at the moment of judgment, or whether their miserable condition could not be conceived as a "resurrection," in the manner intended by the scholars of the apocalypse. It required a long period of reflection on the fact that for *all* men, it is *the entire man* that is to appear before the eschatological Judge, in order for the theology of the new Adam to bear fruit. Another obstacle, perhaps more serious to theological development, was the persistence of millenarian trends, which concealed the positive effects of the redemption by extending it to those exiled from the Kingdom.

As was natural, the apologetic of the resurrection of the body was linked to the resurrection of Christ. The Gnosis and Hellenism attacked both dogmas at once, denying them on the grounds of the inherent imperfection of matter or dissolving them in the subterfuges of Docetism. The special value of the system of Gregory of Nyssa is to have integrated this solidarity into a well-knit notion of the "theandric" unity of humanity, the singular merit of which was not to fall into the groove of the Platonic "Idea" but to maintain the mutual relations of soul and body in this ascent together towards the Father, following the "first-born from the dead."

Throughout the patristic period the doctrine of the resurrection suffered from the inadequacy of the various anthropologies used to interpret it. As a result of gropings oriented more by the theological sense of the redemption of man taken in his integrity than by real progress in the use of philosophical categories for thinking about man, a certain agreement was reached. The anthropologies of Gregory of Nyssa, of Augustine, of Maximus the Confessor, though not without merit, were not completely adequate to their dogmatic role. Some progress was achieved indirectly through angelology, now seen to possess a separate status (the absence of which counted for much in Origen's mistaken ideas). But a pervasive Platonism exercised too great an influence for the Fathers to have been able to abandon completely the idea that man is essentially a spirit and his incarnation a more or less accidental and more or less unfortunate matter of chance. The introduction into the anthropological mixture of a certain dose of Stoic so-matism, after diluting its materialistic virulence, was only an expedient and a risk. The most eclectic of the Fathers arrived at the best results. Because of his inde-pendence and originality, Gregory of Nyssa achieved unusual success, although his achievement is not with-out its weak points. His boldness as an equilibrist made him hard to imitate.

On the nature of the glorified body, a growing unan-imity appears. Minds of as different tendency as Ter-tullian and Cyril of Jerusalem concurred in defining the common belief in similar terms: to the *nec alius sed aliud* of Tertullian, Cyril answers τοῦτο ὀυ τοιοῦτο. Sub-stantial identity thus plainly affirmed, differences in ap-pearance could be variously envisioned, depending upon whether one stressed the mutual recognition preceding the judgment, or the angelic state required to approach God. Many sought a solution in a gradual or a sudden transformation in the resurrected bodies. The bodies of the just would be more or less "spiritualized," while those of the damned would go to "perdition," though this did not signify total destruction.

Taken as a whole, the Greek East remained faithful to the ascetical and mystical line inaugurated by the controversial yet impressive Origen and found in the progressive spiritualization of the resurrected body the prolongation of an ascetical effort to bring about the ascendancy of spirit over matter begun here on earth. From this point of view there is a real continuity be-tween Greeks and Indians as the latter envisage progress toward beatitude as a *yoga* and see in certain ascetics —the great monks—true "living-saints." Monastic life had no other end than the founding of paradise upon earth, and the vigorous beginning of a hidden but real development of the "body of the resurrection," this "interior man" who believes, while the other withers away. The end is reached when "being" and "appearing" succeed in coinciding perfectly, a state which the resurrection brings about. The Latin high Middle Ages, although crossed by many rays from the oriental mystique, remained faithful on the whole to the "dualist" ideas of the apocalypses, still popularly read, to the point that there were "adventist" agitations. Insofar as it concerned the final separation of the good and the wicked, the judgment did not cease to be of importance to popular preaching, which attempted to civilize somewhat the successive waves of barbarians. That the conception of beatitude was not felt differently from that of damnation, the diptychs of Romanesque tympani clearly demonstrate. Ideas of the resurrection sprang naturally from them.

Four

THE LATIN FATHERS

The thought of the Latin Fathers on the resurrection of the body seems less rich perhaps than that of the Greek Fathers. After reviewing the basic statements of their belief, we shall quote some of the texts which we consider most significant and add a very brief commentary.

In its oldest existing form, the Roman baptismal Creed affirms faith in the resurrection of the body:

(I believe) "in the Holy Ghost and the Holy Church and the resurrection of the body" (in Hippolytus, *Trad. Apost.,* 21; text from the beginning of the third century; the creed may go back to the end of the second century).

About the same time, in Carthage, Tertullian admits the resurrection of the body to the number of articles of the rule of faith (*The Veil of Virgins,* 1; *Of the Pre-scriptions against Heretics,* 13). "The resurrection of the body is the hope of Christians" (*The Resurrection of the Flesh,* 1).

"Thus, according to the Christian faith, which is not known to deceive, the body will rise again" (St. Augustine, *The Faith and the Creed,* X, 24). "That the flesh should rise again for all men who have been born or who will be born, who are dead or who will die, no Christian can doubt" (*Enchiridion,* XXIII, 84).

Tertullian confronted heretics (the Gnostics, Marcion) who, despising and condemning the flesh which they made

the work of an evil god, denied the reality of Christ's
flesh and also the resurrection of the body. Against them
Tertullian exalted the dignity of the flesh, created by
God and the instrument of our salvation. By His flesh,
Christ is the Redeemer of our flesh, therefore we shall
rise.

After a section from the *Contra Marcion* we shall quote
several fragments of the treatise *On the Resurrection
of the Body:*

"It is always the resurrection of the flesh that is denied.
For if it is a question of the soul, most of the wise men claim
it is divine and promise it salvation; the common people
themselves render worship to the dead, because they are
confident that their souls continue to exist; but as to men's
bodies, it is evident that they are immediately destroyed by
the flames or by wild beasts and in any case, even if they are
buried with much care, by the work of time. Thus if the
Apostle chides those who deny the resurrection, it is because
they deny what he avers against them, that is, the resurrection of the body. You have his answer in brief (cf. 1 Cor. 15);
as to the rest, here are some elaborations. Even the expression 'resurrection of the dead' requires a defense of the proper
meaning of *dead* and of *resurrection.* He only is dead who has
lost the soul which caused him to be alive; it is the body which
loses the soul and thus becomes dead: thus the word 'death'
is fitting for the body. If there is a resurrection of the dead,
and this death is nothing else than bodily, it is the body which
will have a resurrection. Likewise, the word 'resurrection'
applies only to what is fallen. 'Rise' (*surgere*) may be said
of that which has never fallen, which has always been alive.
But 'rise again' (*resurgere*) can be said only of that which
has fallen; it is when he arises because he had fallen that
one says someone is resurrected (*resurgere*). The syllable *re*
always means to begin again. We say, therefore, that the
body falls into the earth by death, as the Law of God attests.

Of the body it has been said 'Dust thou art and into dust thou shalt return' (Gen. 3:19). What is of the earth goes into the earth, that falls which goes into the earth, that rises which falls. 'For since by a man came death, by a man also comes resurrection of the dead' (1 Cor. 15:21). Here the Body of Christ is pointed out to us by the word 'man,' who consists of a body. If we have life in Christ as we have death in Adam, since in Adam we find the death of the body, it is necessary that in Christ we have the life of the body. Otherwise there would be no comparison, if the life in Christ did not attain to the same substance which found death in Adam" (*Contra Marcion,* V, 9).

" 'And the Lord God formed man of the slime of the earth' (Gen. 2:7). What an honor for the clay, which receives the imprint of the hands of God, which is touched, taken up, drawn out, shaped. Think of God completely taken up and given to this clay, with His hand, His intelligence, His activity, His counsel, His wisdom, His providence, and above all with His love, which traced the lineaments of man. While molding the earth, God thought of Christ who would be man, that is slime, of the Word made flesh, that is earth. Thus the Father said to His Son: 'Let Us make man to Our image and likeness.' And God made man, that is He shaped him; 'He made him in the image of God,' that is, of Christ. . . . Thus the clay clothing the image of Christ who came in the flesh was not only the work of God, it was also the pledge of our salvation" (*The Resurrection of the Body,* 6).

"Thus it is a glory to the earth to have been molded by the hand of God, but it is a greater glory for the flesh to have received the breath of God by which it was separated from the heaviness of the earth and received the adornment of the soul. You are not more wise than God: you will not mount precious stones and lustrous pearls in lead, in bronze, in iron or even silver, but you will set them in choice and very elaborate gold. . . . If God put the shadow of His soul, the breath of His spirit, the work of His mouth, into a cheap casket, lodging it there, did He condemn it? He lodged it there, or rather He inserted it and mingled it with the flesh in such a close union that we do not know whether it is the flesh which supports the soul or the soul the flesh; whether it is the flesh which obeys the soul or the soul the flesh. But we must believe that it is the soul which is borne and which rules, since it is the nearer to God. But this also works to the glory of the body, since it contains the soul which is near to God, and allows it to share in its rule. It is through the body that the soul can make use of the things of nature, enjoy the world, taste the savor of the elements. . . . If all things are subject to the soul through the body, they are also subject to the body. . . . And if the body is the servant of the soul, it is also her associate and coheir. If it is associated with her in the possession of temporal goods, why will it not be in the heritage of eternal goods?" (7).

"Now let us see what is the proper state of the name 'Christian' and let us see also the prerogatives that God has accorded to this low and coarse substance. It will suffice to say first that the soul absolutely cannot obtain salvation if she has not first believed while she was in the flesh. To this extent is it true that the body is the basis of salvation. When the soul binds itself to God, it is the flesh which allows it to bind itself: the body is washed so that the soul may be purified, the body is anointed so that the soul may be consecrated; the flesh is marked with the sign of the cross so that the soul may be strengthened; the body receives the imposition of hands so that the soul may be illumined by the Spirit; the flesh is fed by the Body and Blood of Christ so that the soul may be nourished by God. Those who are united in the act cannot be separated in the recompense . . ." (8).

"To sum up, the flesh that God has modeled in the image of God with His hands, which He has animated by His breath to give it a life like His own, which He has destined to inhabit, to possess, to rule all of His creation, which He has reclothed by His sacraments and His discipline, to whom He has given purity, whose mortifications He has approved, whose sufferings He has appropriated, will not this flesh arise, which belongs to God under so many titles? Far from us, far from us be the thought that God will abandon to eternal death the work of His hands, the fruit of His intention, the envelope in which He enclosed His breath, the queen of His creation, the heir of His liberality, the priest of His religion, the soldier of His witnessing, the sister of His Christ. We know that God is good; His Christ taught us that He alone is very good. He who commands us to love our neighbor according to Him, will Himself do what He commands, He will love the flesh which is His neighbor under so many titles . . ." (9).

After having thus exalted the flesh, Tertullian demonstrates the possibility of the resurrection. He appeals to the divine omnipotence to which nothing is impossible:

"He who made the flesh is able to remake it; it is greater to make it than to remake it, to give existence than to give it back; thus we must believe that the resurrection of the flesh is easier than its creation" (11).

He recalls the legend of the phoenix, already used by St. Clement of Rome (*Epistle to the Corinthians,* 25) and the subject of a poem by Lactantius. He appeals especially to the miracles of Christ and comments at length on the Scripture texts affirming the resurrection, for example the vision of the dry bones in Ezechiel 37, Jesus' discussions with the Sadducees (Matt. 22:23-33) and above all the teachings of St. Paul (1 Cor. 15). His commentary on St. Paul's text, in which he touches the heart of the mystery, is as follows:

" 'For if the dead do not rise, neither has Christ risen; and if Christ has not risen, vain is your faith, for you are still in your sins. Hence they also who have fallen asleep in Christ, have perished,' (1 Cor. 15:16-18). What is the truth by means of which the Apostle instructs our faith?—the resurrection of the dead, you say, which is denied.—Indeed, and he wishes to make us believe in it through the Lord's resurrection. . . . And how did Christ rise? In His flesh or not? Doubtless if you learn from the Scriptures that He died and was buried only in the flesh, you will agree that it is also in the flesh that He arose. And what fell in death, what has lain in the tomb, is what is resurrected, not so much Christ in the flesh as the flesh in Christ. Thus if we are to rise according to the example of Christ who rose in the flesh, we will not arise by the example of Christ if we do not also arise in the flesh. 'For since by a man came death,' says St. Paul, 'by a man also comes resurrection' (1 Cor. 15:21). St. Paul distinguishes Adam, the author of death, and Christ, the Author of the resurrection; but by relating them under the same name of man, he avers that the substance which will arise is the same as that which is dead. If 'in Adam all die, so in Christ all will be made to live' (1 Cor. 15:22), they will be brought to life in Christ in their flesh as in Adam they died in their flesh . . ." (48).

It is our own flesh that will arise, transformed into a "spiritual state," but the same substance:

"For it would be absurd, even iniquitous and thus unworthy of God, to recompense a substance other than that which has labored. This flesh of the martyr is torn and another will be crowned? On the contrary, is this which rolled in filth other than the one which will be damned? Would it not be better to set aside once and for all the hope of the resurrection than thus to mock the majesty and the justice of God?" (56).

"Therefore the flesh will arise, the whole body, and the flesh itself and the flesh in its integrity. It remains in trust somewhere near God, through the mediation of the most faithful mediator of God and man, Jesus Christ, who will give man back to God and God back to man, spirit to flesh and flesh to spirit. In Himself He has already joined the one to the other, He has united the bride to the bridegroom and the bridegroom to the bride. If it is said that the soul is the bridegroom, the flesh will follow the soul at least as its dowry. . . . But the flesh is the bridegroom which in Jesus Christ, by His Blood, has received His Spirit as bridegroom . . ." (63).

Between Tertullian and St. Augustine, there are occasional allusions to the resurrection, for example by St. Hilary, who also comments on St. Paul:

"We are all spiritual if the Spirit of God is in us. But, this Spirit of God is also the Spirit of Christ. And, since the Spirit of Christ is in us, the Spirit of Him who raised Christ from the dead is in us, and He who raised Christ from the dead will also give life to our mortal bodies because of the Spirit of Him who dwells in us (cf. Rom. 8:11). We are vivified, however, because of the Spirit of Christ that dwells in us through Him who raised Christ from the dead" (*The Trinity,* VIII, 21).[1]

"After death has destroyed them, God will remake our bodies, not from some other material, but from the substance that they had from the first. Thus the resurrection of corruptible bodies into the glory of incorruption will not destroy their nature but will change it into a new quality. It is not a different body that will rise, although it will rise in a different condition, according to the Apostle's word: 'What is sown in corruption will rise in incorruption . . .' (1 Cor. 15:42). There is an alteration but not destruction. When that which has been rises to be what it was not, it does not lose its origin, but it increases in honor" (*Homilies on the Psalms* 2, 41).

". . . When the infirmity of our corruptible flesh has been transformed into heavenly glory, the will no longer will desire evil, nor ambition glory, nor pride honor, nor work repose, nor body food, nor the fatigue of the day the sleep of the night: we shall have everlasting nourishment, a life perpetually awake, common use of goods, heavenly satiation by the Word of God, the eternal hymn of praise to God with

[1] *St. Hilary of Poitiers,* Vol. 25, The Fathers of The Church, The Catholic University of America Press, p. 292.

the chorus of angels. That is the reward of faith, the glory of our corporeal resurrection, where there will be nothing to desire because there will be no need of anything . . . there will not be suffering from infirmity or old age, because we shall live on eternally . . ." (*Tr. on the Title of Psalm* 91, n. 10).

Thus, the main difficulty we can have in believing in the resurrection is that, as St. Augustine says later, we cannot imagine "what will be and what the grace of our spiritualized body will be" (*City of God,* XXII, xxi).

Let us listen to St. Ambrose consoling himself upon the death of his brother, Satyrus, by faith in the resurrection. He has quoted Isaias 66:22 ff. on the new heavens and the new earth, on the fire which is not extinguished and the worm that does not die, and he continues:

"If heaven and earth are renewed, how can we doubt the possibility of man's renewal, for whom heaven and earth were made? If the transgressor is kept for punishment, why should not the just man be preserved for glory? If the worm of sinners does not die, how shall the flesh of the just perish? For the resurrection, as the very form of the word indicates, is this: What has fallen shall rise again, what has died shall live again.

It is in full accord with the nature and course of justice that, since body and soul possess activity in common, the body carrying out what the mind has planned, both should come into Judgment and both be committed to punishment or preserved together for glory" (*On His Brother, Satyrus,* II, 87-88).[2]

"Why should we doubt that body will rise again from body? Grain is sown, grain comes up again. The fruit falls to earth, the fruit forms again. But the grain decks itself with blossoms

[2] *The Funeral Orations of St. Gregory Naziansen and St. Ambrose,* Vol. 22, The Fathers of the Church, The Catholic University of America Press, pp. 235-236.

and is clothed with a husk. 'And this mortal body must put on immortality, and this corruptible body must put on incorruption' (1 Cor. 15:53). The blossom of the resurrection is immortality. . . . But some may wonder how decayed bodies can become sound again, scattered members brought together and destroyed parts be restored. Yet no one wonders how seeds softened and broken by the dampness and weight of the earth grow and become green again. . . . Why, therefore, should we wonder whether the earth will restore human beings which she has received, since she gives new life to, rears, clothes, protects, and defends whatever seeds are sown in her? So all doubts should be dropped whether the dependable earth, which restores with compound interest, as it were, the seed entrusted to her, will also return her deposit of mankind. . . . We see a grape decay and a vine shoot forth. A graft is inserted and a tree is reborn. Is there a divine Providence for renewing trees and no concern for men? He who has given these things for man's use has not allowed them to perish. Will He allow man to perish whom He has made to His own image? . . .

"It surely would not be difficult for God to join what has been scattered, and to unite again what has been dispersed. Could it be maintained for a moment that God, whom the universe and the silent elements obey and nature serves, did not perform a greater miracle in giving life to clay than in reconstituting it?" (*Ibid.* 54-58).[3]

But we must turn to St. Augustine, who discussed the resurrection several times, both in his sermons to the faithful (*Sermons* 256, 264, 361, 362) and in his more theological works such as the *Manual* (*Enchiridion*), a complete account of the Christian faith, or especially in *The City of God,* the last books, of which (XX, XXII) on the "end" of the two Cities take up the problem of the resurrection, the Judgment, and the mystery of heavenly

[3] *Ibid.*, pp. 219-221.

beatitude. The teaching of the twenty-second book in particular is repeated sometimes in the same words in sermons 361 and 362 from which we shall quote sections. What engrossed Augustine and his contemporaries was the possibility of the resurrection and all the difficulties it presented to a materialistic outlook, one too concerned with physical things (bodies burned, devoured by wild beasts or cannibals, eaten by fish which in turn were eaten by men . . .), and the state of the resurrected body. The latter problem had already been approached by Origen, who underwent later (543) a posthumous condemnation for having thought that the resurrected body would have the most perfect form, in other words, the spherical. To the first problem Augustine answers as Tertullian and St. Ambrose had before him, by an appeal to the omnipotence of God, to which the perpetual renewal of nature as well as miracles, especially the saints' miracles, bore witness. To the second problem St. Augustine answers with St. Paul that in future the flesh will be "spiritual," entirely transformed and transfigured by its participation in the Spirit.

From The City of God

". . . as there are the two rebirths . . . one in time by faith and Baptism, the other in the last Judgment by the incorruptibility and immortality of the flesh—so there are two resurrections, the first of which is temporal and spiritual and allows no second death, while the other is not spiritual but corporeal and is to be at the end of time. This resurrection, through the last Judgment, will send some into the second death, others into that life which knows no death" (XX, vi. 2).[4]

"Now, the faith to which all these miracles bear witness

[4] *St. Augustine: The City of God, Books 17-22,* Vol. 24, The Church Fathers, The Catholic University of America Press, p. 264.

is the faith that holds that Christ rose bodily from the dead
and ascended with His flesh into heaven, because, of course,
the martyrs were witnesses. That, in fact, is what the word
'martyrs' means. The martyrs were witnesses to this faith.
It was because they bore witness to this faith that they found
the world hostile and cruel. Yet, they overcame the world,
not by defending themselves, but by preferring to die for
Christ. Those whose intercession has the power from the
Lord to work these miracles were killed on account of His
name and died for faith in Him. . . . God may have varying
means to His different ends and these means may be altogether
incomprehensible to the minds of man. But the main point
is that all miracles are witnesses to that faith which pro-
claims the supreme miracle of the resurrection of the flesh
into life everlasting. . . .

"Let us, then, choose to believe those who both proclaim
what is true and perform what is miraculous. For they first
proclaimed the truth and suffered for it before they were
given power to be workers of wonders. And of all the truths
they preached the chief is this: that Christ rose from the
dead and was the first to reveal that immortality of resurrection in the flesh which, as He has promised, is one day
to be ours—whether in the beginning of the world to come
or at the end of this present time."[5]

Here is a section of Sermon 264 on the ascension:

"You also have to lay aside that weak human nature, just
as you heard in the Epistle of the Apostle: 'This corruptible
body must put on incorruption, and this mortal body must
put on immortality,' because, as he says, 'flesh and blood can
obtain no part in the Kingdom of God' (1 Cor. 15:53, 50).
Why will they obtain no part? Is it because the flesh will
not rise again? Far be it! The flesh will rise again, but what
will it become? It is changed; it becomes a heavenly and
angelic body. Do angels have a corporeal body? But there
is this difference—because that body will rise again, that same

5 *Ibid.*, pp. 450-451, 453.

body which is buried, which dies; that same body which is seen and felt; that body which needs to eat and drink in order to live; that body which becomes sick and suffers pain; that same body has to rise again, unto everlasting punishment in the case of the wicked, and to undergo a change in the case of the good. When this change has been made, what will it become? Now it will be called, not a mortal, but a heavenly body, because 'this corruptible body must put on incorruption, and this mortal body must put on immortality.'

"However, people are amazed that God, who made all things from nothing, makes a heavenly body from human flesh. When He was in the flesh, the Lord made wine from water; is it anything wonderful if He makes a heavenly body from human flesh? Do not admit any doubt about God because He is able to do this. . . . Is He who was able to make you when you did not exist not able to make over what you once were? And is He not able to give a greater degree of glory to your faith on account of His own Incarnation? Therefore, when this world will have passed, that reward will be born of which John says: 'Beloved, now we are the children of God, and it has not yet appeared what we shall be. We know that, when He appears, we shall be like to Him, for we shall see Him just as He is' (1 John 3:2). Meanwhile, prepare yourselves for that vision; as long as you are in the flesh, believe in Christ incarnate. . . . His humanity, that is, the Head [of the Mystical Body], has gone before us into heaven; the other members will follow. Why? Because it is fitting for those other members to enjoy rest here for a little while, and for each one to arise in his own time. If the Lord, too, should wish to arise at that later time, there would be no one in whom we would believe. For that reason, He wished, in His own Person, to offer to God the first fruits of those sleeping, in order that, on seeing what has been restored to Him, you might hope for the same reward in your own case. All the people of God will be equal to and associated with the angels. Therefore, let no one say to you, my brethren, 'Those stupid Christians believe that the flesh will rise again. Who rises, or who has risen? Who has come back from the lower regions and has spoken to you?' Christ has come back, O wretched one, O perverse and unreasonable human heart. If his grand-father should rise again, this man would believe him; the Lord of the world has risen, but he is unwilling to believe" (*Sermon* 264, 6).[6]

Before concluding let us quote the last phrases of *The City of God:* "On that day we shall rest and see, see and love, love and praise—for this is to be the unending end, that kingdom without end, the real goal of our present life." Less well-known perhaps are the reflections in Sermon 362, which repeat almost exactly the words from *The City of God* just quoted:

"What shall we do in heaven? . . . all our activity will consist of singing *Amen* and *Alleluia.* What do you say of that, brethren? I see that you understand me and that you are happy in what you understand. But do not begin again to be saddened by a carnal thought . . . and believe that this life will be contemptible and not very desirable, saying to yourselves: we shall always be singing *Amen* and *Alleluia,* who can bear it? But it is not with ephemeral sounds that we shall sing *Amen* and *Alleluia,* but with our whole soul. What does *Amen* mean? What does *Alleluia* mean? *Amen* means so be it; *Alleluia,* praise God. And as God is unchanging Truth . . . perpetual, stable, always incorruptible . . . we shall say: So be it; and in saying this, we shall say *Amen,* but with insatiable satiety. We shall lack nothing and this will be satiety; but what we do not lack will always be attractive to us and there will be, so to speak, an insatiable satiety. And as you fill yourselves insatiably with the Truth, you will say with truth insatiable: *Amen,* so be it. . . . And as we shall be one and in perpetual delight we shall see the truth and so shall contemplate it with absolute certainty, inflamed with love for this truth, and adhering to it with mild and chaste

[6] *St. Augustine: Sermons of the Liturgical Seasons,* Vol. 38, The Church Fathers, The Catholic University of America Press, pp. 405-407.

and incorporeal embrace, then we shall praise it and we shall say: *Alleluia.* And all the citizens of this blessed city, moved to one praise together and exulting together in the most burning love for one another and for God, will say *Alleluia,* because they will say *Amen"* (*Sermon* 362, XXVIII, 39).

To conclude with the words of this sermon which contain the whole essence of the doctrine:

"Let us hope that what has already happened to Christ's Body will happen to ours. And if we do not yet see it in fact, awaiting it, let us hold it by faith" (*Sermon* 362, XV, 17).

"When the last hour has come, when God has determined to awaken the elect from their sleep, a voice will come from the throne and from the very mouth of the Son of God, who will command the dead to arise: Dry bones, dry bones, hear the Word of the Lord. . . . At the sound of this all-powerful voice which will make itself heard at the same moment from the east even to the west and from the north even to the south, the dead bodies, the dry bones, the cold and insensible ashes and dust will be moved in the hollow of their graves; all nature will begin to stir; and the sea and the land and the depths will prepare to yield up their dead, that some believe they had swallowed up as a prey but whom they had only received as a repository, to deliver them faithfully, perfectly preserved. For, my brethren, Jesus who loved His own and loved them unto the end will take care to gather together to Himself their precious remains from all parts of the world. Do not be astonished at such a great deed; it is of Him that it is written, upholding all things by the word of His power (Hebr. 1:3). All the vast extent of the earth, all the depths of the sea and all the immensity of the world is only a trifle before His eyes. He bears up with His finger the foundations of the earth, the whole universe is under His hand. And He, who knew how to find our bodies in the very nothingness from which He drew them by His Word will not let them escape from His power, among His creatures. For this matter of our bodies is not less to Him because it has changed its name and shape; and He will indeed bring together again the scattered remains of our bodies, which are always precious to Him because He once united to them a soul which is His image, because He filled them with His grace and they are always protected by His powerful hand, in some corner of the universe where the law of alteration has thrown these precious remains. And if a violent death has almost destroyed them completely, God has not let them be lost for He calls what is not as if it were. . . . And Tertullian was right in saying that nothingness is to Him as though it were everything . . ." (Bossuet, Sermon for All Souls' Day).

Five

THE FAITH AND CHRISTIAN THOUGHT

Let there be no confusion: this attempt to understand and to define the dogma of the Catholic theology of the resurrection of the body is not meant to be a kind of anticipated description of heaven nor to give even an approximate idea of what heaven will be for us.

On the one hand, "Eye has not seen nor ear heard, nor has it entered into the heart of man, what things God has prepared for those who love him" (1 Cor. 2:9). Heaven is a divine mystery. Every divine mystery is full of meaning, luminous, enlightening, and it summons us to meditation; but because the infinite is one of its elements, it infinitely surpasses our faculties. We realize this at the outset of our study, and will see it more and more clearly as we go on. But we know only as much of the mysteries as God has willed to reveal of them. Not much is revealed on this mystery. Cajetan was surprised by overly bold questions in such an area: "Let us postpone to the future," he said, "knowledge which, until that time, will be beyond nature."[1]

That was a wise course. We shall try not to lose any of the light that revelation affords us, by paying attention to the main thing, the heart of the mystery.

On the other hand, Our Lord said in His great prayer to the Father: "Now this is everlasting life, that they may know thee, the only true God, and him whom thou hast sent, Jesus Christ" (John 17:3). Heaven will be for

[1] Card. Cajetan, O.P., *In. III,* 57, 4.

us essentially the possession of God through the face-to-face vision of the One God in His Trinity, and the beatitude we shall experience in the immediate presence of Spirit to spirit. We shall not discuss the subject here; our aim is limited.

Moreover, the human soul is immortal; it subsists beyond the separation from its fleshly companion; thus separated, it is judged a first time in the particular judgment—and it immediately receives the recompense it deserves. For a period which (neither in time nor eternity) is inscribed in human history—from the moment of death until the Lord's return, when He comes to judge the living and the dead—the holy and just souls who need no purification, are, according to the Catholic faith, admitted to the beatific vision though their bodies have not been resurrected. We shall not take up this matter either. Our silence is not due to forgetfulness or denial. Obviously, we believe what the Church believes on this point. But it is not the concern of the present inquiry.

One might, finally, consider the Lord's return itself and meditate on the general judgment where all the resurrected will be brought together at the time of the reunion of their souls and bodies. We shall also omit this topic.[2] We shall restrict our subject to the eternal state and condition of the resurrected in the corporeal part of their nature.

Millions of Christians express their faith on this point every day when they recite the Apostles' Creed, the "I believe in God," which concludes by affirming the resur-

---

[2] What we have to say on these questions can be found in M. A. Genevois, O.P., *Entre dans la Joie. Catéchèses sur l'au-delà.* Paris, Editions du Cerf.

rection of the flesh, or when they sing in the Nicene Creed every Sunday, "I look for the resurrection of the dead and the life of the world to come." During the course of the centuries, an impressive list of Creeds has expressed the same meaning,[3] as have some of the most solemn documents of the magisterium.[4] Here we would like to give a very precise idea, although we are concerned with a mystery, of what is meant by this "resurrection of the body," this "resurrection of the dead." Our faith is able to hold to the verbal expression of a formula: by means of a thought it clings to a reality which the images imply. What should we and what can we honestly think when we pronounce these words?

The first to be resurrected was Our Lord Jesus Christ. "He arose from the dead, ascended into heaven, and sitteth at the right hand of God," the first one to arise in a real resurrection, that is, a total and definitive resurrection.

"The resurrection," says St. Thomas ". . . is a restoring from death to life. Now a man is snatched from death in two ways: first of all, from actual death, so that he begins in any way to live anew after being actually dead; in another way, so that he is not only rescued from death, but from the necessity, nay more, from the possibility of dying again. Such is a true and perfect resurrection, because so long as a man lives, subject to the necessity of dying, death has dominion over him in a measure. . . . Furthermore, what has the possibility of existence, is said to exist in some respect, that is,

---

[3] Including the Creed of St. Epiphanius, the *Fides Damasi*, the *Libellus* of Pastor, the Rule of Faith of Toledo, the Creed of St. Athanasius, that of the eleventh Council of Toledo, the professions of Faith of St. Leo IX, Innocent III and Pius IV. Cf. Denz. 14, 16, 20, 30, 40, 287, 347, 427, 994.

[4] The Councils of IV Lateran, II Lyon, the famous bull *Benedictus Deus* of Pope Benedict XII. Cf. Denz. 242, 429, 464, 531.

in potentiality. Thus it is evident that the resurrection where-
by one is rescued from actual death only, is but an imperfect
one."[5]

The resurrections effected by Elias and Eliseus were
not perfect and neither was the resurrection of the wid-
ow's son of Naim, of the daughter of Jairus, of Lazarus.
They were only signs and portents, partial and provisional, of the true and perfect resurrection brought to us
by faith and hope. Jesus' resurrection was perfect; it was
total and definitive.

Historical, exegetical, apologetical discussions of Jesus'
resurrection are not of interest to us here. We assume
that the problem is solved—as indeed it is—in the affirma-
tive. But what does it mean, what does it mean now,
for the Body of Christ, this total, absolutely irreversible
return to life? What is the meaning of the ascent to
heaven and the sitting at the right hand of the Father?
What is the meaning of these events when we study them
less for their own sake than in connection with the resurrection of our own body?

Certainly the resurrection of Jesus is primarily and
especially a mystery. The New Testament documents
expressly leave to it the character of mystery. Let us
take care not to forget this as we humbly strive to build
our synthesis from them. Father Lagrange wrote these
admirable phrases at the beginning of such a chapter:

"None of the Evangelists says a word about the resurrection
of Jesus. A great artist, François Rude, sculptured Napoleon
in stone rising from the bed of his tomb to awaken to glory.
The Evangelists have not attempted to express the animation
of the livid and bruised flesh animated by the breath of the

[5] St. Thomas, III, qu. 53, a. 3.

soul, the human body which has caused the Son of God to suffer, transfigured by glory in beatitude, the voice of the Father pronouncing in His eternal dwelling, 'Thou art My Son, this day have I begotten Thee,' Jesus Christ thanking His Father for having given Him the nations as an inheritance. All these things are ineffable, remaining hidden in God.[6]

Before and after theological speculation, one must wait attentively in the silence of prayer for the touches of the Holy Spirit alone.

According to the Gospel, the mystery lies primarily in the fact that Christ arose in His Body, which was both the same as and different from what it had been.

The same, because visible, tangible, recognizable. He breathes, He eats, He speaks. "See my hands and feet, that it is I Myself" (Luke 24:39). Different, in the sense that He is not always there, visible and tangible, but that He suddenly appears—sometimes through closed doors—and disappears, or ascends into heaven.

St. Paul envisages the mystery of the resurrection of Jesus above all from the point of view of the salvation brought by Christ. Undoubtedly this is the right approach if we are concerned with the mystery itself. Seen from below, it is the principle of moral and supernatural justification. The final resurrection will be its result and its manifestation in the Mystical Body. But the wonderful thing in St. Paul's eyes is precisely that the Christ, whose fulness we are, is inseparable from the personal Christ. The destiny of the Mystical Body rests on what occurs in the physical Body—thus the importance of the fact itself. ". . . if Christ has not risen, vain then is our preaching, vain too is your faith" (1 Cor. 15:14).

[6] M. J. Lagrange, O.P., *L'évangile de Jésus-Christ,* Paris, Gabalda, p. 581.

Without retelling the story, Paul expressly notes the evidence he has received, and he adds his own to it. He himself also saw the risen Christ: "And last of all, as by one born out of due time, he was seen also by me" (1 Cor. 15:8). He saw Him and he understood.

Nevertheless, a new condition must be added to the certainty of the identity. Paul knows that "Christ, having risen from the dead, dies now no more, death shall no longer have dominion over him" (Rom. 6:9), that He has not undergone and will not undergo the corruption of the grave, that on His countenance shines "the glory of God" (2 Cor. 4:6). And, of course, we are not speaking of the revelation of His kingship or of the fact that He "was foreordained Son of God by an act of power in keeping with the holiness of his spirit" (Rom. 1:4) and of "the spirit which gives life" (1 Cor. 15:45), which are prerogatives of the divine Person.

In his treatise on the life of Jesus, St. Thomas several time quotes St. Gregory the Great: "The Body of Christ, after the resurrection, was the same in nature, but different in glory," *Ejusdem naturae sed alterius gloriae.*[7] This is the principle which should underlie all Catholic reflection on the mystery.

". . . that is said to rise, which fell. But Christ's Body fell by death; namely inasmuch as the soul which was its formal perfection was separated from it. Hence, in order for it to be a true resurrection, it was necessary for the same body of Christ to be once more united with the same soul. And since the truth of the body's nature is from its form, it follows that Christ's Body after His resurrection was a true body, and of the same nature as it was before. But had His been

---

[7] St. Gregory the Great, *Homiliae XL in evang.,* 26, 1. Cf. St. Thomas, III, qu. 28, a. 2, obj. 3; qu. 54, a. 2, 2nd reply; qu. 54, a. 3; qu. 55, a. 6.

an imaginary body, then His resurrection would not have been true, but apparent."[8]

". . . whatever goes with the nature of a human body, was entirely in the Body of Christ when He rose again. Now it is clear that flesh, bones, blood, and other such things, are of the very nature of the human body. Consequently, all these things were in Christ's Body when He rose again; and this also integrally, without any diminution; otherwise it should not have been a complete resurrection, if whatever was lost by death had not been restored. Hence Our Lord assured His faithful ones by saying (Matt. 10:30): 'The very hairs of your head are all numbered' and (Luke 21:18): 'A hair of your head shall not perish' . . . in His resurrection He resumed unto an everlasting life, the Body which in His conception He had assumed for a mortal life."[9]

"That it was a true resurrection He shows first on the part of the Body; and this He shows in three respects; first of all, that it was a true and solid Body, and not fantastic or rarified, like the air. . . . Secondly, He shows that it was a human Body, by presenting His true features for them to behold. Thirdly, He shows that it was identically the same Body which He had before, by showing them the scars of the wounds. . . .

". . . He showed them the truth of His resurrection by showing that His soul was reunited with His Body: and He showed this by the works of the threefold life. First of all, in the operations of the nutritive life, by eating and drinking with His disciples. . . . Secondly, in the works of the sensitive life, by replying to His disciples' questions, and by greeting them when they were in His presence, showing thereby that He both saw and heard. Thirdly, in the works of the intellective life by their conversing with Him, and discoursing on the Scriptures. And, in order that nothing might be wanting to make the manifestation complete, He also showed that He had the divine nature, by working the miracle of the draught

[8] St. Thomas, III, qu. 54, a. 1.
[9] St. Thomas, III, qu. 54, a. 3.

of fishes, and further by ascending into heaven while they were beholding Him. . . ."[10]

Thus Jesus has the same Body now that He had during His earthly life, at Nazareth or on the roads of Palestine. In our way of conceiving Jesus in heaven, let us beware of reviving the old heresies which once falsified the mystery of His Incarnation: Docetism, in which His Body was only an appearance; Monophysitism which submerged His humanity in His divinity; Apollinarianism, which separated this humanity from His soul on the pretext that divinity could take its place. *Ejusdem naturae:* the same nature; therefore corporeal, material, at the same time informed, moved, animated, by the same soul. A completely human Body; the Body of Jesus, born of the Blessed Virgin. The heart of Jesus invoked in the litany is not a myth. The soul of Jesus, so intelligent, so free, so sensitive and loving. . . . To diminish the true humanity of Jesus in heaven is to end by denying the reality of His resurrection, to cast a slur on the reality of the Incarnation.

Another glory: the fact that Jesus appeared to His disciples but did not remain with them is already an indication that His life was not going to be as it had been. The suddenness of these appearances and disappearances is especially surprising. It can only be said: ". . . Christ on rising did not return to an ordinary human life, but to a kind of immortal and Godlike condition, according to Rom. 6:10: 'For in that He liveth, He liveth unto God.' "[11]

All this moves us to make comparisons. The closed

[10] St. Thomas, III, qu. 55, a. 6.
[11] St. Thomas, III, qu. 55, a. 2.

doors remind us of the Church's traditional thought on the Savior's virgin birth. Other points evoke the mastery of Jesus' body over the elements—when He walked upon the waters, even giving St. Peter the same power, then, scarcely having reboarded the boat, transports it to its destination. Especially we are reminded of the transfiguration, so obviously presented by St. Luke as an anticipation of the glorious coming of the Son of Man. These events reveal the omnipotent presence of the divinity in Jesus.

But during His whole mortal life, the divinity was in Him, and He gave witness to it. What was there new about His Body after the resurrection? The fact that the humanity, in these particular episodes, showed extraordinary properties is, one sees upon reflection, less unusual than that it ordinarily did not show them. From His conception, Jesus—true God—had enjoyed the beatific vision. From the first, His soul was in glory. It required a special divine disposition to prevent this glory of His soul from flashing out through the Body with which it was one: Jesus had to be passible and mortal for the work of redemption. But given the hypostatic union, it was natural (so to speak) that His Body was glorious. A real miracle suspended the overflow of His glory during the time of His redemptive pilgrimage. The miraculous transfiguration was not a new miracle, but a momentary suspension of the first miracle. Normally, without a particular providential design, the Body of the Word Incarnate would have been impassible and incorruptible. Normally, the happiness of His Body would have arisen from His blessed soul. Normally, His flesh should have appeared shining with light, before and after the resurrection, and not only on Thabor. Normally, He would not have had to die; He fully consented to it. On Holy Saturday He remained "free among the dead" (Ps. 87, 6 Greek and Vulgate). ". . . therefore He abode a while in death, not as one held fast, but of His own will, just so long as He deemed necessary for the instruction of our faith."[12]

The resurrection established the Man-God in the fulness of His prerogatives. It brought about the triumphal accession to His Body of all its congenital rights, as a return to its normal condition. Here a problem arises from the persistence of certain things from the past: Why did He eat, being now incorruptible? Why did He retain the wounds of Calvary's nails and lance in the marvellous integrity of His members? (He truly ate, but not from necessity, only in order to show His true nature. As to the marks of the wounds, they were not and are not deformities in Him, but titles to honor and the greatest glory. . . . To say nothing of other ways they are appropriate.)

The main cause of the independence from physical laws manifested by Jesus' glorified Body was the power of divinity, but this power properly and rightly belonged to Him. His glorious soul itself could move His Body according to His will. It was this that gave Him the agility which bore Him to heaven on the day of the ascension.

Under those conditions, and considering the number of His conversations about the Kingdom of God as the Acts reports them "during forty days" (Acts 1:3), it does not seem that Jesus then lived continuously with

[12] St. Thomas, III, qu. 53, a. 2, 2nd reply.

His disciples: would they not have believed that He had returned to a life exactly like that He had led before?

Where was He? An idle question: His empire extends "unto every place" (cf. Ps. 102:22). Wherever He was, even very near His own, invisible, was already "the new heaven and the new earth" announced by the Apocalypse (21:1). He was there "in His glory" (Luke 23:26). He was "the glory of God" shining there (Apoc. 21:23). The ascension, which was the last departure, until the time of the great return, manifested only an exaltation comparable to the resurrection.

Where was He from then on? Where is He now? Where is the heaven He ascended to? . . . This has not been revealed either. Has humankind understood this? It has formed different ideas according to the state of its knowledge. If the angels, Cajetan thinks, were charged with announcing the ascension, it was precisely because man could not conceive its outcome. But the notion of space must be retained, because the Body of Christ was not a body if it was not "dimensioned," localized: it is somewhere, in the measureless space which our languages call —by the human scale—the heavens. The heavens are a real place for a real body, the real Body of Christ.

There, He is "such as He was when He ascended there," says St. Augustine;[13] thus, such as He was at His resurrection. Therefore, also identical to what He had been previously—in all His elements and with the Blood that the Eucharist makes present to us—and glorious.

The expression of St. Mark, taken into the creed, "He . . . sits at the right hand of God" (16:19), should not

[13] *Epistola 205, ad Consentium,* Quoted in III, qu. 54, a. 4, 3rd reply, St. Thomas.

be taken in a materialistic sense or understood as a physical posture. The saying affirms the Lord's repose in glory, in the place of honor in the divine joy, and alludes to the power of judgment, such as Jesus had promised to the Apostles. We would not go so far as to say with Cajetan that the positions of sitting and lying show fatigue, and that Jesus could only be standing in heaven. Certainly to the protomartyr Stephen He appeared standing, as if to welcome him, but He is sovereignly master and free in His attitudes, which would not be human if He were immobile. Let us remember that heaven is a place absolutely without fatigue—and consequently of sleep. Otherwise, it can be conceived in continuity with realistical notions. It is Christ indeed. Let us be careful not to limit the perspectives of His glorification by being too precise. The mystery is surely more rich and beautiful than anything we imagine.

After Jesus, there were others resurrected whose condition should throw light on what our future state may be. There is the Blessed Virgin.

As a matter of fact, the dogmatic definition of November 1, 1950, does not speak of resurrection. It says simply that "the Immaculate Mother of God, the ever-virgin Mary, after having completed the course of her earthly life, was assumed body and soul into heavenly glory."[14] This can mean a resurrection strictly speaking, coming after a real death—according to the thought of Pius XII and what appears to us to be the better theology—or direct passing from life on earth to life in heaven without

[14] Pius XII, Bull, *Munificentissimus*.

undergoing death, through some means of transformation such as will be operative for those still alive when Jesus returns. The defined dogma only states the mystery, which exists in the world beyond: Mary's death, even if it is certain, is connected with her life on earth, which is subject to discussion.

Moreover, Mary's situation is not at all irrelevant to our subject. For Mary, the assumption is her "heavenly glorification after the example of that of her only Son."[15] Among the benefits Pius XII hoped to see from the definition was that "finally, faith in the bodily assumption of Mary into heaven would assert and strengthen faith in our own resurrection also."[16]

Up to 1950 theologians had been concerned almost exclusively with studying the fact and the possibility of dogma's definition. Since then, very little has been done to probe into and develop the subject. We believe that Mary's body is as alive and glorified as her soul in heaven. But what does this entail for her body, and, especially, what is applicable to us in all this?

As a matter of fact, belief in Mary's assumption is tied to her unique predestination, to her virginal divine motherhood and to her unique association with the militant and triumphant Redeemer. These arguments for the assumption are valid only for her. Nothing conclusive from them can be immediately applied to all. We do not hesitate to apply to her body—as we apply to Christ's —a common theology of the glorified body.

Can something relevant to our subject be derived from

[15] *Ibid.*

[16] *Ibid. Actuosiorem reddat* should perhaps be translated "to make more vehement, more passionate."

a Marian interpretation of Chapter 12 of the Apocalypse? This interpretation we know is debated by exegetes. St. Pius X unhesitatingly accepted it. Pius XII added some qualifications; in the bull *Munificentissimus* he does not make a Scriptural argument of this text; he says that the classic writers (*scholastici doctores*) have interpreted it in terms of the assumption, in other words only as an argument from Tradition.[17] This then is the context of the first verse of the Introit of the new Mass for August 15: "A great sign appeared in heaven: a woman clothed with the sun, and the moon was under her feet, and upon her head a crown of twelve stars."[18]

It is always difficult to analyze symbols prosaically and abstractly, since their poetic luster is charged with dream and memory, and their emotional overtones are as important as their meaning. In particular, what is this garment of the sun? Does it suggest anything of the brightness of the resurrected?

Undoubtedly the most partisan exegete of the Marian interpretation of Chapter 12 is Father Braun. He asserts, first: "Definitive examination of the various symbols will require much study, from which we can only expect more or less conjectural conclusions."[19] He says, however:

[17] *Ibid.* We are not saying that Pius XII dismissed the argument from Scripture, but he did not use it as such. A dogmatic bull, like the councils, is not meant to settle matters upon which Catholic writers hold various opinions, within the unity of faith.

[18] The verse also occurs in the sixth response of Matins and in the capitulum for None in the feast of the Immaculate Conception, alluding to the battle of victory against the dragon. In the liturgy of the feast of the apparition of Our Lady at Lourdes (Epistle and second antiphon of Lauds) as in the office of the Miraculous Medal, there is only an accommodation beginning with the word *Apparuit.*

[19] F. M. Braun, O.P., *La mère des fidèles,* Casterman, p. 170.

"The appearance of the sun is reminiscent of Psalm 104
(103), 1-2:
'Bless the Lord, O my soul:
O Lord my God, Thou art exceedingly grand.
Thou hast put on praise and beauty:
And art clothed with light as with a garment.'

And even more so the Apocalypse (21:23) referring to
the heavenly Jerusalem, 'And the city has no need of
the sun or the moon to shine upon it. For the *glory of
God* lights it up.' The passage refers to the heavenly
Jerusalem; that the glory of God replaces the brightness
of the sun makes one think that it is itself a more brilliant sun than the day star."[20]

Here a perspective opens out to us. But a little further
on, the author concludes simply: "Without going into
detail about the symbolism of the sun and the twelve
stars, it can, at the very least, be acknowledged that this
astral appearance is especially fitting, in terms of the
visions of the Lamb and the heavenly Jerusalem, to a
person contemplated in the glory of heaven. The moon
placed under her feet recalls the more naturally that
she does not belong to the temporal order, ruled by lunar
change as the present world is. The three images meet
at the same point. They seem to concur in giving an idea
of the condition in which the Mother of the Child now
finds herself in the place prepared for her."[21]

So we remain unsatisfied. Let us console ourselves
that with this verse it is the same as with the previous
theological reasoning: even if it designated the Virgin

[20] *Ibid.*
[21] *Ibid.*, pp. 173-174.

of the assumption with certainty, it would be to glorify the Mother of the Redeemer as such; if the images were easier to conceive we would not be able to generalize from them.

We will therefore reflect only on the fact. Today, corporeally, there is at least one person in heaven with Jesus, the Blessed Virgin, His Mother.

Are they alone there? A widely attested tradition from the end of the sixth century, especially in the Orient, asserts that Enoch and Elias—and Moses is sometimes added—did not die, but were taken up alive into heaven. The only basis of belief seems to be apocryphal legends. Even if we were more certain of the truth we would not necessarily be dealing with resurrected persons, for these holy men are generally thought of as having to die in the final struggle against anti-Christ. Let us note as a more serious although not conclusive argument the mysterious presence of Moses and Elias at Thabor; "appearing in glory" (Luke 9:31), they are "talking together with" Jesus (Matt. 17:3) at the time of the anticipated manifestation of His glorious Body.

The problem of the resurrected presented by St. Matthew's account of the Passion is more difficult: "And behold, the curtain of the temple was torn in two from top to bottom; and the earth quaked, and the rocks were rent, and the tombs were opened, and many bodies of the saints who had fallen asleep arose; and coming forth out of the tombs after His resurrection, they came into the holy city, and appeared to many" (Matt. 27:51-53).

Is this an imperfect, temporary resurrection or an anticipation of the final resurrection? "A very debatable question which it is impossible to resolve," says Father Fillion, prudently.[22] Father Lagrange thought they "certainly assumed only an ephemeral life";[23] they "appeared to some, but as phantoms, and returned almost immediately to their graves, for there is no longer a question about it."[24] On the other hand, Father Prat wrote: "Whether these privileged ones had to die again or took up their ordinary life at the risk of losing the beatitude of which they were certain, their condition would have had nothing enviable about it. No doubt at the day of the ascension they formed the escort of the Conqueror of death in His triumphal entry into the dwelling place of His glory. Since they were recognized by a number of persons, their death cannot have occurred very long before. . . ."[25]

The older exegetes disagreed as much as the modern ones. But names as important as Clement of Alexandria, Origen, Eusebius of Cesarea, St. Epiphanius, St. Gregory of Nyssa, St. Ephrem, St. Ambrose, St. Jerome, Rufinus of Aquila, St. Bede, on the side of those who accept one perfect resurrection, do make an impression and do not permit us to treat the matter lightly.[26]

Comparing St. Jerome's arguments for a definitive resurrection and St. Augustine's for a temporary one, St. Thomas finds the latter "much more convincing."[27] How-

[22] L. Cl. Fillion, P.S.S., *Vie de Notre Seigneur Jésus-Christ,* Paris, Letouzey, v. III, p. 500, n. 3.

[23] M. J. Lagrange, O.P., *Évangile selon saint Matthieu,* Paris, Gabalda, pp. 532-533.

[24] *Ibid., L'Évangile de Jésus-Christ,* Paris, Gabalda, p. 573.

[25] F. Prat, S.J., *Jésus-Christ,* Paris, Beauchesne, v. II, p. 412.

[26] Cf. M. Jugie, A.A., *La mort et l'assomption de la Sainte Vierge,* Cité du Vatican, pp. 49-54, and the references in it.

[27] *Summa,* III, qu. 53, a. 3.

ever, he is not here discussing the problem in full nor for its own sake, though he approaches it directly in his *Commentary on the Sentences of Peter Lombard* and his *Commentary on the Gospel according to St. Matthew*. In both places, St. Thomas favors a definitive resurrection, for interesting reasons. "This seems more probable, for in order to bear true witness to Christ's true resurrection it was fitting that they be truly risen," he says in the *Sentences*.[28] In the *Commentary on St. Matthew* he repeats this argument and adds another: "If they arose to die again it was not a benefit but rather a misfortune to them. They arose having to ascend to heaven with Christ."[29]

Cajetan gives a third reason. Before discussing (and setting aside without too much difficulty) the exegetical reasoning of St. Augustine, who had carried weight with his master, the illustrious Thomist writes: "Concerning the various opinions on the resurrection of those who arose with Christ, it seems reasonable that they arose perfectly, that is, to a life completely immortal, in order for Christ to have companions in His physical joy. There is less corporeal happiness, it seems, if one is alone. In his corporeal life, man is a social animal, and not only on account of his needs in the world but also for the natural pleasure which comes from physical companionship itself."[30] This could be stated with more finesse, but it is very clear.

The three arguments carry weight. Added to the traditional line of thought pointed out earlier, they seem to

[28] *In IV Sent.*, 43, qu. 1, art. 3, 1 obj., 3rd reply.
[29] c. 17.
[30] Card. Cajetan, O.P., *In III*, qu. 53, a. 3, Comm. II.

us to establish at least a serious probability if not a certainty.

Can we guess the names of any of these risen ones? "A vain conjecture," thought Father Prat.[31] A conjecture, yes, but not so vain. Piety has sensitivities that history lacks; theology should take account of them, because the gift of piety is a gift of the Holy Spirit. His Holiness John XXIII—and not in a *ferverino* but in a solemn homily— gave his endorsement to pious beliefs. After quoting St. Matthew he added: "Thus it is to the dead of the Old Dispensation who were closest to Jesus—we cite two of those most intimate, John the Baptist, the Precursor, and Joseph of Nazareth—it is to them, as we may piously believe, that there came the honor and privilege of leading this admirable escort on the paths to heaven and intoning the first notes of the *Te Deum* without end of the human generations ascending after Jesus the Savior to the glory promised to the faithful, assisted by His grace."[32]

Have others been added to Christ's companions in the glory of the resurrection, to His Mother and these privileged souls? A long and solid tradition includes St. John the Evangelist.[33] St. Thomas categorically agrees.[34] It would not be a right; it is an exceptional privilege, in relation to the general extension of the resurrection up

---

[31] *Loc. cit.*

[32] John XXIII, Homily for the canonization of St. Gregory Barbarigo, May 26, 1960. Transl. from *l'Osservatore Romano,* week of June 10, 1960.

[33] Cf. M. Jugie, *op. cit.,* pp. 710-726.

[34] *Expos. super symbolum; In IV sent.,* 43, qu. 1; art. 3, arg. 2 and obj. 1, 2nd reply; *In ev. s. Ioann.,* 21, 5.

to the end of the world. It is not *de fide* but *pie creditur*.
We cannot assert more.

It is probable, then, that Christ in glory enjoys the
corporeal presence not only of Our Lady of the Assumption, but of a small court of persons. We can conceive
this group, forerunners of the end of time, only with ref-
erence to "physical companionship," as Cajetan calls it;
that is, they know each other and communicate there
not only by means of spiritual contemplation of the divine
Word, but through the mediation of transfigured matter
and beatified senses.

Jesus is the "first-born from the dead" (Col. 1:18).
"Christ has risen from the dead, the first-fruits of those
who have fallen asleep" (1 Cor. 15:20). If He has risen,
we shall rise. This is the fundamental principle that to
St. Paul dominates the whole subject of the resurrection,
the "hope of Israel" (Acts 28:20). However, in analyzing
St. Paul's principle, we emphasize that although he
exploits it more fully than the other inspired writers,
it is not peculiar to him. It is not by accident that St.
Matthew draws attention to the resurrected ones we
have just discussed. Jesus presents Himself often as the
principle of the resurrection of those who were His. Thus
He said at the pool of Bethsaida, "For as the Father
raises the dead and gives them life, even so the Son also
gives life to whom He will" (John 5:21).

In the discourse on the bread of life, He repeated,
". . . this is the will of him who sent me, the Father, that
I should lose nothing of what he has given me, but that
I should raise it up on the last day. For this is the will
of my Father who sent me, that whoever beholds the

Son, and believes in him, shall have everlasting life, and I will raise him up on the last day . . . no one can come to me unless the Father who sent me draw him, and I will raise him up on the last day" (John 6:39, 40, 44).

In His farewell, He confided to His children, ". . . I go to prepare a place for you, I am coming again, and I will take you to myself; that where I am, there you also may be" (John 14:3). And in his priestly prayer, He asks the Father to glorify him "that as Thou hast given him power over all flesh . . . to all Thou hast given him he may give life everlasting" (John 17:2).

Obviously the texts are more concerned with what we call efficient causality than with the exemplary causality we are discussing, but the two causalities are inseparable here. Jesus is at once the source and the type of our final salvation; one cannot say whether He is the source because the type or *vice versa*.

In any case, with St. Paul the idea of a model to reproduce, to imitate as a very conscious ideal of oneself has great importance. Such is the grace received from Christ: ". . . so that I may know him and the power of his resurrection and the fellowship of his sufferings: become *like to him* in death, in the hope that somehow I may attain to the resurrection from the dead" (Phil. 3:10-11).

This is the great hope: ". . . our citizenship is in heaven from which we also eagerly await a Savior, our Lord Jesus Christ, who will refashion the body of our lowliness, conforming it to the body of his glory" (Phil. 3:20-21).

It is clear from this text that our bodies as well as our souls are concerned. On earth, surely, we renew ourselves interiorly in the image of God, when "we all, with faces unveiled, reflecting as in a mirror the glory of the Lord, are being transformed into his very image from glory to glory" (2 Cor. 3:18); the day will come when our predestination will be realized in its fulness, which is "to become conformed to the image of his Son" (Rom. 8:29)—of His Son incarnated and made man, for it is a question of re-creating the "heavenly man" whose likeness we "bear also" (1 Cor. 15:49).

The exemplar is a formal extrinsic cause. Christ's resurrection is the model of ours because it already is, in a way, formally ours. To understand and assimilate St. Paul's view of this resurrection, it would seem necessary to relate it to the center of his whole message, the doctrine of the Mystical Body: ". . . you are all *one* in Christ Jesus" (Gal. 3:28), "this mystery among the Gentiles—Christ in you" (Col. 1:27).

The earliest references to this great vision are in 1 Corinthians, of which Chapter 15 contains St. Paul's thought on the resurrection of the dead. However, at the risk of banality we must return to the apparition on the road to Damascus for the light it offers—a conclusive insight: "I am Jesus whom thou art persecuting" (Acts 9:5). Jesus? He is alive, therefore, whom Saul—like all unbelievers—believed dead. Whom thou art persecuting? Saul thought he was only pursuing the members of a sect. Jesus is living; and the Christians are Jesus. For thirty years Paul never ceased to meditate upon, to propagate, to probe into the relationship between the two mysteries. His entire vision of our predestination, of our redemption, of the Church, is only a confrontation with the truth of the Lord's resurrection and of the fulness of Christ in the whole Christ. This is the keystone of the Apostle's entire ethic, individual and social, and the root of his entire teaching on Baptism and on the resurrection: ". . . we were buried with him by means of Baptism into death, in order that, just as Christ has arisen from the dead through the glory of the Father, so we may also walk in newness of life. For if we have been united with him in the likeness of his death, we shall be so in the likeness of his resurrection also" (Rom. 6:4-5; cf. 3-11).

Paul creates a neologism: we are "conresurrected" (Eph. 2:6; Col. 2:12; 3:1), risen-with-Him. "As to the soul, in fact; as to the body, in hope," St. Thomas further distinguishes.[35] But one requires the other. We are risen here and now, spiritually and mysteriously, while we are awaiting our physical and manifest resurrection.

And the same One will bring about our resurrection who brought about His own: "But if the Spirit of him who raised Jesus from the dead dwells in you, then he who raised Jesus Christ from the dead will also bring to life your mortal bodies because of his Spirit who dwells in you" (Rom. 8:11). "When Christ, your Life, shall appear, then you too will appear with him in glory" (Col. 3:4).

In one sense, Christ's bodily glorification is incomplete as long as His entire Church, His "humanity by addition," is not also risen. His radiance, His splendor has not shone upon all His members. Just as our souls will be happy with the happiness of His soul, "our bodies are made glorious by sharing in the glory of Christ's body."[36]

---

[35] *In epist. ad Ephesios*, chapter 2, line 2.

Now we can realize the full meaning of Christ's words to Martha, "I am the resurrection" (John 11:25).

We also realize more perfectly why Christ presents Himself in the Paschal discourse on the bread of life as the food "which endures unto life everlasting"; "the bread of God . . . that . . . gives life to the world. . . . This is the bread that comes down from heaven, so that if anyone eat of it he will not die. . . . If anyone eat of this bread he shall live forever; and the bread that I will give is my flesh for the life of the world. . . . He who eats my flesh and drinks my blood has life everlasting and I will raise him up on the last day. . . . Your fathers ate the manna, and died. He who eats this bread shall live forever" (John 6:27, 33, 51, 52, 54, 59).

We can understand now the revelation of the Son to the seer of Patmos: "I am . . . *he who lives;* I was dead, and behold I am living forevermore; and I have the keys of death and of hell" (Apoc. 1:18). Finally, we can understand the title Peter gave to Jesus after the cure of the cripple at the Gate Beautiful, "the author of life . . . whom God has raised up from the dead" (Acts 3:15).

The Fathers of the Church have wonderfully developed these texts. Let us glance at some of them. St. Irenaeus:

"We can receive incorruptibility and immortality only by being united to incorruptibility and immortality. And how shall we be united to incorruptibility and immortality, if incorruptibility and immortality do not become what we are, in such a way that what is corruptible in us is absorbed by incorruptibility, what is mortal by immortality, in order that we receive the adoption of children? God willed to be born, to live among us, to descend into hell, to seek the lost sheep which is His creature; He willed to ascend to heaven and thus

---

[36] St. Thomas, III, qu. 56, a. 2, 1st reply.

offer to the Father man whom He found again, making of Himself the first-fruits of the resurrection of man. As the Head has risen, so the rest of the Body of all men—once the punishment of disobedience has been fulfilled—will rise; it will be reformed by reconciliations and reunions; it will be strengthened by a divine increase and each member in the Body will have his own suitable place. There will be many dwellings near the Father because there are many members in the Body."[37]

Origen:

"On the last day, death will be overcome. The resurrection of Christ after the suffering of the Cross in a mysterious way contains the resurrection of the entire Body of Christ. As the visible Body of Christ was crucified, buried, and finally resurrected, thus the entire Body of the saints of Christ is crucified with Him and no longer lives in itself. But when the resurrection of the true and whole Body of Christ comes, then the members of Christ that are now like dry bones will be rejoined, each finding its place, and all of them together will constitute a perfect man, in the measure of the fulness of the Body of Christ, and then the multitude of members will be one Body, for all will belong to the same Body."[38]

St. Gregory of Nyssa:

"Since the resurrection of our entire nature had to be brought about, God in some manner stretched forth His hand; He beheld the corpse we had become; He approached death to the extent of uniting Himself to mortality. Thus He will give to human nature in His own Body the principle of the resurrection; thus He will resurrect man entire in Himself. The flesh that He has put on will have no other origin than that of our race, and it was this flesh that was joined to divinity through the resurrection. Thus, just as in our own bodies what we feel in one sense is felt throughout the whole organism, so, as if our nature constituted only one living being, the

---

[37] *Adversus Haereses,* III, 19, 1 and 3.
[38] Origen, *Comm. In Ioh.,* X, 20.

resurrection of one of its members flows over all, and, because of the continuity and unity of our nature, it proceeds from one part to the whole."[39]

Thus the resurrection of Jesus has indeed become the common patrimony of humanity.

As much must be said (with the obvious distinctions) of the ascension and the seating at the right hand of God: ". . . where I am there also shall my servant be" (John 12:26). And, "He who overcomes, I will permit him to sit with me upon my throne; as I also have overcome and have sat with my Father on his throne" (Apoc. 3:21).

St. Paul speaks not only of coming to life with Christ and rising with Him but of being "seated . . . together in heaven in Christ Jesus" (Eph. 2:6). In his commentary on this epistle, St. Thomas explains that it is "now in hope"—but a very sure hope—that it is so; "in the future, it will be so in reality." In the *Summa* he gives the reason: ". . . Christ's ascension is the direct cause of our ascension, as by beginning it in Him who is our Head, with whom the members must be united."[40]

The theological reason is thus the same as that for the resurrection. As the Head is, so shall the members be; as Christ is, so we shall be.

Two things must be safeguarded in the application of what is written about Christ to other resurrected persons. First, Christ rose insofar as He is Son of God; His omnipotence as Son of God could act in Him for the purpose of His earthly mission and at the behest of His

[39] *Oratio catechetica*, 32.
[40] St. Thomas, III, qu. 57, a. 6, 2nd reply.

will, without necessarily revealing permanent qualities of His glorified Body. Second, Jesus has not shown everything of what He will become; we perceive only the fringes of the mystery; we can only know very little about these marvels.

Examining first the Gospels and St. Paul's thought on the resurrection of Jesus, we were able—with St. Gregory the Great and St. Thomas—to classify them under two headings, identity and transformation. If we then reread what the Apostle writes of our own future resurrection, we are struck by the same distinction: he hopes for us exactly what has occurred in Christ. He has really risen; we shall really rise. He has thus entered into glory; we shall be glorified.

This identification is very strongly shown in the terrible argument *ad hominem* addressed to the Corinthians: ". . . if there is no resurrection of the dead, neither has Christ risen. . . . Hence they also who have fallen asleep in Christ, have perished. If with this life only in view we have had hope in Christ, we are of all men the most to be pitied. . . . If the dead do not rise at all, why then do people receive Baptism for them? And we, why do we stand in jeopardy every hour? . . . If the dead do not rise, 'let us eat and drink for tomorrow we shall die'" (1 Cor. 15:13-32).

This personal numerical identity could not be without identity of nature, and specific identity; that is, it requires individual bodies, sufficiently identical to what they were on earth for the risen to be really human and to be themselves.

This seems to us to be simple common sense; it was

less evident to the Greek mind at the beginning of the Christian era, but our belief goes back to and refines the Judaism in which St. Paul had been brought up.

Insights on the world beyond dawned gradually, we know, in Israelite thought. This hope was at first (providentially) temporal and earthly. From ancient times it foreshadowed later developments: the Hebrews' funeral rites and their conception of the abode of the dead give evidence of a belief in a vague afterlife. The individualization of the religious sense at the end of the kingship, and the scandal—especially after the exile—of the evident injustices of earthly life, brought about (with God's assistance) clearer thinking and a better solution to the problem of personal destiny. The encounter with Greek thought also contributed to this. There is proof even in the Septuagint translation of the Hebrew Bible, which permits an immortalist interpretation of some old texts.[41] The persecution of Antiochus finally compelled the inspired sages' reflection to a categorical affirmation of retribution in the next life.

But it was in their bodies that the *hasidim* suffered. Justice required that they be recompensed in their own bodies. Let us reread the proud answers of the seven martyr brothers to the king in 2 Machabees. They express hope and they threaten: "These [hands] I have from heaven, but for the laws of God I now despise them: because I hope to receive them again from him . . . as to thee, thou shall have no resurrection unto life. . . . But stay patiently a while, and thou shalt see his great

[41] Cf. **Is.** 26:19; Job 42:17.

power, in what manner he will torment thee and thy seed" (2 Mach. 7:11, 14, 17).

The seven brothers and their mother, moreover, would have been surprised and perhaps shocked, as if it were an invidious Hellenism, at the distinction between body and soul which underlies our insistence upon their faith in corporeal retribution. For them, judgment of the good and the evil was unimaginable without the resurrection of the body because, like all men of the Old Testament, they regarded a human being as absolutely one. Between them and St. Paul, who receives the complete and total heritage of Christ, the idea (in Wisdom) of an immortality for "naked" man, to use St. Paul's expression,[42] that is for the soul no longer associated with its body, is revealed. And the Church has preserved unbroken the double truth: on the one hand, the metaphysical unity of the living body and the soul which animates it, and on the other, the distinction between them, a distinction which permits a time of joyful waiting or of temporary purification for the souls of the dead before the resurrection.

But while it is clear that St. Paul—as does the New Testament generally—admits the immortality of the soul in this sense, it is all the more clear that he is completely without any dualism in the Platonic or Stoic sense. We do not separate what we distinguish. Faithful (like ourselves) to a more sublime and more ancient revealed truth into which a distinction was later introduced without contradicting it, St. Paul thought primarily of judgment, reward, and punishment as a retribution to man

---

[42] Cf. 2 Cor. 5:3.

in his physical-spiritual totality, and not of the exceptional state of a soul temporarily separated from the body.

Thus he expressly inherits from the purest Judaism faith in the resurrection of the body. The body, for him, meant man, and man not otherwise specified was man with a body. This is the object of the resurrection to which he returns so often.

We have heard the martyrs of Antiochus appeal, against the apparent impossibility of rising from the corruption of the tomb, to the "great power" of God. St. Paul does likewise,[43] as do the early apologists.[44] There is value in the argument, although since the time of Celsus and Porphyry unbelievers have found it too facile. To the omnipotent God, it is no more difficult to resurrect His creatures than it was to draw them out of nothingness. The God who in procreation can raise a total living person from a humble cell will no more be hindered by decomposed elements—even digested and redigested ones; He will know how to find them again regardless of their present state in order to make of them the seed of glorified bodies.

A certain number of contemporary theologians believe that God can dispense even with this "seed." Let us agree with them that philosophically speaking the seed is not an indispensable requirement for identification. Since the formal element subsists, the same being, the same man, subsists even without the seed.

Father Congar writes, "The general principles of Tho-

---

[43] Cf. 1 Cor. 15:35-38.

[44] Cf. H. I. Marrou, "La résurrection des morts et les apologistes des premiers siècles," in *Lumière et Vie,* 1952, pp. 83-92.

mist philosophy allow of the thesis of a physical identity deriving from the soul. The body need not be thought of as something pre-existing into which the soul enters as tenant into his lodging. It is the soul which creates its body, and constantly creates it by borrowing the elements of the exterior world. Their perpetual changing does not prevent the soul from maintaining the identity of the total corporeal and spiritual personality which assumes them."[45]

All this is quite true, and that is why we shall not renew these rather dated discussions of the subject. But should philosophy have the final word? We believe that if St. Thomas—as Father Congar also recalls—required no more of it, this was through fidelity to what Father Wébert called "an instinct of the Christian faith that the thesis of resurrection only by action of the informing power of the soul offends more than it satisfies."[46] We may prefer to be faithful to the letter of St. Paul who originated the image of the seed, in which, from the metaphysical point of view as well as from that of modern physics, we see nothing that would require us to reject the most obvious meaning.

The integrity of risen bodies is a corollary of their identity. From the supplement to the *Summa* the robust realism of the medieval theologians on this point emerges: all the members of the human body will rise again, including the hair and the fingernails and all the body fluids, though not necessarily having all that they had

---

[45] Y. Congar, O.P., *Vaste monde ma paroisse*, Paris, Éd. du Témoignage chrétien, p. 208.

[46] J. Wébert, O.P., annotation on the resurrection in the *Summa*, *Revue des Jeunes*, p. 323.

on earth. Human beings will rise as they are, masculine or feminine. Too much insistence on this point may cause us to forget the transformation we are going to discuss, but the theological reasoning is certain:

". . . 'the soul stands in relation to the body not only as its form and end, but also as efficient cause' [De Anima, II]. For the soul is compared to the body as art to the thing made by art . . . and whatever is shown forth explicitly in the product of art is all contained implicitly and originally in the art. In like manner whatever appears in the parts of the body is all contained originally and, in a way, implicitly in the soul. Thus just as the work of an art would not be perfect, if its product lacked any of the things contained in the art, so neither could man be perfect, unless the whole that is contained enfolded in the soul be outwardly unfolded in the body, nor would the body correspond in full proportion to the soul. Since then at the resurrection it behooves man's body to correspond entirely to the soul, for it will not rise again except according to the relation it bears to the rational soul, it follows that man also must rise again perfect, seeing that he is thereby repaired in order that he may obtain his ultimate perfection. Consequently all the members that are now in man's body must needs be restored at the resurrection."[47]

They rise as adults, even though they did not attain to full growth on earth.

A too materialistic Aristotelianism? The Plotinian St. Augustine (twenty-second book of the City of God) is no more restrained. It is a matter of the common, traditional thought of Christianity.

The transformation upon which St. Paul next insists was not itself in the Old Testament heritage. It came solely from the Gospel, from the example and words of Christ.

[47] St. Thomas, Supplement, qu. 80, a. 1.

We recall the Sadducees' insidious question about the woman who had seven husbands. Jesus's answer is expressed this way by St. Luke: "The children of this world marry and are given in marriage. But those who shall be accounted worthy of that world and of the resurrection from the dead, neither marry nor take wives. For neither shall they be able to die any more, for they are equal to the angels, and are the sons of God, being sons of the resurrection" (Luke 20:34-36).

The text specifically excludes sexual relations from the life of the resurrected: *neque nubent neque nubentur*. It also gives three reason for the exclusion, (1) immortality, making unnecessary the successors men seek here on earth through the procreation of posterity, (2) spirituality, the immediate cause of this immortality, and (3) divine sonship, source of the spirituality and the immortality.

It would be well to be able to scrutinize the term "sons of God" to grasp what it means in this passage. "Sons of the resurrection" is a Semitism which cannot be transcribed "born of the resurrection." May one say "born of God"? Perhaps this filiation means only literally a resemblance, such as exists between son and father; the resurrection will bring about a participation in the spirituality and immortality of God. Its full meaning, however, turns on the mystery of grace, divine adoption.

Then one thinks of what St. John and St. Paul wrote, "Beloved, now we are the children of God, and it has not yet appeared what we shall be. We know that, when he appears, we shall be like to him, for we shall see him just as he is" (1 John 3:2). "For you have died and your life is hidden with Christ in God. When Christ, your life,

shall appear, then you too will appear with him in glory"
(Col. 3:4). According to St. Matthew and St. Mark, Jesus
said the risen would be "like the angels." The term probably invented by St. Luke and rendered exactly in the
Vulgate is more precise—not only like or similar but
"equal to the angels." The risen will not be angels and
will have none of their appearance but they will equal
them in resemblance to the spirituality and the immortality of God.

This teaching and the state of Jesus Himself as He
enters through the resurrection into the full possession
of His divine prerogatives are the background of St.
Paul's famous explanation: "What is sown in corruption
rises in incorruption; what is sown in dishonor rises in
glory; what is sown in weakness rises in power; what
is sown a natural body rises a spiritual body" (1 Cor.
15:42-44).

These are the four classic properties of the glorified
body: impassibility, clarity, agility, spirituality. The main
one is spirituality; it could be said that the others derive
from it. Calling this property "subtlety" is too narrow
a way of contrasting it with the opacity of earthly matter and finding an explanation of how Jesus appeared
through closed doors. St. Thomas believes this movement
could only be a miracle. Glorified bodies would ordinarily
have their usual size and be in their usual place. But the
spirituality illustrated by Jesus and referred to by St.
Paul means the kind of participation in and analogy to
the spirit manifested in the body through the mastery
over it possessed and exercised in their union by the soul.

The "spiritual body" will not be subtle because it is
penetrable by other bodies. It will be worthy of respect

by other bodies. But it will be penetrable by the spirit, permeable by it, malleable to it, because it is wholly subject to the spirit.

St. Augustine points out: "For as, when the spirit serves the flesh, it is fitly called carnal, so, when the flesh serves the spirit, it will justly be called spiritual. Not that it is converted into spirit, . . . but because it is subject to the spirit with a perfect and marvellous readiness of obedience, and responds in all things to the will that has entered on immortality—all reluctance, all corruption, and all slowness being removed."[48]

The tenuousness of the "spiritual body" will not make it more ethereal than earthly bodies. There is no point in trying to draw a parallel with the modern equation of matter with light. Light to us is material; scholasticism knew this long before mechanical wave lengths were discovered. The most subtle musical harmony is still material. The spirituality of the glorified body is a different thing entirely. Created to serve the spirit, to serve it completely, it finds itself perfectly disposed for this function in every way.

The term "spirit" should not deceive us, either. It is a question of the soul, but of the supernaturalized soul, that is, of the soul itself spiritualized by its own submission to and absolute openness to the glory of being supremely possessed by shared divine life. St. Paul contrasts the spiritual body and the natural body, that is,

---

[48] *City of God*, I, 13, 20. G. Combes uses the variant reading *voluptatem* for *voluntatem* and translates the passage, "because it will be obedient to the spirit with a sovereign and wonderful ease, to the extent of deriving from it the joy of an indissoluble immortality: it will not experience suffering or corruption, nor the least constraint." Bibliothèque Augustinienne, v. 35, Paris, Desclée de Brouwer, p. 309.

one animated by the soul inhabiting it. The spiritual body will be such because it will be animated by a soul completely possessed by the Holy Spirit.

We come back again to the total divine filiation which Jesus put at the center of everything in His reply to the Sadducees. The spirituality of our risen bodies will come to them from their "divinization," through the "divinization" of their blessed souls.

The impassibility or incorruptibility of glorified bodies is therefore only a result of this "divinization." The body perfectly subject to the soul, itself totally subject to God, will be unassailable. It will be completely conditioned by the soul and only by the soul. Any passibility whatever, whether by invasion from without or from some disorder within, will be unthinkable from now on:

". . . since in corruptible things form does not perfectly overcome matter, it cannot tie it completely so as to prevent it from sometimes receiving a disposition contrary to the form through some passion. But in the saints after the resurrection, the soul will have complete dominion over the body, and it will be altogether impossible for it to lose this dominion, because it will be immutably subject to God, which was not the case in the state of innocence. Consequently those bodies will retain substantially the same potentiality as they have now to another form; yet that potentiality will remain tied by the triumph of the soul over the body, so that it will never be realized by actual passion."[49]

Suffering comes about through deformation. But the "information" of the senses from the exterior world is not a suffering but an enrichment when the senses are alert to their true head. This enrichment is a pleasure which the elect will enjoy insofar as it is fitting to their

[49] St. Thomas, *Supplement to the Summa,* qu. 82, a. 1, 2nd reply.

state. Sense experience will lose only its quality of being forced and will come to spiritual maturity by taking initiative toward the world, psychologically speaking.

Another important point is:

"If impassibility is considered in itself, since it denotes a mere negation or privation, it is not subject to be more or less, but will be equal in all the blessed. On the other hand, if we consider it in relation to its cause, it will be greater in one person than in another. Now its cause is the dominion of the soul over the body, and this dominion is caused by the soul's unchangeable enjoyment of God. Consequently in one who enjoys God more perfectly, there is a greater cause of impassibility."[50]

It will be so "unchangeably," that is, by means of the soul the blessed body will share the very eternity of God.

Clarity—glory, luminosity, or beauty—of the glorified body is (according to the Biblical expression)[51] the manifestation of spirituality and of divine filiation.

One is immediately reminded of the dazzling brightness of the face and even the garments of Jesus at the transfiguration. In this there was obviously a lesson and a promise. The human body is not luminous by nature, but it will be so, in some manner.

Clarity is also the result of spirituality. It is the supernatural glory of the soul which, in the person of the children of God, overflows into the body and gives it the measure of its definitive beauty:

"For whatever is received into anything is received not according to the mode of the source whence it flows, but according to the mode of the recipient. Wherefore clarity which in the soul is spiritual is received into the body as

[50] St. Thomas, *Supplement to the Summa,* qu. 82, a. 2.
[51] Cf. Col. 3:3-4; 1 John 3:2.

corporeal. And consequently according to the greater clarity of the soul by reason of its greater merit. . . . Thus in the glorified body the glory of the soul will be known, even as through a crystal vessel is known the color of a body contained in a crystal vessel. . . ."[52]

By the same fact, the final, eternal beauty of the body is merited, like the splendor of the soul:

"It is by divine appointment that there is an overflow of glory from the soul to the body, in keeping with human merit; so that as man merits by the act of the soul which he performs in the body, so he may be rewarded by the glory of the soul overflowing to the body. And hence not only the glory of the soul, but also the glory of the body falls under merit, according to Rom. 8:11, 'He . . . shall quicken also our [Vulg., your] mortal bodies, because of his spirit that dwelleth in us [Vulg. you].'"[53]

We cannot help thinking of Christ, "beautiful above all the sons of men" (Ps. 44:3) and of the woman "blessed amongst women" (Luke 1:42).

The gift of agility is the last aspect of the glorified soul's marvellous mastery over the body. It is a final consequence of the spirituality which ineffably subjects it to the form from which it holds its specific being. Action follows being: the body henceforth obeys with unspeakable docility and promptness, for no law of the material world holds back the impulses of the soul which moves it at will.

In St. Paul's text, agility is a strength. Think of the suppleness that an athlete's vigor shows. It seems to require no effort and to do anything required of it. Likewise, the glorified body will have to make no more effort

52 St. Thomas, *Supplement,* qu. 85, a. 1.
53 St. Thomas, III, qu. 19, a. 3, 3rd reply.

to overcome resistance, to slow up, to break down barriers, in order to rule and traverse the material universe.

Now that men are making their first steps into outer
space let us reread what St. Thomas wrote seven centuries ago:

"It is necessary to suppose that the glorified bodies are
moved sometimes, since even Christ's Body was moved in
His ascension, and likewise the bodies of the saints, which
will arise from the earth, will ascend to the empyrean. But
even after they have climbed the heavens, it is likely that
they will sometimes move according as it pleases them; so
that by actually putting into practice that which is in their
power, they may show forth the excellence of divine wisdom,
and that furthermore their vision may be refreshed by the
beauty of the variety of creatures, in which God's wisdom
will shine forth with great evidence. . . ."[54]

This seems to anticipate the marvels of science-fiction!
Surely one may be permitted a smile; nevertheless, it
is not foolishness—and we shall be filled with God
alone. With the elect there will be neither vain curiosity
nor egoistic dilettantism, still less any need for distraction and escape. But their agility will proclaim the divine
power, and their contemplation of the physical heavens
in visits to the galaxies will not add anything interior
to their essential vision of God. Again it is His glory
they will see unfolded there.

Guy de Larigaudie, modern chevalier of faith and
adventure, will achieve his desires:

"I have walked across the world as if it were a walled
garden. I have sought adventure on all five continents, I have
accomplished all my childhood dreams one after another. The
park of the old Perigord house where I took my first step

[54] St. Thomas, *Supplement to the Summa*, qu. 84, a. 2.

has become enlarged to the limits of the earth and I have played the game of my life in both hemispheres. Nevertheless the walls of the garden have only receded, and I am always caged up.

> But some day I shall come where I can sing my song of love and joy.
> All barriers will be broken.
> And I shall possess the Infinite."[55]

We can even presume that the cosmonauts will receive a recompense adapted to their special heroism (originated, of course, by Christ). A serious theologian wrote recently, though with only aviators in mind:

"If we grant that philosophers, theologians, savants, taste a special joy in finally seeing in reality—whether by *connaissance du matin* (vision in *Verbo*) or by *connaissance du soir* (intuitive knowledge of creatures *extra Verbum*)—the truths they laboriously ponder on earth, why should not the conquerors of the air . . . have a special (secondary but real) joy in exercising in heaven their gift of agility, being transported now not by powerful but fragile machines but by the very force of the soul filled with God, leading the body where it wills?"[56]

This final point may be noted. We proceed no further than theology. In all this there is only an attempt to conceive a little of what results for the body, in the union of the person, from the fact that a soul is "filled with God."

Here a digression is necessary. St. Paul's great passage on the resurrection of the dead—1 Cor. 15—and consequently all we have just said, applies only to those who

[55] P. Croidys, *Guy de Larigaudie,* Paris, Plon, p. 234.

[56] M.-B. Lavaud, O.P., "Le corps dans la glorie," in *La Vie Spirituelle,* v. LV (May, 1938), p. 131.

are saved. In passing, we have alluded to differences in degree in regard to merit and reward, and St. Paul also wrote: "All flesh is not the same flesh, but there is one flesh of men, another of beasts, another of birds, another of fishes. There are also heavenly bodies and earthly bodies, but of one kind is the glory of the heavenly, of another kind the glory of the earthly. There is one glory of the sun, and another glory of the moon, and another of the stars; for star differs from star in glory. So also with the resurrection of the dead" (1 Cor. 15:39-42).

But what of those who are not saved? We are taught much less about the damned. The Apostles—inspired by the Holy Spirit—are not given to pessimism and intimidation. In their outlook there is nothing of the sadism which characterizes the artists of troubled periods and some preachers moved more by good intentions than prudence. In what the New Testament has to say about the chastisement of the wicked it is difficult to distinguish between what is meant literally and the images and expressions inherited from the prophets and the apocalyptics. Moreover, a theology of hell is not presented. Yet Scripture is clear, and the faith of the Church categorical: the damned will also rise.

When Jesus speaks of "those who shall be accounted worthy of that world and of the resurrection from the dead" (Luke 20:35), this saying shows the optimistic spirit we have pointed out.[57] He does not contradict what He teaches elsewhere—". . . the hour is coming in which all who are in the tombs shall hear the voice of the Son of God. And they who have done good shall come

[57] See also St. Paul, Phil. 3:11.

forth unto resurrection of life; but they who have done evil unto resurrection of the judgment" (John 5:28-29).

St. Paul declares before Felix that "there is to be a resurrection of the just and unjust" (Acts 24:15). And when he refers to the judgment seat of God or of Christ, he sees us there, consistently with all of Jewish thought, "in the flesh."[58] This means in the strict sense of the word that "*every knee* should bend of those in heaven, on earth and under the earth, and *every tongue* should confess that the Lord Jesus Christ is in the glory of God the Father" (Phil. 2:10-11; cf. Rom. 14:10-11). All death will be destroyed (1 Cor. 15:26).

The Fathers of the Church entirely agree on this point. All subscribe to St. Augustine's very explicit statement: "This in any case no Christian ought to doubt: that the bodies of all men who have been born and are to be born, and have died and are to die, will rise again."[59]

The magisterium has not often had to intervene, since the traditional teaching was clear. The major document is that of Pope Benedict XII in 1336: "Moreover we define that, in accordance with the common providence of God, the souls of those who die in the state of mortal sin descend into hell after death, and suffer infernal punishment; and that, moreover, on the day of Judgment all shall appear in the flesh before the Judgment seat of Christ to render an account of their deeds 'so that what each one did when in the body, whether good or evil, appears again.' "[60]

Although what has been said about the identity of the

---

[58] Cf. 2 Cor. 5:10; Rom. 14:10-11; Daniel 12:2; 2 Mach. 7:14-15.
[59] *Enchiridion,* 84.
[60] Const. *Benedictus Deus,* Denz. 531.

resurrected applies to the damned also, what has been said of their transformation does not. St. Thomas makes a clear distinction:

"The resurrection of all men will bear some resemblance to Christ's resurrection, as regards that which pertains to the life of nature, in respect of which all were conformed to Christ. Hence all will rise again to immortal life, but in the saints who were conformed to Christ by grace, there will be conformity as to things pertaining to glory."[61]

Neither the bodies nor the souls of the damned will be glorified. Their bodies will possess neither spirituality nor impassibility nor clarity nor agility, as we have described these qualities in the elect. The reason is clear: these qualities result only from the beatific presence of God in the souls of all the members of Christ's Mystical Body. The application, when we think of it, is tragic. St. Hippolytus writes, "The unjust will not receive a transformed body. It will be free from neither attachments nor disorders, nor will it be glorified; in coming to life again, they will suffer the maladies in which they died."[62]

Nevertheless, though the bodies of the damned do not possess impassibility they will possess at least a certain incorruptibility, since they will be immortal and their punishment eternal. "They will arise incorruptible in order to burn forever," St. John Chrysostom says.[63] We are not going to examine here the nature of the fire of hell and its instrumental action (more spiritual than

---

[61] Supplement to the *Summa*, qu. 76, a. 1, 4th reply.
[62] *Adversus Graecos*, 2.
[63] *De resurrectione mortuorum*, 8.

material) on bodies it does not change. Let us note, however, that the fact that the fire does not destroy the bodies it consumes is not due to some inferiority in the quality of the fire—whatever its exact nature, it will be superior to the fire of this life—but to the immortality of the bodies it is burning.

What is the source of this immortality? St. Thomas answers above: the resurrection of Christ, by which men will have the same nature even though they do not have His glory. All risen bodies will be in some manner conformed to the Body of Christ. Even the damned will owe this mercy to Christ—for it will be an act of mercy as well as justice. They will realize this intensely, even as they despairingly refuse to accept it. Their refusal cannot tie God's hands.

Let us think of the resurrection of the flesh, which our faith promises, in the broadest and most inclusive terms. Even though nothing explicit is said about it in revelation, we need not hesitate to conclude that it applies to stillborn infants. To be immortal their souls do not need Baptism to elevate them to supernatural life; their souls are immortal from the time they are created. By virtue of Christ's resurrection, and in the likeness of Christ and for His glory, their bodies will arise in the fulness of growth. They will not be glorified, strictly speaking, and we do not know anything about the qualities of their bodies in relation to those of glorified bodies. A certain impassibility seems to be called for by the immortality of the soul with which their bodies are united. It would not be just for them to suffer when they have not personally sinned. Being deprived of the gratuitous gift of the divine vision—for mankind the result of original sin—is a suffering of nature, not a punishment of individuals, and they are able to bear it in utter serenity.

Let us return now to our more pleasant reflections upon the glorified body. These bodies will be both identical to what they were on earth and yet as different as possible. The same soul will animate them naturally which supernaturally communicates to them its blessedness and its glorification.

Supernaturally, everything arises from the divine sonship henceforward manifest, and the soul is only the instrument of a gift descending from above her. But the supernatural first raises nature to its perfect stature. It cannot be out of place to try to deduce what we will be like in heaven when the soul has full mastery over the body. The resurrection of the body is a kind of consummated hylomorphism.

For a Platonic spirituality, the union of soul and body is something forced; for Christian philosophy the reverse is true. The Ecumenical Council of Vienne was completely in the line of Biblical thought about the oneness of the human being when it defined, against the errors of the Franciscan, P. J. Olivi, that "the rational or intellective soul is of itself and essentially the form of the human body."[64] Christ had to rise again in order that human nature might be perfect in Him. It is a very strong argument from fitness for the resurrection that without it our nature would remain imperfect forever; our soul could not be fully and finally happy if it were not one day reunited to our body.

[64] Denz. 481.

St. Thomas writes:

"It is also manifest . . . that the soul is united to the body naturally: since it is by its essence the form of the body: wherefore it is unnatural for the soul to be without the body. Now nothing unnatural can last forever and consequently the soul will not remain forever without the body. Therefore, since the soul is immortal, it must needs be reunited to the body: and this is to rise again. Hence the immortality of the soul would seem to demand the future resurrection of the body.

"Again it has been proved that man's natural desire tends to happiness. Now ultimate happiness is the perfection of the happy one. Consequently whosoever lacks something for perfection is not yet perfectly happy, since his desire is not yet wholly at rest; and all imperfect things naturally seek to attain to perfection. Now the soul when separated from the body is, in a way, imperfect: even as any part is when severed from its whole: and the soul is naturally part of human nature. Therefore man cannot obtain ultimate happiness, unless his soul be reunited to his body: and this is all the more true, seeing that as we have shown, man cannot reach ultimate happiness in this life."[65]

St. Bonaventure derives from this an argument in favor of the bodily assumption of the Blessed Virgin into heaven: "There would not be supreme happiness if she were not there personally. The person is not the soul; it is a composite of body and soul. Thus it is clear that Mary is in heaven as a composite of body and soul, otherwise she would not have perfect joy."[66]

We cannot undertake to describe the ideal psycho-physiological relations of the human body and the human soul. It is, however, important, to note that it will be

---

[65] *Summa Contra Gentiles*, IV, qu. 79.
[66] *De assumptione B. M. V.*, sermon I. Cited by Pius XII in the bull *Munificentissimus*.

like this in every way: the perfect state of a body which is not merely a good instrument of the soul but its proper "matter"; the body, in its entirety, of a soul; a body that "materializes" a soul not to abase it but to make it itself —human—in the meeting of two kinds of substance; a body that the soul marvellously utilizes for its consummated human life.

Examining our Lord's psychology, St. Thomas inquires whether He had discursive knowledge: "The soul of Christ possessed knowledge in the manner of the elect, who, according to the Gospel, resemble the angels; but with the angels, knowledge does not include discursive thought or reasoning." And he answers: "The blessed are likened to the angels in the gifts of graces; yet there still remains the difference of natures. And hence to use reasoning is connatural to the souls of the blessed, but not the angels."[67]

The argument may be continued: it is connatural to human intelligence to abstract ideas from images provided by the senses; indeed it can draw them immediately out of the reservoir of the imagination and the memory; but it is connatural to the latter to refresh themselves unceasingly through the activity of the external senses. Consequently, in the intellectual life of the blessed—and the same is true of their psychic life—there is a place for the perfect and integral use of the senses. They will not be useless for those enjoying the beatific vision: Christ's divine knowledge did not make either His infused or His acquired knowledge useless.

And the ideal human body of an ideal human being

[67] St. Thomas, III, qu. 11, a. 3, 3rd reply.

receives not less but rather more from the soul than it gives—on the natural plane only. During life on earth, the body is as it were physically molded by the unique experience of the free soul to which it is united. This is true of the resurrected body a fortiori even aside from the clarity which accompanies its "glorification." As we have seen, the resurrected body is identical to the one we have on earth; after the resurrection it will be more ours, more fully and more perfectly possessed by the person because the soul, which now has greater mastery over it, will be better expressed in it. In a perfect human nature, the body would be transparent to the soul, the expression, the showing forth of its spiritual reality. After the resurrection this will be true to the fullest extent.

All of this places a new value upon the body which earthly asceticism (and very rightly so) chastises and brings into subjection (cf. 1 Cor. 9:27). Mortification is not masochism; it is illuminated by hope and suffused with esteem and respect for the very body which for the time being it causes to suffer. The body will be rewarded, and more than a hundredfold. It will be won because it has been lost. The body will triumph, and in it matter will have its triumph.

Here we have been concerned with the future and with ourselves but it goes without saying that we are not forgetting that the resurrection has begun; in Christ and (proportionately) in the Blessed Virgin, the human body and even matter have achieved supreme honor.

The great opposition of the early centuries to the dogma of the resurrection of the body arose from contempt of the body. Despite appearances, it is the same today. Whether as a result of cheap eroticism, of dialectical materialism, of scientific and experimental positivism or—at the other extreme—of Cartesianism or a more or less exaggerated idealism, the body is universally degraded. Would it be presumptuous to ask whether the kind of distaste so many modern Christians feel before the act of pure faith in the resurrection of the body required by the Credo arises from this climate of low regard for the body? Is the timidity even of theologians the result of the lack of a theology of the body?

St. Paul had the courage to write, ". . . do you not know that your members are the temple of the Holy Spirit? . . . Glorify God and bear him in your body" (1 Cor. 6:19-20).

The whole sacramental and liturgical order works through the body to sanctify the soul. It is by virtue of Baptism, in which water streams over it, that the body will arise.

The Eucharist is the Body of Christ coming to sanctify our souls and our bodies. Jesus Himself made the connection between communion and resurrection on the last day, mentioned in so many of the postcommunion prayers of the missal.

St. Cyril of Alexandria has said:

"It is impossible that He Who is Life by nature did not totally overcome corruption and conquer death. That is why, although the death which assails us because of sin has power to reduce our bodies to corruption, nevertheless, because Christ comes among us by His flesh, we shall truly rise. It would be unbelievable or almost impossible if life did not vivify those to whom it comes. Just as we cover a spark with a great deal of straw to preserve the seed of the fire, so in us Our Lord Jesus Christ by His flesh hides His life in the depths of our being; He deposits it as a germ of immortality which must consume all the corruption in us."[68]

Think of the anointings of the body in Baptism, in Confirmation, in Ordination, the Last Anointing. Think of the part played by the body in the love consecrated by the sacrament of Marriage.

The realism of our mysteries presupposes an accurate anthropology. The body and the soul are not separate beings but principles of the unique being that is man, in his absolute unity. If, in the state of fallen nature, our present state, a dissociation seems to appear when "the flesh lusts against the spirit and the spirit against the flesh" (Gal. 5:17), and if its wages are death—"it was not so from the beginning" (Matt. 19:8). And it will not be so at the end.

In the resurrection the glorified body will be first of all a real body, authentically and fully human.

"It was not so from the beginning. . . ." The fruit of the tree of the knowledge of good and evil was forbidden under pain of death; it was by disobedience and sin that death entered the human world. Before sin, there was no question of a resurrection because there was no question of death. God planted "the tree of life in the midst of paradise" in Eden (Gen. 2:9); man had only to reach out and pluck from it to live forever. Can the state of immortal man in the earthly paradise throw any light on his state in the resurrection? Yes and no.

Obviously, history cannot help us. Neither can prehistory as we know it from the discoveries of paleontology. Paradise existed before prehistory; or, if a certain continuity is established between human history and natural

[68] St. Cyril of Alexandria, *In Ioh.* IV, 2.

history, it would be necessary to conceive paradise as one of the parentheses called mutations, in which nature (contrary to the adage) leaps forward. Science establishes the result of the mutation: real mutants escape it. Science can only ignore the Adam and Eve of our holy books; with even more reason, the supernatural elevation of these absolutely first real human beings and its brief preternatural consequences, in the course of a part of their existence, have left no traces in fossils. There is a gap between Adam and Eve and the animal ancestors of their bodies—if there were any; there is the abyss of the fall between them and their descendants, the primitive men of our excavations and our hypotheses. Only revelation and faith teach us anything about the too short period of paradise itself. It is a rather delicate undertaking to examine Scripture and Tradition on this point, but the worst source of error is anxiety about parallels with science.

Moreover, we are concerned here with only a small part of the theology of the first man. We are leaving out of consideration the results of his being the first man, father, and head of the human race, and are directing our attention only to the effects of original innocence upon him. We need not delay over the gifts of the soul from the viewpoint of supernatural grace with its train of virtues and the preternatural privilege of immunity from concupiscence or from the viewpoint of intelligence and science, which also resulted. Only the physical state of man will be relevant to our inquiry.

A treatise on man's origins should distinguish between what comes from pure nature and what derives from the state of grace through preternatural privilege. We can dispense with this; it is not nature as such we wish to understand, it is nature transformed. The glorification of the resurrected body does not come from nature but from the state of glory; thus an a fortiori based on the radiance of the state of original grace seems valid.

St. Augustine's description of the earthly paradise, quoted and commented on from century to century by the noblest Doctors of the Church and the humblest preachers, expresses exactly the mind of the faithful of today and always on this subject. If it is not *de fide,* it is close to it.

"In paradise, then, man lived as he desired so long as he desired what God had commanded. He lived in the enjoyment of God, and was good by God's goodness; he lived without any want, and had it in his power so to live eternally. He had food that he might not hunger, drink that he might not thirst, the tree of life that old age might not waste him. There was in his body no corruption, nor seed of corruption, which could produce in him any unpleasant sensation. He feared no inward disease, no outward accident. Soundest health blessed his body, absolute tranquillity his soul. As in paradise there was no excessive heat or cold, so its inhabitants were exempt from the vicissitudes of fear and desire. No sadness of any kind was there, nor any foolish joy; true gladness ceaselessly flowed from the presence of God, who was loved 'from a pure heart, and a good conscience, and faith unfeigned' [1 Tim. 1:5]. The honest love of husband and wife made a sure harmony between them. Body and spirit worked harmoniously together, and the divine commandment was kept without difficulty. No languor made their leisure wearisome; no sleepiness interrupted their desire to labor."[69]

The heavenly paradise will demand at least this much. At least . . . but this is to say far too little. It is strange

[69] *City of God,* 14, 26.

that St. Paul does not introduce the comparison between Adam and Christ in order to deduce the physical qualities of the latter from the physical properties of the former, as we would do, but to contrast them. Adam's was the "animal body" which, perfect as it is, the "spiritual body" of the risen must transcend.

"If there is a natural body, there is also a spiritual body. So also it is written, 'The first man, Adam, became a living soul'; the last Adam became a life-giving spirit. But it is not the spiritual that comes first but the physical, and then the spiritual. The first man was of the earth, earthy; the second man is from heaven, heavenly. As was the earthy man, such also are the earthy; and as is the heavenly man, such also are the heavenly" (1 Cor. 15:44-48).

If one can say then that in its original innocence the body was "completely subject to the soul,"[70] this still was not—and by far—a perfect subjection, or even a positive and active one, such as we outlined in connection with the spirituality of the glorified body.

From the physical standpoint, the state of innocence requires immortality and impassibility. These also are transposed several levels higher if we wish to form an idea of the resurrected body. St. Augustine is slow to contrast the *de facto* immortality of the first man (as doubtful, and dependent upon the sacrament of the tree of life) with the rightful immortality of the risen, for the first man was not made so that he could not die, yet practically speaking, except for sin, he would not die.[71]

Scheeben writes, similarly:

[70] St. Thomas, I, qu. 94, a. 2.
[71] *City of God,* 13:20, 23.

"In a certain way integrity achieved what this glorification achieves, but only because it also rested on a sort of glorification effected by the Holy Spirit. However, it was not a glorification that radically sublimated the body and its life, or made impossible the revival of its natural shortcomings, and hence its complete dissolution. The natural defects were merely covered up and suspended, but were not eliminated by an interior transformation. Such transformation takes place only in heavenly glorification; and therefore Adam's immortality was only a *posse non mori* (a power of avoiding death), not a *non posse mori* (impossibility of dying). Hence the mystery of glorification transcends the mystery of integrity as greatly as the *non posse mori* excels the *posse non mori.*"[72]

In the state of original justice, the clarity of the glorified body did not exist either. This was in no way a privation or an evil; even if the beauty of the soul was expressed more perfectly than now, in a body it possessed more fully, this beauty could not communicate a splendor that it lacked.

The same thing is true of agility. Adam in innocence surely enjoyed the privilege of possessing a body that did not sluggishly resist his will, but within the framework of natural laws. The agility of "spiritual bodies" will place it above all the laws of quantified matter.

In short, the evocation of paradise gives us few details about the resurrection of the body, but it provides a springboard for a leap of our imaginations far beyond anything they can conceive.

The risen Christ ascended into heaven, and only there has He found a proper setting for His Body in its new state.

[72] M. J. Scheeben, *The Mysteries of Christianity*, trans. Cyril Vollert, S.J., Herder, 1947, section 95, p. 679.

Ancient physics misled the meditations of the masters of scholasticism on this point. They acknowledged a substantial difference between earthly bodies and celestial bodies. For the former, matter is in potency to many forms; these bodies can change from one to another and are corruptible. With celestial bodies in their "quintessence" matter is capable of only one form and these bodies are not corruptible. This incorruptibility of celestial bodies permitted the scholastics to satisfy themselves by imagining an ascent of Jesus to the existing heavens without transforming them. The scholastics noted only that He was beyond the skies. Changes in knowledge have had the advantage of forcing theology not to trust itself further but to reconsider its own principles. Revelation is not silent regarding the context of Christ's new risen life, which is the same as that promised for men after His return.

"And I saw a new heaven and a new earth. For the first heaven and the first earth passed away, and the sea is no more," writes the seer of the Apocalypse (21:1). Even though the apocalyptic images are not to be taken literally—and even here, the sea, at least, certainly has an allegorical meaning—the expression has left its mark on Christian thought.

The Second Epistle of St. Peter presents his view: ". . . the day of the Lord will come as a thief; at that time the heavens will pass away with great violence, and the elements will be dissolved with heat, and the earth, and the works that are in it, will be burned up . . . await and hasten toward the coming of the day of God, by which the heavens, being on fire, will be dissolved and the elements will melt away by reason of the heat of the fire! But we look for new heavens and a new earth, according to His promises, wherein dwells justice" (2 Peter 3:10-13).

What promises? Some word of Jesus which was not recorded? The allusion to the "many mansions" where He is preparing a place for us? Or, more simply, a recollection of the prophecies of Isaias and the figurative language of Judaeo-Christian theology? These points need discussion.

One leans toward a realistic interpretation, on account of the opening of the paragraph: "For of this they [deceitful scoffers] are willfully ignorant, that there were heavens long ago, and an earth formed out of water and by water through the Word of God. By these means the world that then was, deluged with water, perished. But the heavens that now are, and the earth, by that same Word have been stored up, being reserved for fire against the day of judgment and destruction of ungodly men" (2 Peter 3:4-7).

The deluge was not an image. Is the fire that corresponds to it any more so?

St. Paul presents the clearest vision: "For the eager longing of creation awaits the revelation of the sons of God. For creation was made subject to vanity—not by its own will but by reason of him who made it subject —in hope, because creation itself also will be delivered from its slavery to corruption into the freedom of the glory of the sons of God. For we know that all creation groans and travails in pain until now" (Rom. 8:19-23).

Through the clarity of the body itself the resurrection will show forth the "children of God," that is, those who here on earth live in the very life of the Son of God by spiritual and invisible grace. Their shining forth will not take place in shadowy surroundings like the chiaroscuro of Caravaggio. Around them will be as it were the spirituality and clarity of the world.

When St. Paul tells us that creation awaits this manifestation sorrowfully, he is, of course, personifying the inanimate universe. The universe did not know original sin and will have no part in the return of the Lord. The state of disorder that developed in it does not indicate any change whatever in the laws that govern it.

It is true that Yahweh said to Adam, ". . . cursed is the earth in thy work. . . . Thorns and thistles shall it bring forth to thee" (Gen. 3:17-18). But this did not make the earth unproductive where it had formerly been fruitful for tillage; everything happened in man alone; the effort of tillage, formerly a joyful task assigned by the creator, now becomes an affliction. Likewise, St. Thomas calls the opinion that the animals now became wild and began to devour each other "completely unreasonable."[73] As a carnivorous animal does not change its nature when it is domesticated, it remains what it is if it returns to wild state. Animal instinct—which causes a crane to spontaneously align itself with the one who is leading the flight, the gazelle to tremble all over when it hears a lion's roar for the first time, or the bee to serve the queen of the hive—predisposed beasts to obey the king of creation. However, this mastery was in man and emanated from him. God said, ". . . let him have dominion over the fishes of the sea, and the fowls of the air, and the beasts, and the whole earth, and every

[73] I, qu. 96, a. 1, 2nd reply.

creeping creature that moveth upon the earth" (Gen. 1:26). By causing man to lose the effulgence which subdued to him a universe that was or could easily be domesticated, sin disordered this universe only in relation to him, not in itself. That a pebble, a thorn, a mosquito wounds the images of God is abnormal in relation to the ideal, is a metaphysical disorder and a religious misfortune. When our divine sonship is manifested and when it radiates from the soul into the human body, it will restore—and more than restore—to man his primitive dominion over creation. And it will be a good thing! Everything will be restored to order. The "redemption of our body" (Rom. 8:23) will have been the signal of a cosmic liberation.

When Jesus was transfigured on Thabor, not only His Body appeared in its glorious clarity, His garments also "became white as snow" (Matt. 17:2). "Spiritual bodies" will spiritualize creation by their reflection and as it were their reverberation in the same way that they themselves are spiritualized, by being wholly at the disposal of the spirit, as we have indicated.

A master of contemporary exegesis has written: "In Christ . . . there has already come about the cosmic renewal which will mark the eschatological era. The Body of Christ is the first cell of the new cosmos. In Him the Spirit has already taken possession of matter, as it will with all creation after the Parousia when Christ will definitely 're-establish' all things."[74]

We are not thinking therefore of an annihilation of

[74] P. Benoit, O.P., *Exégèse et théologie,* Paris, Éd. du Cerf, v. I, p. 386.

the universe in flames; we take the expression to be a symbol of extreme intensity and the clearest of the metaphors for the final stage of the world in the fullness of time. The universe will not be destroyed but in its own way spiritualized and divinized. We do not—in the line of Aristotle's physics and Ptolemy's cosmology—envision a fixing of the stars nor a cessation of all inferior life in a magnificent and terrible universe turned to stone. To make a new earth, God need not begin His creative work over again and make something else. It will be in itself what it is: for it is good, it is very good. What will be incommensurably new will be the degree, the fulness, the authencity of its domination by the human and the spiritual.

The technical progress so justly admired today will astound our descendants (if there are any) some centuries and millennia from now. But the results of this progress by the end of the world will be only child's play in comparison to the power over the world and the extent of it that God wishes for His sons of the resurrection. Matter is ennobled in our laboratories, factories and industries, marked as it is by the intelligence which makes use of it: it will be so to a marvellous extent and for the whole universe in the final heaven.

Will people accuse us of granting to the world by that fact a kind of eternity? Yes, in man and for man, in the children of God and for the children of God, through God's omnipotence, matter itself will be made eternal, "freed from the slavery of corruption" and nothingness. Whether one conceives it in terms of cyclic return or constant expansion, it will be matter, created, inanimate, unconscious and crumbling in its incomplete elements; but on account of man, the son of God, its totality will endure into a new era.

Impeded by the physics of his time and doubtless also by a poor translation of the Apocalypse, St. Thomas wrote, ". . . after the resurrection the time which is the measure of the heaven's movement will be no more"; he adds, however, "there will nevertheless be time resulting from the before and after in any kind of movement."[75] We can be this positive and more so. There will be no more history in the resurrection, since all the divine ends will have been achieved, but there will be duration, in the final flowering.

What will be for us, already exists, let us repeat—the state of Christ, of the Virgin of the assumption, and, if God has willed it, our ancestors near them. The promised new heaven and new earth are not only for the future.

In these pages we have carefully avoided all debate and polemic, although specialists will note some preferences. Let us frankly admit this. We should like to make three remarks in closing.

It is surely important not to forget that life eternal consists essentially in the beatific vision. The light of glory is a gift to the soul. Its refulgence which will transfigure the body is only a secondary result. However, certain ways of presenting the heaven of our faith as a simple synonym of the spiritual world which is the divine world seem to us purely and simply to eliminate the mystery of the immortalization of matter such as the resurrection

[75] *Supplement to the Summa,* qu. 84, a. 3, 5th reply.

of the body implies. We do not absolutely need a completed cosmology in order to imagine heaven, nor need we attempt a new concordism by utilizing the findings of physical science and modern astronomy. But the heaven of the unanimous Catholic tradition is not a vague symbol, it is somewhere on high. It is not a subjective state, it is an objective place. It has not merely an anthropological meaning, it is an extrahuman reality.

We must also be careful of simplifications and excessive antitheses. It is true, very true, that faith gives us the substance of things hoped for. It is true, very true, that the end of time began with the resurrection of Christ, our Head, and with our filial adoption in Him. It is true, very true, that the risen Christ is with us henceforward throughout all time. It is true, very true, that even our temporal tasks, supernaturally oriented, bear here and now a reflection of eternity. But hope is not possession. What we shall be is not yet manifest. Christ will be with us even to the end of time, the hour of which has not yet sounded. Excellent and necessary as it may be to apply the Gospel to the world of today, the figure of this world will pass, and our activities are effective in gaining the universe only if our hearts are turned toward eschatological perspectives. And, under the pretext of "demythologizing" the world beyond, Christians do not assume an attitude of scorn toward other Christians who believe in the resurrection of the body and await the return of the Lord, not forgetting that the Last Day will mark the coming of the world's golden age. He is no less mature in his faith and hope who, aspiring above all to a real face to face meeting, believes no less in the resurrection of the body and lives radiantly turned toward the eternal city. "And the Spirit and the bride say, 'Come!' And let him who hears say, Come!" (Apoc. 22:17). This is not necessarily an opiate; it should be, it is, a ferment.

Finally, we have discussed the resurrection of the body only in terms of the individual's last end. We cannot, obviously, ignore the social dimensions of the new Jerusalem. But it is souls, not bodies, that weld and solder societies; thus this is not a relevant aspect of our theme. From this standpoint we have not said everything about heaven! However, even this omission points to a truth. Even in the community of love supremely achieved in the Church triumphant, even swept on by the torrent of the life of the Trinity, each individual will retain his inalienable ontological and teleological primacy as a unique image of God uniquely loved by Him.